ActionScript® 3.0 for
ADOBE® FLASH® PROFESSIONAL CS5
CLASSROOM IN A BOOK®

The official training workbook from Adobe Systems

www.adobepress.com

Adobe

Adobe Press books are published by Peachpit, a division of Pearson Education located in Berkeley, California. For the latest on Adobe Press books, go to www.adobepress.com. To report errors, please send a note to errata@peachpit.com. For information on getting permission for reprints and excerpts, contact permissions@peachpit.com.

Writer: Chris Florio   Technical Editor: Angela Nimer
Project Editor: Rebecca Freed   Compositor: Danielle Foster
Development Editor: Judy Ziajka   Indexer: Rebecca Plunkett
Production Editor: Danielle Foster   Cover design: Eddie Yuen
Copyeditor: Scout Festa   Interior design: Mimi Heft

Printed and bound in the United States of America

ISBN-13: 978-0-321-70447-4
ISBN-10: 0-321-70447-9

9 8 7 6 5 4 3 2

WHAT'S ON THE DISC

Here is an overview of the contents of the Classroom in a Book disc

The *ActionScript 3.0 for Adobe Flash Professional CS5 Classroom in a Book* disc includes the lesson files that you'll need to complete the exercises in this book, as well as other content to help you learn more about ActionScript 3.0 and use it with greater efficiency and ease. The diagram below represents the contents of the disc, which should help you locate the files you need.

Lesson files

Each lesson has its own folder inside the Lessons folder. You will need to copy these lesson folders to your hard drive before you can begin each lesson.

Online resources

Links to Adobe Community Help, product Help and Support pages, Adobe certification programs, Adobe TV, and other useful online resources can be found inside a handy HTML file. Just open it in your Web browser and click on the links, including a special link to this book's product page where you can access updates and bonus material.

Adobe Press

ADOBE PRESS Find information about other Adobe Press titles, covering the full spectrum of Adobe products, in the Online Resources file.

CONTENTS

10 WORKING WITH AN XML PLAYLIST

11 USING ACTIONSCRIPT AND COMPONENTS TO CONTROL VIDEO

12 DELVING DEEPER INTO GRAPHICS AND ANIMATION WITH ACTIONSCRIPT

GETTING STARTED

Adobe Flash Professional CS5 provides a comprehensive authoring environment with tools for working with 2D and 3D animation, sound, vector and bitmap graphics, text, and video. Adobe ActionScript 3.0 is a sophisticated programming language that is totally integrated into Flash CS5 to develop rich interactive projects. The ActionScript techniques that you will learn in this book can be used with the great design and animation tools in the Flash interface to create rich interactive applications, games, e-learning content, and e-commerce tools for the web, the desktop, and mobile devices.

About Classroom in a Book

ActionScript 3.0 for Adobe Flash Professional CS5 Classroom in a Book is part of the official training series for the Adobe Flash platform, developed with the support of Adobe product experts. The lessons are designed so that you can learn at your own pace. If you're new to ActionScript, you'll learn the fundamental concepts and features you'll need to accomplish a wide range of techniques covered in the book, but also gain enough understanding of the language to be able to learn additional techniques on your own. Each lesson in the book includes suggestions for continuing to develop your skills. Classroom in a Book teaches many advanced features, including tips and techniques for using the latest versions of ActionScript and Flash.

The lessons in this book include opportunities to use new features in Flash Professional CS5 such as Code Snippets, working with TLF Text, interacting with Adobe's Pixel Bender Toolkit 2, and developing for the Adobe AIR 2 platform.

Prerequisites

Before you begin to use *ActionScript 3.0 for Adobe Flash Professional CS5 Classroom in a Book*, make sure that your system is set up correctly and that you've installed the required software. You should know how to use the mouse and standard menus and commands, and also how to open, save, and close files. If you need to review these techniques, see the printed or online documentation included with your Microsoft Windows or Apple Mac OS software.

This book is geared toward Flash users who are already comfortable with the interface and basic design and animation features of Flash. If you are new to Flash entirely, you may want to go through the lessons in *Adobe Flash Professional CS5 Classroom in a Book*.

This book assumes no programming experience. If you are a designer wishing to learn ActionScript 3.0, but perhaps are a little daunted by code, this book is for you. It also is helpful for Flash users who may have worked with earlier versions of ActionScript but have not yet made the transition to ActionScript 3.0.

Installing Flash

You must purchase the Adobe Flash Professional CS5 software either as a stand-alone application or as part of Adobe Creative Suite. Both products come with Flash Player 10, Adobe AIR 2, Adobe Media Encoder CS5, Adobe Extension Manager, Adobe Device Central, Adobe Bridge CS5, and the Pixel Bender Toolkit 2 in addition to the actual Adobe Flash CS5 application. Flash CS5 requires Apple QuickTime 7.6.2 or later. For system requirements and complete instructions on installing the Flash software, see the Adobe Flash ReadMe.pdf file on the application DVD.

Install Flash from the Adobe Flash Professional CS5 application DVD onto your hard disk. You cannot run the program from the DVD. Follow the onscreen instructions. Make sure that your serial number is accessible before installing the application. You can find the serial number on the registration card or on the back of the DVD case.

Optimizing performance

Flash Professional CS5 requires a minimum of 1 GB of RAM. The more RAM available to Flash, the faster the application will work for you. A broadband Internet connection is required for access to the online services offered by Adobe.

Copying the lesson files

The lessons in this book all revolve around a Flash project contained in an FLA file. Most of the lessons use additional resources such as audio, video, image, and text files. To complete the lessons in this book, you must copy these files from the *ActionScript 3.0 for Adobe Flash Professional CS5 Classroom in a Book* CD (located inside the back cover of this book) to your computer.

Copy the Lessons folder (which contains folders named Lesson01, Lesson02, and so on) from the *ActionScript 3.0 for Adobe Flash Professional CS5 Classroom in a Book* CD onto your computer by dragging it to your hard drive.

When you begin each lesson, you will be instructed where to navigate within the Lessons folder to find all the assets you need to complete the lesson.

If you have limited storage space on your computer, you can copy each Lesson folder individually as you need it and delete it afterward if desired. As mentioned before, some lessons build on preceding lessons but even then, the assets in each lesson folder are self-contained and don't require materials from other lesson folders. You do not have to save any finished project if you don't want to or if you have limited hard disk space.

How to use these lessons

Each lesson in this book provides step-by-step instructions for creating a project that illustrates essential ActionScript techniques. Some lessons build on projects created in preceding lessons; others stand alone. All the lessons build on each other in terms of concepts and skills, so the best way to learn from this book is to proceed through the lessons in sequential order. Some techniques and processes are explained and described in detail only the first few times you perform them. Many of the most essential ActionScript processes are repeated throughout the exercises so that you can build a familiarity as well as a level of comfort with the basic tools in the language.

Each of the lesson folders contains a Start folder with the files that you will use to create the lesson as well as a Complete folder with a sample version of the completed lesson for reference; you can compare your work in progress against these samples of finished, working ActionScript. Some of the lessons also include other files and folders with media and resources needed to complete the lesson's project. Be sure to keep each folder's contents together.

Standard elements in the book

Boldface text: Words that appear in **boldface** indicate text that you must type while working through the steps in the lessons.

Boldface code: Lines of code that appear in **boldface** within code blocks help you easily identify changes in the block that you are to make in a step.

```
function moveUp(e:Event):void {
  if (jt0.position.y>165) {
    var pt0:Point=new Point(jt0.position.x-5,jt0.position.y-5);
    mover0.moveTo(pt0);
  } else {
    stage.removeEventListener(Event.ENTER_FRAME, moveUp);
    snapshot_btn.visible = true;
  }
}
```

Code in text: Code or `keywords` appear slightly different from the rest of the text so you can identify them.

Code and wrapped code lines: To help you easily identify ActionScript, XML, and HTML code within the book, the code has been styled in a special font that's unique from the rest of the text. Single lines of code that are longer than the margins of the page allow wrap to the next line. They are designated by an arrow at the beginning of the continuation of a broken line and are indented under the line from which they continue. For example:

```
var variables:URLVariables = new URLVariables();
```

```
var mailAddress:URLRequest=new
  ¬URLRequest("http://www.actionscript.tv/email.php");
```

Italicized text: Words that appear in *italics* are either for *emphasis* or are *new vocabulary.*

Italics are also used for placeholders, in which the exact entry may change depending on your situation. For example:

```
mailto:yourName@yourISP.com?subject=From Lesson 13 link&Body=
  ¬This message was sent from Flash
```

Menu commands and keyboard shortcuts: Menu commands are shown with angle brackets between the menu names and commands: Menu > Command > Subcommand. Keyboard shortcuts are shown with a plus sign between the names of keys to indicate that you should press the keys simultaneously; for example, Shift+Tab means that you should press the Shift and Tab keys at the same time.

Checking for updates

Adobe periodically provides updates to software. You can easily obtain these updates through Adobe Updater, as long as you have an active Internet connection.

1 In Flash Professional CS5, choose Help > Updates. The Adobe Updater automatically checks for updates available for your Adobe software.

2 In the Adobe Application Manager dialog box, select and download the updates you want to install. A message tells you if your application is already up to date. If the application is up to date, click Quit to close the Application Manager dialog box and return to Flash.

▶ **Tip:** Alternative ways to perform tasks and suggestions to consider when applying the skills you are learning.

● **Note:** Additional background information to expand your knowledge and advanced techniques you can explore to further develop your skills.

● **Note:** To set your preferences for future updates, click Preferences in the Adobe Updater dialog box. Select how often you want Adobe Application Manager to check for updates, for which applications, and whether to download them automatically. Click OK to accept the new settings.

Flash Player version

The lessons in this book (with the exception of Lesson 14 which uses Adobe AIR) are created to work with Flash Player 10 or higher. While most web users have a recent version of the Flash Player, it is always a good idea before beginning your own Flash based projects to identify the target audience and determine which version of the Flash Player to develop for before starting the process. For information on Flash Player version penetration visit:

www.adobe.com/products/player_census/flashplayer/

Additional resources

ActionScript 3.0 for Adobe Flash Professional CS5 Classroom in a Book is not meant to replace documentation that comes with the program or to be a comprehensive reference for every feature. Only the commands and options used in the lessons are explained in this book. For comprehensive information about program features and tutorials, refer to these resources:

Adobe Community Help: Community Help brings together active Adobe product users, Adobe product team members, authors, and experts to give you the most useful, relevant, and up-to-date information about Adobe products. Whether you're looking for a code sample or an answer to a problem, have a question about the software, or want to share a useful tip or recipe, you'll benefit from Community Help. Search results will show you not only content from Adobe, but also from the community.

With Adobe Community Help you can:

- Access up-to-date definitive reference content online and offline
- Find the most relevant content contributed by experts from the Adobe community, on and off Adobe.com
- Comment on, rate, and contribute to content in the Adobe community
- Download Help content directly to your desktop for offline use
- Find related content with dynamic search and navigation tools

To access Community Help: If you have any Adobe CS5 product, then you already have the Community Help application. To invoke Help, choose Help > Flash Help. This companion application lets you search and browse Adobe and community content, plus you can comment on and rate any article just like you would in the browser. However, you can also download Adobe Help and language reference content for use offline. You can also subscribe to new content updates (which can be automatically downloaded) so that you'll always have the most up-to-date content for your Adobe product at all times. You can download the application from www.adobe.com/support/chc/index.html.

Adobe content is updated based on community feedback and contributions. You can contribute in several ways: add comments to content or forums, including links to web content; publish your own content using Community Publishing; or contribute Cookbook Recipes. Find out how to contribute: www.adobe.com/community/publishing/download.html.

See http://community.adobe.com/help/profile/faq.html for answers to frequently asked questions about Community Help.

Adobe Flash Professional CS5 Help and Support: www.adobe.com/support/flash where you can find and browse Help and Support content on adobe.com.

Adobe TV: http://tv.adobe.com is an online video resource for expert instruction and inspiration about Adobe products, including a How To channel to get you started with your product.

Adobe Design Center: www.adobe.com/designcenter offers thoughtful articles on design and design issues, a gallery showcasing the work of top-notch designers, tutorials, and more.

Adobe Developer Connection: www.adobe.com/devnet is your source for technical articles, code samples, and how-to videos that cover Adobe developer products and technologies.

ActionScript Technology Center: www.adobe.com/devnet/actionscript is a special section of the Adobe Developer Connection designed specifically for ActionScript users.

Resources for educators: www.adobe.com/education includes three free curriculums that use an integrated approach to teaching Adobe software and can be used to prepare for the Adobe Certified Associate exams.

Also check out these useful links:

Adobe Forums: http://forums.adobe.com lets you tap into peer-to-peer discussions, questions, and answers on Adobe products.

Adobe Marketplace & Exchange: www.adobe.com/cfusion/exchange is a central resource for finding tools, services, extensions, code samples, and more to supplement and extend your Adobe products.

Adobe Flash Professional CS5 product home page: www.adobe.com/products/flash.

Adobe Labs: http://labs.adobe.com gives you access to early builds of cutting-edge technology, as well as forums where you can interact with both the Adobe development teams building that technology and other like-minded members of the community.

Adobe certification

The Adobe training and certification programs are designed to help Adobe customers improve and promote their product-proficiency skills. There are four levels of certification:

- Adobe Certified Associate (ACA)
- Adobe Certified Expert (ACE)
- Adobe Certified Instructor (ACI)
- Adobe Authorized Training Center (AATC)

The Adobe Certified Associate (ACA) credential certifies that individuals have the entry-level skills to plan, design, build, and maintain effective communications using different forms of digital media.

The Adobe Certified Expert program is a way for expert users to upgrade their credentials. You can use Adobe certification as a catalyst for getting a raise, finding a job, or promoting your expertise.

If you are an ACE-level instructor, the Adobe Certified Instructor program takes your skills to the next level and gives you access to a wide range of Adobe resources.

Adobe Authorized Training Centers offer instructor-led courses and training on Adobe products, employing only Adobe Certified Instructors. A directory of AATCs is available at http://partners.adobe.com.

For information on the Adobe Certified programs, visit www.adobe.com/support/certification/main.html.

Accelerate your workflow with Adobe CS Live

Adobe CS Live is a set of online services that harness the connectivity of the web and integrate with Adobe Creative Suite 5 to simplify the creative review process, speed up website compatibility testing, deliver important web user intelligence and more, allowing you to focus on creating your most impactful work. CS Live services are complimentary for a limited time* and can be accessed online or from within Creative Suite 5 applications.

Adobe BrowserLab is for web designers and developers who need to preview and test their web pages on multiple browsers and operating systems. Unlike other browser compatibility solutions, BrowserLab renders screenshots virtually on demand with multiple viewing and diagnostic tools, and can be used with Dreamweaver CS5 to preview local content and different states of interactive pages. Being an online service, BrowserLab has fast development cycles, with greater flexibility for expanded browser support and updated functionality.

Adobe CS Review is for creative professionals who want a new level of efficiency in the creative review process. Unlike other services that offer online review of creative content, only CS Review lets you publish a review to the web directly from within InDesign, Photoshop, Photoshop Extended, and Illustrator and view reviewer comments back in the originating Creative Suite application.

Acrobat.com is for creative professionals who need to work with a cast of colleagues and clients in order to get a creative project from creative brief to final product. Acrobat.com is a set of online services that includes web conferencing, online file sharing and workspaces. Unlike collaborating via email and attending time-consuming in-person meetings, Acrobat.com brings people to your work instead of sending files to people, so you can get the business side of the creative process done faster, together, from any location.

Adobe Story is for creative professionals, producers, and writers working on or with scripts. Story is a collaborative script development tool that turns scripts into metadata that can be used with the Adobe CS5 Production Premium tools to streamline workflows and create video assets.

SiteCatalyst NetAverages is for web and mobile professionals who want to optimize their projects for wider audiences. NetAverages provides intelligence on how users are accessing the web, which helps reduce guesswork early in the creative process. You can access aggregate user data such as browser type, operating system, mobile device profile, screen resolution and more, which can be shown over time. The data is derived from visitor activity to participating Omniture SiteCatalyst customer sites. Unlike other web intelligence solutions, NetAverages innovatively displays data using Flash, creating an engaging experience that is robust yet easy to follow.

You can access CS Live three different ways:

1   Set up access when you register your Creative Suite 5 products and get complimentary access that includes all of the features and workflow benefits of using CS Live with CS5.

2   Set up access by signing up online and get complimentary access to CS Live services for a limited time. Note, this option does not give you access to the services from within your products.

3   Desktop product trials include a 30-day trial of CS Live services.

CS Live services are complimentary for a limited time. See www.adobe.com/go/cslive for details.

INTRODUCTION TO ACTIONSCRIPT 3.0

Before you begin working through the lessons, it is worth taking a little time to understand the history of ActionScript and address a few topics that may clarify for you how Adobe ActionScript 3.0 works with Adobe Flash and the Flash platform.

A brief history of Flash and ActionScript

Flash and ActionScript have evolved together since Flash was originally released in 1996. Today, the combination of the design and animation tools in Flash CS5 and the advanced interactive capabilities of ActionScript 3.0 offers one of the most powerful, most versatile, and certainly most popular development environments available, but the origins of ActionScript as part of Flash were fairly humble.

In the first three versions of Flash, there were no programming tools available, and interactivity meant selecting from a few simple drag-and-drop options in the Actions panel. These actions allowed for navigation of the Flash Timeline and creating links to URLs, but not much more.

Flash 4 was the first version that allowed for entry of code using a simple scripting language, which became informally known as ActionScript. In Flash 5, ActionScript evolved even more and became an official scripting language. With each version of Flash since that time, the capabilities of ActionScript have become richer, offering interactive control of animation, text, sound, video, data, and much more. In 2003 ActionScript 2.0 was introduced, and its capabilities were on par with object-oriented languages such as Java and C#. You will learn more about object-oriented programming (OOP) starting in Lesson 4, "Creating ActionScript in External Files."

Serious programmers started becoming more interested in ActionScript as a development tool, but they found that even though ActionScript 2.0 rivaled the features of other languages, it did not rival their performance. This was because each version of ActionScript was built on the foundation of the previous one, going all the way back to its very simple beginnings. Flash Player was not originally designed for creating high-performance applications and games, but developers began using it for those purposes. It became clear that a new version of ActionScript needed to be written from the ground up.

In 2006, Adobe introduced ActionScript 3.0, which offered significant new functionality as well as dramatic performance increases. Flash CS3 was the first version of Flash to incorporate ActionScript 3.0. Flash CS4 added functionality to ActionScript 3.0, including new 3D capabilities, new animation controls, and ActionScript classes for working with Adobe AIR (see Lesson 14, "Creating Adobe AIR Applications with Flash and ActionScript"). Flash CS5 continues the evolution of ActionScript 3.0 and has added lots of new ActionScript for working with advanced text features; enhancing the AIR platform; and working with a variety of devices and controllers, including multitouch and touch-screen devices. Flash CS5 also has a number of new features to help you learn and work with ActionScript, including the new Code Snippets panel, which lets you reuse common ActionScript code with the click of a mouse. Other new ActionScript features, such as code completion and tooltips for custom classes, will show their worth as you begin working with the language.

ActionScript 3.0 for new programmers

Having the power and sophistication of ActionScript 3.0 within Flash is wonderful, but with these capabilities comes more complexity and a steeper learning curve. Many designers and animators who use Flash regularly are daunted by the prospect of learning ActionScript 3.0, and the majority of books on the subject are written for those with programming experience. The truth is that with a little patience at the beginning, you can quickly learn enough ActionScript to be able to add lots of interactive features to your Flash work.

The lessons in this book are geared toward designers who have little or no programming experience. Some knowledge of ActionScript 1.0 or 2.0 is of course useful, but should not be necessary to successfully complete the lessons.

By working through these lessons, you will gain a comfort with the syntax of ActionScript 3.0. More importantly, you will gain a large repertoire of interactive tools to add to your existing Flash skills. You'll also build a foundation that will allow you to continue your ActionScript education using the material at the Adobe Flash Developer Center (adobe.com/devnet/flash) and the many other books and resources available.

For users of ActionScript 1.0 and 2.0

Much has changed in ActionScript 3.0 compared with ActionScript 1.0 and ActionScript 2.0, and some advanced ActionScript 1.0 and 2.0 programmers are still intimidated by the prospect of learning ActionScript 3.0. The next sections cover some points that may help you to make the transition and convince you that the benefits of ActionScript 3.0 will justify the effort.

First, the bad news

There is no doubt that ActionScript 3.0 is more verbose than earlier versions of the language; this means that, especially in the beginning, you have to type more code to get the same results. The payoff becomes apparent fairly quickly, but at first glance, ActionScript 3.0 can be a little scary for new users.

Also, Flash applications written in ActionScript 3.0 cannot be simply integrated with Flash projects created with earlier versions of ActionScript. This is because there are actually two ActionScript players inside Flash Player 9 and later.

Flash Player contains ActionScript Virtual Machine 1 (AVM1), which plays files created with ActionScript 1.0 and ActionScript 2.0, and Virtual Machine 2 (AVM2), which plays files created with ActionScript 3.0. While it is possible for files to communicate between the two virtual machines, it is not as simple as communicating with files created with the same version of AVM. In this book, we will focus exclusively on ActionScript 3.0, but if you plan on integrating new ActionScript 3.0 projects into older Flash websites or applications, you should thoroughly study the resources in Flash Help on integrating ActionScript 3.0 with older files.

...and now the good news

ActionScript 1.0 and ActionScript 2.0 developers who have made the transition to ActionScript 3.0 very quickly appreciate its advantages, especially:

- Better performance. As mentioned, ActionScript 3.0 code executes much faster than earlier versions of the language—usually 2 to 10 times, but sometimes up to 100 times, faster. This makes Flash viable for creating high-performance games, simulations, 3D interfaces, and data-driven applications.

- More consistent syntax. Because everything up to ActionScript 2.0 was built on top of previous versions, there were often many ways to do similar things. This could be extremely confusing. For example, in ActionScript 1.0 and 2.0 something as simple as responding to an event or creating a new object could be dramatically different, depending on what the event or object was. As you will see beginning in Lesson 2, "Working with Events and Functions," once you learn how to do something in ActionScript 3.0, the syntax will remain consistent throughout the language. For example, there is one way to listen for and respond to an event in ActionScript 3.0, regardless of the type of event.

- Better error checking and feedback. Everyone makes mistakes, so it is a blessing that ActionScript 3.0 offers much better feedback to help you identify and correct errors in your code.

- Lots of new features. ActionScript 3.0 has introduced dozens of new classes that offer functionality that was previously unavailable, including ways of working with sound, video, text, XML, 3D, and lots more. As you progress through the lessons you will become comfortable with many of these features.

Formats for playing back Flash and ActionScript 3.0 files

Usually, creating a website or application in Flash means publishing your finished work as a SWF file that can be played using Flash Player, most typically in a web browser. This is the most common use of Flash for most developers.

Flash has also always provided the option of creating platform-specific projector versions of your projects. These are self-running executable files that can be created for either Macintosh or Windows.

Not long ago, Adobe introduced its Adobe AIR technology, which allows creation of true cross-platform desktop applications that run on Macintosh, Windows, or Linux. Adobe AIR applications can be made using Flash CS5, which includes a number of new features for AIR 2.0. In Lesson 14, "Creating Adobe AIR applications with Flash and ActionScript," you will learn to use ActionScript 3.0 to create desktop applications that can access the user's operating system and printer.

Flash CS5, Flash Builder 4, and Flex

Many Flash users have heard of Adobe Flash Builder and Flex but are not sure how or if they fit into their development process. Flash CS5 and Flash Builder 4 are both commercial applications from Adobe. Flash Builder 4 is the new name for what formerly was called Flex Builder. You can use Flash CS5 and/or Flash Builder 4 to create SWF files for Flash Player as well as stand-alone Adobe AIR applications. Another option for experienced programmers is to use the free Flex SDK that is available from Adobe at www.adobe.com/products/flex/flex_framework/.

All of these programs support the entire ActionScript 3.0 language. Flash Builder is more geared toward people with a programming background and includes a number of features that support the development of large-scale rich-media applications and data-driven projects. Flash CS5 on the other hand includes tools and an interface adapted to the needs of designers and animators.

If you do projects that integrate a lot of design, video, animation, and media but also have lots of interactivity that requires serious amounts of coding, you may wish to consider developing your Flash projects using both Flash CS5 and Flash Builder 4. Both tools ship with the Adobe CS5 Web Collection and are very well integrated. Many developers or teams will create the visual parts of an application in Flash CS5 and then from within Flash CS5, launch and use Flash Builder 4 to write their ActionScript code. Of course this is an optional step—code can also be written exclusively in Flash CS5.

This book focuses on the use of ActionScript 3.0 in Flash CS5, but all the concepts and nearly all the code would work equally well in Flash Builder 4.

ActionScript in the Flash Timeline vs. external ActionScript files

Traditionally, ActionScript in Flash has been placed on keyframes in the Timeline. In earlier versions of Flash, ActionScript could also be placed directly on an object such as a button or a movie clip, but this is no longer the case with ActionScript 3.0.

ActionScript can also be used in a more standardized OOP (Object Oriented Programming) environment. ActionScript 3.0 is based on the ECMA standard and has many similarities to other languages including Java, C#, and C++. ActionScript is a true object-oriented language, which makes it very good for building larger and more complex projects. While this book does not put an emphasis on OOP, the later lessons will lay a foundation that will allow you to delve more deeply into OOP development in ActionScript 3.0 if you wish. An alternative to placing code on the Timeline is to create dedicated ActionScript files that can be used in any Flash project. This is the foundation for OOP in Flash.

In the early lessons of this book, you will be placing all your code in the Flash Timeline. Starting in Lesson 4, "Creating ActionScript in External Files," you will begin working with external ActionScript class files and begin to learn to take advantage of OOP principles.

That's enough background for now...

Let's get started in Lesson 1, "Using Code Snippets and Navigating the Flash Timeline," where, as you may guess by the title, you will learn to work with the new Code Snippets features in Flash CS5 and use ActionScript 3.0 to navigate the Flash Timeline.

1 USING CODE SNIPPETS AND NAVIGATING THE FLASH TIMELINE

Lesson overview

In this lesson, you'll learn to do the following:

- Use the Code Snippet panel in Flash CS5.

- Navigate to a URL using a code snippet.

- Add ActionScript to the Timeline via the Actions panel.

- Add labels to frames on a timeline.

- Control playback with ActionScript you've added to the Timeline.

- Preview your Flash project as a SWF file in the testing environment.

- Change the content of a dynamic text field in ActionScript.

- Use an ActionScript variable to keep track of a changing number.

- Use a conditional statement to respond to the looping of an animation.

 This lesson will take approximately 2 hours.

The Flash Timeline is an extremely useful tool for creating animations. It is also a great environment for setting up a website or simple application that requires navigation between different sections of content. This lesson introduces the techniques for adding code to the Flash Timeline to control playback; it also introduces a few essential ActionScript 3.0 programming concepts.

First, though, this chapter introduces you to a great new feature in Flash CS5 called code snippets. Code snippets are designed to help new programmers learn ActionScript 3.0 and to speed up the work-flow for experienced ActionScript 3.0 developers.

Coordinating the Flash CS5 Stage, Timeline, and
Actions panel.

Getting started

To begin this lesson, from the Lessons > Lesson01 > Start folder, open the lesson01_start.fla file in Flash CS5. This file has layers, graphics, and animation. If you scrub (that is, click the playback head and drag to the left or right) through the Flash Timeline, you'll see that the first 30 frames contain an animation and that Frame 50 contains the background for an interactive interface.

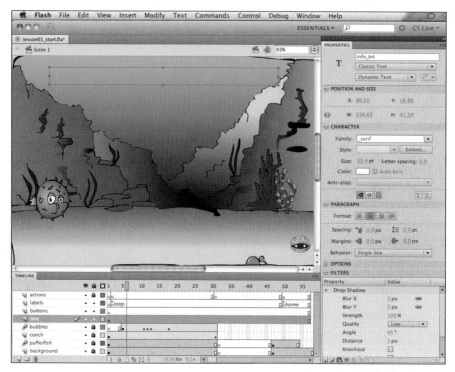

● **Note:** The artwork in Lessons 1 and 2 was created by the animator Rattana Ouch (rattana. ouch@gmail.com).

If you ran the movie at this point, it would just play through the whole Timeline from start to end, showing a brief glimpse of the interface before returning to the beginning. You will soon add ActionScript directly to this file to alter the playback of the Timeline, but first you will make use of the Code Snippets panel to add a link to a URL when a button is clicked.

Adding ActionScript using code snippets

You can create ActionScript on any keyframe in the main timeline of a Flash movie. You can also create it on any keyframe within a movie clip symbol. During playback of the compiled Flash project, the code on each frame will execute when that frame plays.

All timeline code in Flash is written in the Actions panel, accessible in Flash from the Window menu or by pressing F9 (Windows) or Option+F9 (Mac).

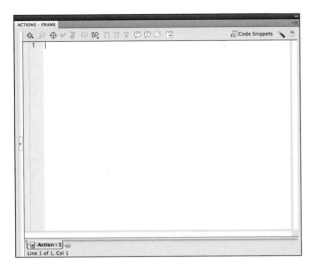

Later, you will see that you can also write ActionScript in external ActionScript files, but for now, you will create code exclusively in the Actions panel.

In addition to typing code directly in the Actions panel, you can add code to this panel using the new Code Snippets panel. Code snippets, as their name implies, are prebuilt chunks of ActionScript 3.0 code that can easily be added to your projects and modified to suit your purposes. Code snippets provide a wonderful way to begin working with ActionScript and can be very useful for increasing the range of tasks that you can accomplish.

Adding a code snippet to navigate to a URL

The Code Snippets panel is found on the Window menu in Flash CS5. When you add a code snippet to your project, the code snippet is written in the Actions panel, saving you the trouble of typing it yourself. After the code snippet is placed in the Actions panel, it is fully editable, allowing you to customize and modify that code.

To see how code snippets work, you will add some code that will link to the Flash support page at www.Adobe.com when a button is clicked.

Begin by adding a button to the Stage:

1   With the lesson01_start.fla file open and the Stage and Timeline visible, select the first frame in the buttons layer.

2   If it is not already visible, open the Library panel (Window > Library).

3   From the Library panel, drag an instance of the item named Button to the lower-right area of the Stage.

4   If it is not already visible, open the Property inspector (Window > Properties).

5   Give your new button instance an instance name by selecting the button onstage and typing **help_btn** in the instance name field in the Property

Note: The Property inspector is also sometimes called the Properties panel.

inspector. In Flash, it is essential that all objects onstage that will be controlled with ActionScript be given instance names.

Note: The button that you are working with is a component that ships with Flash CS5. In previous versions of Flash, component parameters, such as the label property of the button that you just modified, could be modified in a panel called the Component inspector. This panel has been deprecated in Flash CS5, and component parameters are now modified in the Property inspector instead. You will learn more about components in coming chapters and will see that component parameters can also be controlled using ActionScript.

6 With your button instance still selected, give it a label by typing the label **Flash Support** in the Label Name field of the Property inspector, found in the Component Parameters area.

Applying a code snippet

Depending on the functionality needed, code snippets can be applied in a few different ways. For a code snippet that is intended to execute when the user interacts with a button, as is the case here, you apply the snippet by first selecting the button onstage and then applying the code snippet. You will do this now with help_btn:

1 If they are not already visible, open the Code Snippets panel (Window > Code Snippets) and the Actions panel (Window > Actions).

2 Select the help_btn instance onstage.

3 In the Code Snippets panel, open the Actions folder.

4 In the Code Snippets panel, double-click the snippet named Click to Go to Web Page. Notice that the keyframe in Frame 1 of the `actions` layer of the Timeline now has a lowercase *a* in it. This indicates that the ActionScript written by the code snippet has been stored in this frame. You should also see the following code appear in the Actions panel:

```
/* Click to Go to Web Page
Clicking on the specified symbol instance loads the URL in a
¬new browser window.

Instructions:
1. Replace http://www.adobe.com with the desired URL address.
   Keep the quotation marks ("").
*/

help_btn.addEventListener(MouseEvent.CLICK,
¬fl_ClickToGoToWebPage);

function fl_ClickToGoToWebPage(event:MouseEvent):void
{
 navigateToURL(new URLRequest("http://www.adobe.com"),
 ¬"_blank");
}
```

5 Test the movie by choosing Control > Test Movie > in Flash Professional.

6 In the testing environment, click `help_btn`. The code should cause the Adobe home page to open in the computer's default browser when the button is clicked.

Modifying the code snippet

Because code snippets are pure ActionScript code, they can easily be modified to change their functionality. If you examine the code snippet that was written in the Actions panel, you will notice that the first section of code is gray and contains a description of the code that was written and some instructions for modifying it. All of the code snippets that ship with Flash CS5 come with comments like this that

Note: If you are used to playing the Flash Timeline by pressing Enter (Windows) or Return (Mac) or choosing Control > Play, then you should switch to Control > Test Movie > in Flash Professional or Control+Enter (Windows) or Command+Return (Mac). When you preview in this manner, your files will play in the same way as they will for your end users, with all of the ActionScript executing. From this point on, the instruction to test your movie refers to this method of previewing Flash files.

help you understand the ActionScript written by the code snippet. Comments will be discussed in more detail soon and are good elements to add to your own code as notes for yourself and others.

For now, follow the instructions in the code snippet to modify the URL in the ActionScript:

1 Locate the line that reads:

```
navigateToURL(new URLRequest("http://www.adobe.com"),
¬"_blank");
```

2 Modify the URL between the quotation marks to read:

```
http://www.adobe.com/support/flash
```

3 Test the movie by choosing Control > Test Movie > in Flash. This time when you click the button, you should be taken to the support section for Flash on the Adobe website. You can substitute any URL in this code, and clicking the button will cause the browser to navigate to that location.

By the end of these lessons, you will know the ActionScript necessary to write all of this code from scratch, and that knowledge will open infinite creative possibilities. In the meantime, you can use the actions available in the Code Snippets panel to immediately start adding interactivity to your projects. Using this panel will also aid in your learning process by giving you insight into how to create working code and how to modify it to suit your needs.

You will work with the Code Snippets panel again in the next lesson, but now you will begin to write your own ActionScript code.

Placing code on the Flash Timeline

Working with frame labels

Before you start adding ActionScript, notice that among the layers in the Timeline is one called labels. In this layer, Frame 2 has the label loop and Frame 50 has the label home. You can add labels to any keyframe on any timeline in Flash—labels can be very useful for identifying significant locations. ActionScript can reference labels to control navigation. If you haven't worked with labels before, you may want to practice adding an additional label to the Timeline on Frame 30:

1 In the labels layer of the Timeline, select Frame 30.

2 Add a keyframe to this frame by pressing F6 or choosing Insert > Timeline > Keyframe.

3 With the new keyframe selected, find the Label section in the upper-left corner of the Properties panel, and in the Name field, type **endLoop**. (If the Properties panel is not visible, open it by choosing Window > Properties.)

4 Press Enter (Windows) or Return (Mac). You will see the label name appear in the Timeline on Frame 30.

Looping playback with ActionScript

There are many situations in which you may want to play a section of the Timeline repeatedly. For example, an animation might loop while waiting for additional content to load or while the user is deciding which section of a website to go to next.

Creating looping animation

For your first foray into writing your own ActionScript, you will loop the animation that plays from Frame 2 to Frame 30. At first, you will write ActionScript that loops this section indefinitely, and then you will add code that controls the number of times that this section repeats before jumping to the home interface on Frame 50:

1 Arrange your work area so that both the Timeline and the Actions panel (Window > Actions) are visible.

2 In the `actions` layer, select Frame 30 and press F6 to add a new keyframe in that layer.

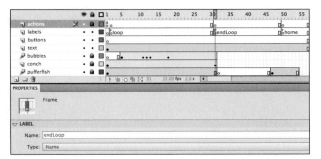

3 Select the new keyframe in the `actions` layer in Frame 30.

4 Click in the Actions panel so that the insertion point appears in Line 1 of the panel. If you do not see line numbers, you can turn them on by choosing Line Numbers from the Actions panel menu in the upper-right corner of the panel.

5 In the Actions panel, type the following code:

```
gotoAndPlay("loop");
```

6 Save your work and test your movie (Control+Enter in Windows or Command+Enter in Mac). Notice that the movie no longer reaches the home frame but instead plays the opening animation over and over. This behavior occurs because every time the playhead reaches Frame 30, the action you just wrote sends it back to Frame 2.

Using gotoAndStop() and gotoAndPlay()

The `gotoAndStop()` and `gotoAndPlay()` methods are about the most venerable ActionScript techniques available and have been virtually unchanged since Flash 2. In the code you just wrote, the ActionScript directs the playback head of the Timeline to go from the current frame to the frame labeled "loop" and continue to play the animation from that point. If instead you want to navigate to a specific frame and pause the Timeline at that location, you could use `gotoAndStop()`, which you will do in the next lesson. In between the parentheses, you could have chosen to use the number of the frame instead of the frame label, as shown here:

```
gotoAndPlay(2);
```

However, use of the frame label as you did in the previous example is highly recommended:

```
gotoAndPlay("loop");
```

This approach allows you to much more easily make changes to the content in your timeline without having to modify your code.

Keeping track of the number of loops

In the next section, you will program your file to jump to the home frame after a specific number of loops, but first you'll add some code to keep track of the number of times that the animation has played. You will do this by storing the value for the number of loops in a variable.

Creating a count variable

The purpose of a variable is to store a reference to data. ActionScript 3.0 can store references to many different types of data in variables, and you will create many of these in the coming lessons. In this lesson, you will create a variable to store a numeric value to keep track of the number of times the animation in Frames 2 through 30 repeats.

To create a variable in ActionScript 3.0, you type **var** and then the name you want to give to your new variable:

1 On the `actions` layer, select Frame 1 and then click in the Actions panel.

2 On a line below the existing code snippet, type the following code:

```
var count:Number = 1;
```

In the next task, you will add some code that changes that value every time the animation loops.

Creating variables in ActionScript 3.0

You will be creating many variables in the lessons to come, so it is worth taking a closer look at the syntax used.

Consider this example:

```
var count:Number = 1;
```

The keyword `var` tells ActionScript that you are creating a new variable. The name of the variable is `count`. You can choose any name you want for your own variables, as long as you follow these three rules:

- Do not use spaces in your variable names.

- Except for underscores, do not use special characters; stick to letters and numbers.

- Do not start your names with numbers. Thus, the variable name `2button` is not valid, but `button2` is fine.

The colon after the variable name indicates that the next piece of information will denote the type of data that will be stored in the variable. In this example, the `count` variable stores a number. You will learn more about data typing in the coming lessons.

An equal sign (=) indicates that what follows is the value to be stored in the variable. You do not need to give a value to a variable when you create it. Often a variable is created so that it can store information at a later time. In our example, the variable `count` is assigned an initial value of 1.

Updating the count variable

To change the value of the `count` variable on each loop, you add some code to change the value each time the animation finishes:

1 On the `actions` layer, select the keyframe on Frame 30.

2 Click in the Actions panel.

3 On a new line below the existing code, type the following code:

```
count++;
```

The characters ++ are a shorthand way in ActionScript to increase a value by 1. The code you just wrote loosely translates to "take the current value of the `count` variable and add 1 to it." The result is that the second time the animation plays, `count` will equal 2, the third time it plays, `count` will equal 3, and so on.

Displaying the count in a text field

At this point, you have a variable keeping track of the number of loops, but when the movie runs, you have no visual feedback telling you how many times the animation has looped. You will now add that feedback in a text field:

1 Select the text field that is onstage in the `text` layer. Notice in the Properties panel that this text field has been given the instance name `info_txt`. Again, it is essential that all objects onstage that will be controlled with ActionScript be given instance names.

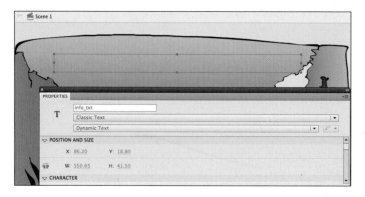

2 On the `actions` layer, select Frame 2, and add a keyframe by pressing F6.

3 With the new keyframe selected in the Timeline, click in the Actions panel.

4 Type the following code:

```
info_txt.text = String(count);
```

5 Save your work and test your movie. The text field should start by displaying the number 1, and this value should increase by 1 each time the animation loops.

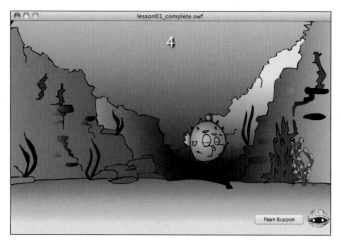

About text fields and strings

Text fields can have many of their properties set using ActionScript. They can even be created and formatted from scratch with ActionScript. You will learn much more about working with text in later lessons.

Consider this example:

```
info_txt.text = String(count);
```

The text field named info_txt has had its `text` property set to equal the current value of the variable `count`. The text field will be updated with the value of `count` each time the Timeline plays Frame 2.

A text field can display only data that is stored as literal text. Literal text in ActionScript belongs to the data type `String`. Because the `count` variable is set to store the data type `Number`, the last bit of code in the example,

```
String(count);
```

tells ActionScript to convert (or *recast*) the `count` number to a text string so that it can be displayed in a text field.

If this is a little confusing, don't worry. You will get plenty of practice with text and data typing in the coming lessons.

Using a conditional statement to control the Timeline

A project that just plays its introduction over and over is not ideal, so let's limit the number of times the introduction loops before jumping to the home frame. For a web project, you might want to set up an introduction that plays over and over until the next section is fully downloaded. You will learn how to create this type of preloader in Lesson 6, "Creating Preloaders in ActionScript 3.0." In this lesson, you will limit the number of times that the introduction plays by making the Timeline jump to the frame with the label home (Frame 50) when the count variable reaches a certain number.

You will accomplish this by adding a conditional statement to your code. A conditional statement in ActionScript checks to see if a condition is true. In this case, if the count variable is more than 4, then code will execute that goes to the home frame.

1 Make sure that both the Timeline and the Actions panel are visible and then select Frame 30 on the `actions` layer.

2 With Frame 30 selected, switch to the Actions panel. Place the insertion point before the code that is already in this window and press Enter (Windows) or Return (Mac).

3   Select and delete the line of code that reads:

```
gotoAndPlay("loop");
```

Then above the line that says count++; add the following code:

```
if(count>4) {
```

4   After typing this line, press Enter (Windows) or Return (Mac). Notice that when you do, Flash automatically adds a new line with a closing bracket for you. This code completion feature is new to Flash CS5 and is a convenience that helps you avoid the common mistake of forgetting to close the brackets of a block of code that needs to be contained within a pair of brackets.

5   Complete the conditional statement so that it reads as shown in the following screen.

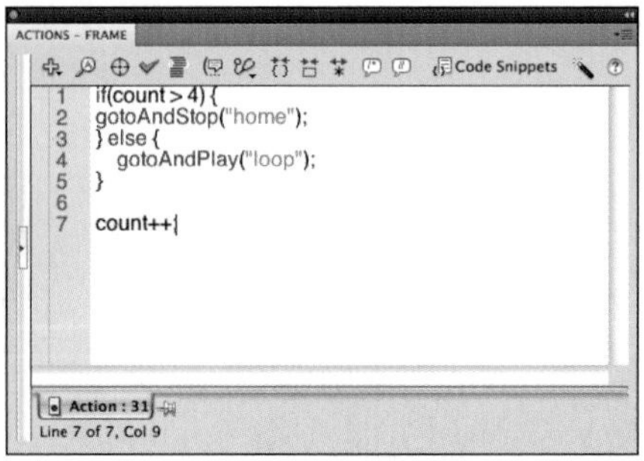

Now each time the animation finishes, the conditional statement checks to see if count has become greater than 4. On the first four loops, when the condition was not true, the playhead goes back to Frame 2 and replays the animation. After the fifth time the animation plays, the condition is true, so the playhead goes to, and stops on, the home frame.

6   Save your work and test your movie. The count should increase to 5 in the text field, and then the Timeline should jump to the home frame.

Updating the text on the home frame

Now you will change the text on the home frame. Since the user is no longer watching the animation loop on this frame, there is no reason anymore to display the count number. Instead, you will add a message to welcome the user to the home frame.

1   Make sure that both the Timeline and the Actions panel are visible and then select Frame 50 on the actions layer.

2   In the actions layer, add a keyframe to Frame 50 by pressing F6.

Conditional statements

Conditional statements are a major reason for the interactive power of ActionScript. They allow your Flash projects to respond differently under different circumstances.

Conditional statements are available in most programming languages and work similarly to the way they do in ActionScript 3.0. Even if you have no experience with programming languages, you are probably familiar with the concept of a conditional statement. You hear an almost-perfect example of one every time you interact with a voicemail system.

For example, you call your friend's house and hear a voicemail system that says:

If you want John, press one,

or,

if you want Mary, press two,

or,

leave a message after the beep.

In ActionScript, the same interaction would look like this:

```
If (wantJohn) {
        pressOne();
} else if(wantMary) {
        pressTwo();
} else {
        leaveMessage()
}
```

Here are some examples of conditions you might want to respond to with ActionScript:

- If a question on a quiz has been answered correctly, then go to the next question.
- If a level of a game has been completed, then update the score and go to the next level.
- If a product has been dragged to the shopping cart, then add its cost to the total purchase and ship the product.

3 Add the following code to the Actions panel for this frame:

```
info_txt.text = "Welcome to the home frame";
```

This code uses the same text field that you used before, but instead of using the count variable to populate the text field, you use the literal words "Welcome to the home frame." When you want to set the text property of a text field to literal words, you enclose the characters you want to use in quotation marks.

4 Test your movie once more; you should see the updated text on the home frame.

Although the application you just created is very simple, it introduced a number of essential ActionScript concepts. Storing and passing data with variables and responding to changing circumstances by using conditional statements are both critical elements in the creation of rich interactivity with ActionScript 3.0. You will be working with these techniques often in the lessons to come.

In the next lesson, you will learn how to respond to events in ActionScript 3.0 by using buttons to add some functionality to the file you created in this lesson.

Some suggestions to try on your own

To get comfortable with the techniques introduced in this chapter, you can try some of the following techniques:

- Change the number of times that the opening animation repeats by altering the conditional statement.

- Change the code on Frame 50 to display different text in the info_txt field.

- Add a new text field to the Stage. Give it an instance name and try to write some ActionScript that will place text in that field.

- In a new file, explore some of the other ActionScript that can be created with the Code Snippets panel. Experiment with modifying this code. Remember that if you cause the code to stop functioning, you can always reset the code snippet.

Review questions

1   What ActionScript code would you use to navigate to a specific frame of the Timeline?

2   What is the keyword that you use to create a new ActionScript variable?

3   What is the purpose of a conditional statement in ActionScript?

Review answers

1   To navigate to a specific frame of the Timeline, you would use `gotoAndPlay()` or
    `gotoAndStop()`. The value between the parentheses describes the specific frame to
    which you want to navigate. For example:

    ```
    gotoAndPlay(1);
    ```

    ```
    gotoAndPlay("home");
    ```

2   A line of ActionScript that creates a variable begins with the keyword `var`.

3   A conditional statement lets you check to see if a condition or conditions are true and,
    if so, execute blocks of code. If the condition is false, you can execute an alternative
    block of code.

2 WORKING WITH EVENTS AND FUNCTIONS

Lesson overview

In this lesson, you will learn to do the following:

- Use code snippets to create ActionScript that navigates the Flash Timeline in response to button clicks.

- Add code to a function created by a code snippet.

- Write event listeners to listen for mouse events.

- Write event-handling functions that respond to mouse events.

- Combine strings of text with variable values to populate a text field.

- Create and call a function that sets the language in a text field.

- Use buttons to change the value of a variable.

 This lesson will take approximately 2 hours.

In the previous lesson, you created code directly in frames of the Timeline that ran automatically when the frame containing the code played. You also began working with events when you added the code snippet to the Lesson 1 file. In this lesson, you will get a deeper understanding of events in ActionScript. Understanding the event model in ActionScript 3.0 is probably the biggest step in mastering the basics of the language and being able to create rich interactive applications.

ActionScript 3.0 has many built-in events, and many actions can occur when an event takes place. A large part of learning ActionScript is learning what events are available and determining how to respond when an event takes place. And as you get more comfortable with ActionScript, you can create your own custom events.

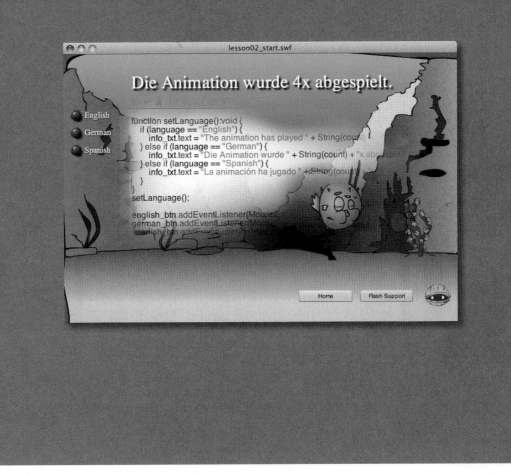

ActionScript events and functions create more
interactive possibilities for you and your users.

The process of working with events is not complex. You write code that tells an object to listen for an event, and you write a function that occurs in response to that event. Unlike in ActionScript 1 and 2, the basic syntax for listening and responding to events is the same throughout ActionScript 3.0. However, mastering this syntax can challenge many beginners. The good news is that in Flash CS5, you can use the Code Snippets panel to write the syntax to create basic event listeners. This panel also provides a terrific way to become familiar with ActionScript syntax.

In this lesson, you will first use code snippets to write an event listener that navigates the Flash Timeline when a button is clicked. You will then gradually transition to writing your own event listener functions.

Working with event-handling functions

Listening to and responding to an event in ActionScript is a two-part process. One piece of code, called an `addEventListener()` method, gives the instruction to listen for a specific event from a particular object. Another piece of code, called an *event-handler function*, responds when that event takes place.

For example, if you have a button onstage, you might want it to do three things:

- Display a menu when the user rolls over the button.

- Hide the menu when the user rolls off the button.

- Navigate to a frame on the Timeline when the user clicks the button.

This example uses only one button, but there are three separate events to listen for (ROLL_OVER, ROLL_OUT, and CLICK), and three separate sets of actions that may occur, depending on which event took place.

For the first event in our example, if the instance name of the button were button1, you would tell ActionScript to listen for the ROLL_OVER event, like this:

```
button1.addEventListener(MouseEvent.ROLL_OVER, showMenu);
```

There would be a similar line of code for the ROLL_OUT and CLICK events.

You use an `addEventListener` method to tell an object in ActionScript 3.0 to begin listening for a specific event. Once `addEventListener` is called, it continues to listen until it is removed. The first element inside the parentheses of the `addEventListener` method indicates which event to listen for. In this case, from the category MouseEvent, we are specifically listening for ROLL_OVER. Notice that the actual event names are all uppercase with underscores between words. The convention of using the uppercase constants for event names may give you a little extra to remember when you are beginning, but it also helps identify errors when compiling the files and is worth the effort to memorize.

After the event name, and separated by a comma, is the name of the function that occurs when the ROLL_OVER event takes place. A *function* is just a block of code that performs one or more, usually related, tasks. An *event-handler function* is one that responds to an event.

Functions can be created and given any name that you like, following the same three rules that we saw for naming variables in Lesson 1, "Using Code Snippets and Navigating the Flash Timeline." In the example, the function name is showMenu. It is a good idea to name functions so that they describe what they are supposed to do.

Reviewing the naming rules in ActionScript

Remember that when you are naming variables, functions, classes, and instances in ActionScript, you should follow these three rules:

- Use only letters, numbers, and underscores in your names; avoid other special characters.
- Do not begin a name with a number.
- Avoid spaces in your names; use underscores rather than spaces.

The basic syntax for our function looks like this:

```
function showMenu(e:MouseEvent):void {
//all the ActionScript to show the menu would go here between the
//left and right curly braces.
}
```

When creating a function in ActionScript 3.0, always start with the lowercase word function and then the name you choose to give your function. After that, you add a set of parentheses that contains what are called *parameters*. You will work with parameters more in the coming lessons; for now, it is enough to know that the required parameter for an event-handling function contains a reference to the event that triggered the function.

After the parentheses, a colon precedes information about the type of data that the function returns. In this case, void means that the function does not return data. You will learn much more about functions in coming lessons.

After that, a pair of curly braces contains all the code that will take place each time an event triggers the function.

If all this is not absolutely clear, don't worry. After a little practice, it begins to make more and more sense, and pretty soon the process will be second nature. And the payoff will be worth it. As already mentioned, becoming comfortable working with

Note: ActionScript is always case sensitive. You may notice in the function and variable names in this book and other places the odd convention of starting with a lowercase character and then beginning subsequent words in the name with uppercase characters, as in showMenu(). While this convention is by no means required, it is a common programming practice, sometimes referred to as "camel case," that helps indicate what type of item is being dealt with. You may want to consider adopting this convention in your work.

event listeners and event-handling functions is probably the biggest step in learning ActionScript 3.0, and the technique is consistent through the entire language. So what you learn in this lesson will be your entryway into many of the interactive possibilities with ActionScript 3.0.

As you saw in Lesson 1, code snippets can be used to create functions that respond to mouse events. You will begin this lesson by using a code snippet that creates an `eventListener` function that navigates the Flash Timeline when a button is clicked. After this, you will gradually make the transition to writing `eventListener` code yourself.

In your own work, you may prefer to continue to use code snippets as a starting point, or you may find that you can eventually work more efficiently by typing your code yourself.

Using code snippets to create navigation

This lesson will start with the file from Lesson 1. You can start this exercise with your completed version of that file; otherwise, in Flash CS5, open the lesson02_start.fla file in the Lessons > Lesson02 > Start folder.

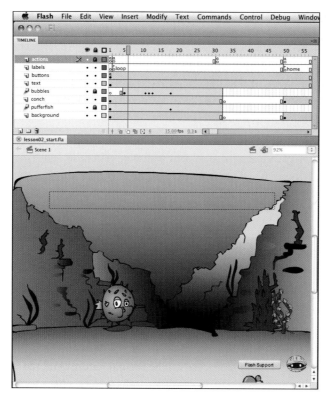

Creating button instances to control navigation

For many simple Flash web projects, most interactivity consists of navigation triggered by button clicks. The ability to write ActionScript that responds to a button CLICK event is also the foundation for understanding much of the rest of the ActionScript language, since all other ActionScript events work in similar ways.

To get you started with this important functionality, Flash CS5 ships with a collection of code snippets that write code to create timeline navigation triggered by button clicks. You will soon use one of these snippets, after we add a new button to the project.

1 In the Flash Timeline, select Frame 1 of the buttons layer.

2 If it is not already visible, open the Library panel (Window > Library).

3 From the Library panel, drag an instance of the Button component and place it next to the existing Flash Support button at the lower-right corner of the Stage.

4 Select the new button onstage, and in the Component Parameters section of Property inspector (Window > Properties), locate the label property.

5 In the field to the right of the label property, type **Home** and press Enter (Windows) or Return (Mac).

   You should see the label on the button update to "Home." You will use this button to allow the user to navigate to the home frame.

   Now give the button an instance name.

6 With the Home button selected, go to the Property inspector, place the cursor in the instance name field, and give the button the instance name **home_btn**.

> **Note:** Instance names follow the naming rules already discussed for variables and functions.

The importance of instance names

It is essential to give an instance name to all onstage buttons, movie clips, and other objects that you wish to control with ActionScript. One of the most common mistakes made by new ActionScript programmers is writing their code correctly but forgetting to give their objects instance names. Checking your instance names is often a good place to start when troubleshooting code that is not working.

Adding a code snippet for navigation

The intended purpose of the Home button you just added is to allow the user to jump to the frame of the Timeline labeled home when the button is clicked. You can use the Code Snippets panel to add some code to make this work.

1 If they are not already visible, open the Actions panel (Window > Actions) and the Code Snippets panel (Window > Code Snippets).

2 In the Timeline, select Frame 2 of the Actions panel. This is the frame where you will place the code snippet.

About code in the Timeline

In the first two lessons, you are placing code in multiple frames of the Flash Timeline. This is a common technique in simple Flash websites. However, for more complex projects, many ActionScript developers often avoid putting ActionScript in multiple frames but instead try to write all of their ActionScript in a single frame or use external ActionScript files with no timeline code at all. As you get comfortable enough with ActionScript to make these choices, you can determine what works best for you and for each individual project. You will learn how to work with external ActionScript files in Lesson 4, "Creating ActionScript in External Files," and you will create an interactive project that loads content into a single frame in Lesson 5, "Using ActionScript and Components to Load Content."

3 On the Stage, select the button with the label Home. Remember that this button has been given the instance name home_btn.

4 In the Code Snippets panel, open the Timeline Navigation folder and double-click the snippet named Click To Go To Frame And Stop.

CODE SNIPPETS

▶ ☐ Actions
▼ ☐ Timeline Navigation
　☐ Stop at this Frame
　☐ Click to Go To Frame and Stop
　☐ Click to Go To Frame and Play
　☐ Click to Go to Next Frame and Stop
　☐ Click to Go to Previous Frame and Stop
　☐ Click to Go to Next Scene and Play
　☐ Click to Go to Previous Scene and Play
　☐ Click to Go to Scene and Play
▶ ☐ Animation
▶ ☐ Load and Unload
▶ ☐ Audio and Video
▶ ☐ Event Handlers

You should now see the following code in the Actions panel below the code that was already there:

```
/* Click to Go to Frame and Stop
Clicking on the specified symbol instance moves the playhead
¬to the specified frame in the timeline and stops the movie.
Can be used on the main timeline or on movie clip timelines.

Instructions:
1. Replace the number 5 in the code below with the frame
¬number you would like the playhead to move to when the symbol
¬instance is clicked.
*/


home_btn.addEventListener(MouseEvent.CLICK,
fl_ClickToGoToAndStopAtFrame);

function fl_ClickToGoToAndStopAtFrame(event:MouseEvent):void {
  gotoAndStop(5);
}
```

The code snippet that was created added an event listener for the Home button instance. Now, when the button is clicked it will automatically call the function that is somewhat verbosely named fl_ClickToGoToAndStopAtFrame (changing the function name in a code snippet does not modify its behavior, and you will change this function's name in the next section).

When a function is called, all the code between the curly braces is executed. In this case, that means that when the user clicks the Home button, the function will send the Timeline to Frame 5. The goto action is the same as we used in Lesson 1. The only difference is that now it is triggered by a button event. You will modify the frame that this function navigates to in the next section.

Modifying the code snippet

Code snippets provide a very easy way to create correct ActionScript syntax, but rarely does any given code snippet perform exactly the function that you want. More typically, you choose that snippet that most closely matches your needs and then customize the code to suit your purpose. You will make a few modifications to the code snippet you just created to make it perform the way you want and make it easier to read.

Remember that the light gray characters in the code snippet are descriptive and nonfunctional comments. If you read the Instruction comments, you will see that to make this code navigate to a desired frame, you replace the number 5 in the line that reads

```
gotoAndStop(5);
```

with a reference to the frame that you actually want the user to go to. One way to do this is to simply replace the 5 with a different number. In the case of the home frame, this would be Frame 50. However, a better way to refer to this frame in the code would be by its label name. Using label names instead of frame numbers in your scripts makes it much easier to make changes to the content in the frames of your Timeline without having to modify your code. You use frame labels in a `goto` method by typing the label name in quotation marks between the parentheses that now contain the number 5.

1 In the Actions panel, modify the line that reads:

```
gotoAndStop(5);
```

so that it now reads:

```
gotoAndStop("home");
```

2 Save your work and test your movie (Control > Test Movie). If you click the Home button while the opening animation is playing, the Timeline should skip directly to the home frame.

3 Close the lesson02_start.swf file to leave the testing environment.

You can see how easy it is to modify the code snippet to achieve the desired navigation.

It would be no problem to leave this code as it is in your project. However, a couple of additional modifications to the code snippet will make it easier to work with as your project develops.

One change you may wish to make to the code snippet is renaming the function. Right now the function has the long and generic name fl_ClickToGoToAndStopAtFrame. It is a good practice to name your functions in a way that describes their specific purpose. Let's change the snippet's default function name to the shorter and more descriptive name goHome. You will need to change this name in two places: in the addEventListener method and in the function itself.

4 In the Actions panel, locate the line that reads:

```
home_btn.addEventListener(MouseEvent.CLICK,
¬fl_ClickToGoToAndStopAtFrame);
```

5 Change this line to:

```
home_btn.addEventListener(MouseEvent.CLICK, goHome);
```

6 Next locate the line that reads:

```
function fl_ClickToGoToAndStopAtFrame(event:MouseEvent):
¬void {
```

7 Change this line to:

```
function goHome(event:MouseEvent):void {
```

Changing the function name in this way has no effect on the code's behavior, but it does make it more succinct and easier to understand.

After you have used a code snippet a few times and understand the included comments (in gray), you may want to delete the comments; doing so does not affect the behavior of the code.

8 Delete the comments.

Here is the code so far for Frame 2 with comments removed:

```
info_txt.text = String(count);

home_btn.addEventListener(MouseEvent.CLICK, goHome);

function goHome(e:MouseEvent):void {
  gotoAndStop("home");
}
```

As you get more comfortable with ActionScript, you will probably want to make a few additional modifications to this code to make it still easier to read, but for now let's move on.

Having successfully created button navigation with a code snippet, you will now try creating similar code by typing it yourself.

Creating event listeners

Although code snippets are convenient, to get the most out of ActionScript 3.0 it is important to be thoroughly confident in your understanding of basic ActionScript syntax. This competence comes only with time, study, and practice. Once you have mastered the syntax for an ActionScript task, you may still find that code snippets are often a great time-saving tool. Now, though, it's time to begin writing ActionScript code on your own. You'll start by creating another event listener, writing your own code from scratch.

Adding a restart button

Now let's add some functionality on the home page to enable the user to restart the animation.

1   Add a keyframe (F6) to the `buttons` layer on the home frame.

2   Click somewhere on the Stage away from the two buttons to deselect them, and then select just the Home button.

3   With the Home button selected, go to the Property inspector (Window > Properties) and change the label name from Home to **Restart**.

4   Also in the Property inspector, with the button still selected, change the button's instance name from `home_btn` to `restart_btn`.

5   With the Actions panel visible, select the home frame of the `actions` layer.

6   Add the following code in the Actions panel below the existing code:

```
restart_btn.addEventListener(MouseEvent.CLICK, goStart);
```

Note: It doesn't matter how many empty lines you place between sections of your code. Many programmers like to leave space between sections of code for clarity; others like to keep things concise by starting new blocks of code on every line. As you start to get comfortable with ActionScript, you will find a style that you prefer.

Be careful to match the capitalization exactly, and notice that `addEventListener` and `MouseEvent.CLICK` turn blue when typed correctly. The color-coding of ActionScript as you type provides useful feedback to let you know you are typing things correctly. Keywords in ActionScript 3.0 turn blue by default. If you type something that is part of the ActionScript language and it appears as black text, double-check your spelling and capitalization.

After this code has been added, when the Restart button is clicked it will try to call a function named `goStart`. So, let's add this function to make the code work.

7   In the Actions panel, on a line below the code you just added, insert the following code:

```
function goStart(e:MouseEvent):void {
count=1;
gotoAndPlay("loop");
}
```

This function will be the one that responds to a click of the Restart button. When the function is called, the Timeline will be sent back to the beginning of the animation, and the variable count will be reset to 1. Remember that count is the variable that keeps track of the number of times that the opening animation has played, so by setting count to 1, you are restarting the movie with its initial setting.

8 Save your work and test your movie.

When you reach the home frame in the testing environment, the button that previously said "Home" should now say "Restart." The Restart button should respond to the code you added by replaying the opening animation, with the button again reading "Home." Notice that the Flash Support button works the same throughout. Because you did not change its instance name, it always responds to the listener and function that you created for it on Frame 1.

If everything is working, congratulations! You are well on your way to being comfortable with ActionScript 3.0. If you had problems with your code, compare it carefully with the example code. If there are errors in the code, the Output panel should appear with descriptions of the errors, and it will show on which lines they appear. Note which line numbers contain the errors, and check your spelling and the color-coding of your ActionScript on those lines. Especially make note of capitalization, and be sure that the instance names of your buttons match the names in your event listeners.

Modifying the text field dynamically

Right now, when your movie loops over the opening animation, the text field is instructed to display the number representing the number of times the animation has played. The number is currently accurate, but the user feedback is not elegant.

Let's make the information in the text field more useful by adding some prose to the field to make a complete sentence.

1 With the Actions panel and the Timeline visible, select the loop frame (Frame 2) in the actions layer of the Timeline.

2 In the Actions panel, change the code that currently reads:

```
info_txt.text = String(count);
```

so that it reads:

```
info_txt.text = "The animation has played " + String(count) +
¬"x.";
```

The plus signs are used to concatenate (or join) the literal text (in quotation marks) with the value of the count variable to form a sentence.

3 Save your work and test the movie once more. The text field should now read "The animation has played 1x (2x, 3x, and so on)."

Adding buttons to control language

To solidify what you've covered so far, add a few more buttons to the Stage to let the user control the language that is displayed in the text field. You will begin by adding a variable that keeps track of the user's language choice and sets a default language to the first frame of the movie.

1 With the Actions panel and the Timeline visible, select Frame 1 of the actions layer.

2 Add the following code below the existing code:

```
var language:String = "English";
```

Now you'll add code that checks the value of the language variable before adding text to the text field.

3 With the Actions panel and the Timeline visible, select Frame 2 of the actions layer.

4 In the Actions panel on Frame 2, select the line of code that reads:

```
info_txt.text = "The animation has played " + String(count) +
¬ "x.";
```

and cut it (Control+X for Windows or Command+X for Mac) to the clipboard.

5 Place the cursor in the Actions panel below the final line of existing code.

6 Create a new function to check which language has been set by adding the following code in the Actions panel:

```
function setLanguage():void {
 if(language == "English") {
 }
}
```

7 In the line above the first right curly brace (}), paste the code that you cut, so that the function now reads:

```
function setLanguage():void {
 if(language == "English") {
 info_txt.text = "The animation has played " + String(count) +
 ¬ "x.";
 }
}
```

When the function is called, it will now check to see if the language variable is set to "English" (which is the default because of the code you added in step 2). If the language is English, then the text field will display your message.

Soon you will add buttons that will let the user choose German or Spanish as well as English, so let's put those two additional possibilities into the conditional statement.

8 Add to the setLanguage() function so that it reads:

```
function setLanguage():void {
 if(language == "English") {
  info_txt.text = "The animation has played " + String(count)
  ¬ + "x.";
 } else if(language == "German") {
  info_txt.text = "Die Animation wurde " + String(count) +
  ¬ "x abgespielt." ;
 } else if(language == "Spanish") {
  info_txt.text = "La animación ha jugado " + String(count)
  ¬ + "x." ;
 }
}
```

Note: The conditional statement in the setLanguage() function checks to see if the language has been set to English. Note that it performs this comparison by using two equals signs (==).

In ActionScript 3.0, you check to see if one value matches another value with two equals signs. In this case, you are checking to see if language is equal to "English."

It is especially important to remember to use two equals signs when comparing values, because a single equals sign (=) is what is used to set one value to equal another. In other words, a single equals sign in this example would be used to set language to English, not to check to see if language is English.

Note: In a Flash project that has large amounts of content for different languages, the translations will more likely be stored in an external location, such as an XML file, and loaded into Flash at runtime. You will learn about working with external XML files in later lessons.

Unlike the functions that we created earlier, the setLanguage() function is not an event-handler function, meaning it is not intended to respond to a specific type of event. This is because this function needs to run at the very start of the application as well as any time the user changes the language selection.

To call this type of freestanding function, you just refer to it by name and add a pair of parentheses after the name. If there were any parameters to pass to the function, they would go between the parentheses. This particular function does not have any parameters.

9 In the Actions panel, select the line after the setLanguage() function.

10 Call the setLanguage() function, so it sets the text correctly at the beginning of the animation loop, by typing the following code:

```
setLanguage();
```

Finally, you will add buttons that let the user change the language.

11 Select Frame 1 of the buttons layer in the Timeline.

12 In the Library panel (Window > Library), you will see three buttons named English Button, German Button, and Spanish Button. Drag one instance of each button to the upper-left corner of the Stage. These are just stock buttons with some text added to them.

13 In the Properties panel, name the instances of the new buttons **english_btn**, **german_btn**, and **spanish_btn**, respectively.

14 Continuing in Frame 2 of the actions layer, add a listener to each button by typing the following code below the last line that you added:

```
english_btn.addEventListener(MouseEvent.CLICK, setEnglish);
german_btn.addEventListener(MouseEvent.CLICK, setGerman);
spanish_btn.addEventListener(MouseEvent.CLICK, setSpanish);
```

When one of these three buttons is clicked, it needs to do two things:

- Set the language variable to the language that was chosen.
- Call the setLanguage() function, which will change the contents of the text field.

Remember, the conditional statement in the setLanguage() function uses the value of the language variable to determine what gets written in the text field.

15 On the lines below the listeners you just created, add the following code:

```
function setEnglish(e:MouseEvent):void {
language = "English";
setLanguage();
}
function setGerman(e:MouseEvent):void {
language = "German";
setLanguage();
}
function setSpanish(e:MouseEvent):void {
language = "Spanish";
setLanguage();
}
```

16 Save your work and test your movie.

The text field will always display English first. While the opening animation is playing, you should be able to use the new buttons to switch the contents of the text field between English, German, and Spanish. If you click the Restart button, the currently selected language should be retained until it is changed (by clicking a different button).

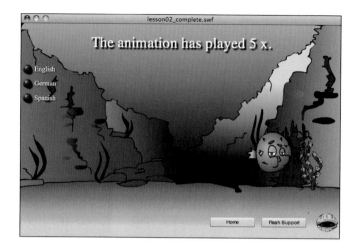

Some suggestions to try on your own

If you made it all the way through this lesson, congratulations! You can now consider yourself a serious student of ActionScript, and you may be amazed at what you can accomplish using just the techniques we have covered in these first two lessons.

To practice and become more comfortable with the techniques covered in this lesson, you can try to add a few more features to the lesson02_start.fla file. Here are some examples:

- Add additional languages. This will involve adding new buttons, as well as new listeners and functions, to the existing ActionScript. Use any languages that you happen to know, use a translation site such as www.freetranslation.com, or just make up your own translation.

- Translate the text in the home frame. Right now you have translated only the content of the text field during the opening animation, but you could write a similar function for the text in the home frame to translate that text based on the language the user chooses.

- Using ActionScript similar to what you added on the Flash Support button, add buttons with links to other URLs.

- Using ActionScript similar to what you added on the Home button, add buttons that go to and stop at specific frames or go to and play specific frames of the animation.

Review questions

1 Describe how the addEventListener() method is used in ActionScript 3.0.

2 What is one way to describe a mouse click in the addEventListener() method?

3 Which character is used in ActionScript 3.0 to join or concatenate strings of text and variable names?

4 What is the syntax for checking to see if one value is equal to another? What is the syntax for setting a variable to a given value?

Review answers

1 The addEventListener() method is used to listen for a specific event on a specific object and to respond to that event by calling an event-handling function.

2 In an addEventListener() method, a mouse click could be described as MouseEvent.CLICK, as in:

```
Button1.addEventListener(MouseEvent.CLICK, doSomething);
```

3 The plus sign (+) is used to concatenate text with evaluated code. This is commonly used to set the text property of a dynamic text field. Here is an example:

```
someTextField.text = "Hello" + userName;
```

4 Two equals signs are used to compare values to see if they are the same, as in:

```
if(password == 3456789) {
 enterSafely();
}
```

A single equals sign is used to set the value of a variable, as in:

```
var firstUSPresident:String = "Washington";
```

3 CREATING ANIMATION WITH ACTIONSCRIPT

Lesson overview

In this lesson, you will learn to do the following:

- Change the properties of a movie clip using ActionScript.
- Use the ENTER_FRAME event to animate movie clip properties.
- Use a conditional statement to detect Stage boundaries.
- Use a variable to store a reference to a movie clip.
- Use buttons to control property changes.
- Use the Tween and easing classes to animate movie clip properties.
- Create custom reusable code snippets.

This lesson will take approximately 2 hours.

Flash has always been a great animation tool, and Flash CS5 includes many animation capabilities, including 3D animation, built-in inverse kinematics with springing, and a robust Motion Editor. When you are creating a cartoon or some other type of linear animation, the Flash Timeline and interface offer great and easy-to-use animation features. However, by learning to control animation with ActionScript, you can create animation that is very interactive and responsive. This capability is essential in most game development and also in training applications, simulations, and creative interface design.

The previous lesson introduced event listeners and event-handling functions. This lesson assumes that you are familiar with adding listeners and functions to respond to mouse clicks. To review these techniques, see Lesson 2, "Working with Events and Functions."

Lesson 3 project interface.

Reviewing the starting file

This lesson will use the lesson03_start.fla file from the Lessons > Lesson03 > Start folder.

Open the file and look at the contents. Onstage there are four movie clips that contain static graphics of musical instruments. Notice that these movie clips have instance names of `violin`, `trumpet`, `banjo`, and `glock`. There is also a movie clip of a star with the instance name of `star_mc`.

● **Note:** Flash CS5 has an entirely new text engine that uses Adobe's Text Layout Framework (TLF). TLF offers many new text formatting and layout capabilities. TLF text is now the default text type for Flash CS5 projects. With the `instrument_txt` field instance selected, notice in the Property inspector that the text type is set to TLF. The type of text that was available in older versions of Flash is now known as Classic Text and is still available as an option in the Property inspector. The new text features in Flash will be examined more closely in Lesson 8.

In addition, the `text` layer has a single text field with the instance name of `instrument_txt`, and the `buttons` layer has a row of buttons, each with a descriptive instance name.

Right now, there is no ActionScript in this file, but we'll change that very soon. In Frame 1 of the `actions` layer, you will add ActionScript to bring some animation into this project.

Controlling movie clip properties with ActionScript

Most Flash designers are used to working with movie clip symbols in the Flash interface. All of the features that can be accessed for movie clips in the Flash interface can also be controlled with ActionScript. You can even create new movie clips from scratch in ActionScript. By using ActionScript in addition to or instead of the Flash interface, you can create many more interactive possibilities in your projects.

For example, it is very easy to control the properties of a movie clip or any display object (more on display objects soon) with ActionScript.

The basic syntax to change any property of a movie clip is to type the path to the clip's instance name, then a dot, followed by the property name that you want to change, and then an equals sign (=), followed by the new value, like this:

```
movieClipInstanceName.propertyName = value;
```

For example, if you have a movie clip with an instance name of `clip1` and you want to rotate it 90 degrees, the code would read:

```
clip1.rotation = 90;
```

If you know the possible properties that you can control and their range of values, then this simple technique can accomplish quite a bit. For the full range of properties and values, see Flash CS5 Help. The following table contains a few of the most common properties and their ranges.

Note: The Flash Stage is measured from the upper-left corner. A movie clip with an x position of 0 means that the registration point of the clip is on the exact left of the Stage. A position of 0 for the y value means that the clip is at the top of the Stage. Values greater than zero for x and y refer to positions to the right and down, respectively. Negative x and y values indicate positions offstage to the left and above the Stage.

Common properties and their ranges

PROPERTY	VALUES	DESCRIPTION
x	–infinity to +infinity	Horizontal position
y	–infinity to +infinity	Vertical position
rotation	–180 to 180 (degrees)*	Rotation
alpha	0 to 1 (0 = transparent, 1 = opaque)	Transparency
scaleX	–infinity to +infinity	Horizontal scale
scaleY	–infinity to +infinity	Vertical scale
visible	true (visible) or false (invisible)	Visibility

*For the `rotation` property, you can use any number, but ActionScript will convert it to the range –180 to +180 degrees.

Changing a property value

You will now use ActionScript to change the horizontal position of the `star_mc` movie clip.

1 With the Timeline and Actions panel both visible, select Frame 1 of the `actions` layer.

2 Click to place the insertion point inside the Actions panel, and type the following code:

```
star_mc.x = 275;
```

3 Save and test the movie. The star clip should appear in the center of the Stage horizontally.

Now we'll change a few other properties of the star.

Note: Transparency and most values that are measured in percentages usually range from 0 to 1 in ActionScript 3.0, rather than from 0 to 100. The scaleX and scaleY properties are designated similarly: A scale value of 1 means that the object is set to 100 percent of its original size; a scale value of 2 means that it's set to 200 percent, or twice its original size; and a value of .5 means that it's set to 50 percent, or half its original size.

4   Add the following below the code you just inserted:

```
star_mc.rotation = 90;
star_mc.alpha = .5;
```

5   Save and test the movie. The star should appear rotated and 50 percent transparent.

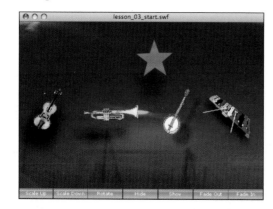

Increasing or decreasing a property's value

Rather than setting a property to a specific value, you can add to or subtract from the property's current value. For example, rather than rotating the star by 90 degrees, you could write code that would take the current amount of rotation and add to or subtract from it.

Let's create some code that adds five degrees to the star's rotation every time it's clicked.

Note: If you have completed the first two lessons, you should be comfortable adding event listeners for MouseEvent.CLICK using the Code Snippets panel. Feel free to continue to use code snippets when CLICK events are called for in the lessons. However, to become more confident with ActionScript syntax, you may find it more helpful to begin typing this code yourself. Unless otherwise stated, the lessons from this point on assume that you are writing the example code from scratch.

In your own work, continue to use code snippets any time that they are helpful to you. At the end of this lesson, you will learn how to create your own code snippets so that you can reuse chunks of your own customized code.

1   Select and delete all the code that you typed in the Actions panel and replace it with the following:

```
star_mc.addEventListener(MouseEvent.CLICK, rotateStar);
function rotateStar(e:MouseEvent):void {
  star_mc.rotation += 5;
}
```

2   Save and test the movie. Each time you click the star, it should rotate an additional five degrees.

Note: Using += is a shorthand way of saying "take the current value of the object on the left and add the value on the right to it." The longhand way to do the same would be:

```
star_mc.rotation = star_mc.rotation + 5;
```

Using an ENTER_FRAME event to animate a movie clip property

Now that you know how to increment a movie clip property, all you need to do to create animation is to increment the property repeatedly at a speed fast enough to make the eye believe that the object is moving.

Because the Flash Timeline moves at a default frame rate that is intended to move graphics fast enough to fool the human eye, creating code that repeats at that frame rate is an easy way to create animation.

The ENTER_FRAME event is ideal for this purpose. The ENTER_FRAME event occurs repeatedly while a Flash movie is playing, even when there is only a single frame in the Timeline.

The process for creating an ENTER_FRAME event listener and function is similar to the process you have already followed for a mouse event.

Try using the ENTER_FRAME event to animate the horizontal position of the star clip using its x property.

1 Below the existing code in the actions layer, add the following code:

```
addEventListener(Event.ENTER_FRAME, starMove);
function starMove(e:Event):void {
 star_mc.x += 2;
}
```

2 Save and test the movie. The star should now move slowly from left to right. It should also still rotate five degrees each time it is clicked.

   At this point, when your movie runs, the star will continue to move to the right off into infinite virtual space. Once it is offstage, it is no longer visible, so let's add some code to keep the star within the Stage bounds. You will add a conditional statement that checks to see if the star has gone offstage to the right.

3 Close the lesson03_start.swf file to return to the authoring environment.

4 Modify the code from step 1 so that it reads:

```
addEventListener(Event.ENTER_FRAME, starMove);
function starMove(e:Event):void {
 if (star_mc.x < stage.stageWidth) {
  star_mc.x += 2;
 } else {
  star_mc.x = 0;
 }
}
```

5 Save and test the movie once more.

Now, as long as the star is still within the bounds of the Stage, it will continue to move to the right, but if the conditional statement detects that the star's horizontal position is greater than the `stageWidth` value, then the star will be moved back to the far left to begin again. This will keep the animation visible and playing forever.

Notice the syntax that describes the width of the Stage: `stage.stageWidth`. The Stage height can be described similarly, with the syntax `stage.stageHeight`. Both `stageWidth` and `stageHeight` are useful properties of the Stage.

6 Close the lesson03_start.swf file to return to the authoring environment.

Creating a variable to store a movie clip reference

In this section, you will create code to make the buttons at the bottom of the Stage change the properties of the four instruments. Which instrument the user selects determines which movie clip the buttons affect. You will achieve this interactivity by creating a variable to keep track of which instrument the user clicked most recently.

● **Note:** The automatic insertion of `import` statements works with the code hints setting in the Flash preferences. If your version of Flash CS5 does not automatically create this or any other `import` statements for you, do not worry. You will be specifically instructed to type any `import` statements needed for the lesson files to work. Any others that may or may not be automatically added are optional. For more information on Flash Preference settings, see Flash Help.

1 On a new line below the existing code in Frame 1 of the `actions` layer, add a new variable called `instrument`:

```
var instrument:MovieClip = banjo;
```

When creating a variable, you set the data type by typing a colon after the variable's name and then indicating the type of data that will be stored in this variable. Notice that the data type of this variable is set to `MovieClip`. This means that the value of `instrument` will always be a reference to a movie clip.

Notice that after you typed the last line of code, Flash may have automatically added this line to your Actions panel:

```
import flash.display.MovieClip;
```

This automatic insertion of `import` statements is a new feature added in Flash CS5. Any time you create a variable of a certain data type for the first time, Flash imports the class that describes that data type (you will learn more about classes in the next lesson). In previous versions of Flash, these `import` statements needed to be typed manually. Although this new auto-insertion is a great convenience, you will see soon that there are still situations in Flash CS5 in which you need to type an `import` statement manually.

The instrument variable you just created was given a default value of `banjo`. If you prefer a different default instrument (but who wouldn't choose the banjo?), feel free to set the value of the variable to the instance name of one of the other instruments.

Next, give the user some feedback in the text field to show which instrument is selected.

2 Below the existing code in the Actions panel, supply some information to the user by setting the `text` property of the text field whose instance name is `instrument_txt`.

```
instrument_txt.text = "The Banjo has been selected.";
```

3 Save and test the movie. You should see "The Banjo has been selected" appear onstage in the text field.

Now add listeners and functions to the four instrument clips to let the user choose the instrument.

4 In the line below the existing code, add the following listeners and functions:

```
violin.addEventListener(MouseEvent.CLICK,onViolin);
banjo.addEventListener(MouseEvent.CLICK,onBanjo);
trumpet.addEventListener(MouseEvent.CLICK,onTrumpet);
glock.addEventListener(MouseEvent.CLICK,onGlock);

function onViolin(e:MouseEvent):void {
 instrument = violin;
 instrument_txt.text = "The Violin has been selected.";
}
function onBanjo(e:MouseEvent):void {
 instrument = banjo;
 instrument_txt.text = "The Banjo has been selected.";
}
function onTrumpet(e:MouseEvent):void {
 instrument = trumpet;
 instrument_txt.text = "The Trumpet has been selected.";
}
function onGlock(e:MouseEvent):void {
 instrument = glock;
 instrument_txt.text = "The Glockenspiel has been selected.";
}
```

5 Save and test the movie. When you click any of the instruments, you should see the text change onstage to indicate your selection.

Now we will use the value of the `instrument` variable to select the movie clip that the buttons at the bottom of the Stage control.

Changing movie clip properties with buttons

The code in this exercise, which changes the values of the instrument properties, should be starting to look familiar to you.

First, for each of the blue buttons at the bottom of the Stage, add an event listener to listen for a CLICK event.

1 In the Actions panel below the existing code for Frame 1, add a listener for each button, using the following code:

```
grow_btn.addEventListener(MouseEvent.CLICK, grow);
shrink_btn.addEventListener(MouseEvent.CLICK, shrink);
rotate_btn.addEventListener(MouseEvent.CLICK, rotate);
hide_btn.addEventListener(MouseEvent.CLICK, hideClip);
show_btn.addEventListener(MouseEvent.CLICK, showClip);
fadeOut_btn.addEventListener(MouseEvent.CLICK, fadeOut);
fadeIn_btn.addEventListener(MouseEvent.CLICK, fadeIn);
```

Now add a function to correspond to each button's listener.

2 Add the `grow` function, which increases the size of the selected instrument by 10 percent each time the Scale Up button is clicked:

```
function grow(e:MouseEvent):void {
 instrument.scaleX += .1
  instrument.scaleY += .1;
}
```

3 Add the `shrink` function, to decrease the size of the selected instrument by 10 percent when the Scale Down button is clicked:

```
function shrink(e:MouseEvent):void {
 instrument.scaleX -= .1;
  instrument.scaleY -= .1;
}
```

4 Add the `rotate` function to rotate the selected instrument by five degrees each time the Rotate button is clicked:

```
function rotate(e:MouseEvent):void {
 instrument.rotation += 5;
}
```

5 Add the `hideClip` function to hide the selected instrument by setting its `visible` property to `false` when the Hide button is clicked:

```
function hideClip(e:MouseEvent):void {
 instrument.visible = false;
}
```

6   Add the `showClip` function to display the selected instrument by setting its `visible` property to `true` when the Show button is clicked:

```
function showClip(e:MouseEvent):void {
 instrument.visible = true;
}
```

7   Add the `fadeOut` function to set the selected instrument's opacity level to 50 percent when the Fade Out button is clicked:

```
function fadeOut(e:MouseEvent):void {
 instrument.alpha = .5
}
```

8   Add the `fadeIn` function to set the selected instrument's opacity level to 100 percent when the Fade In button is clicked:

```
function fadeIn(e:MouseEvent):void {
 instrument.alpha = 1
}
```

9   Save and test your movie. Try selecting different instruments and then click various buttons to see the results of changing the instrument properties.

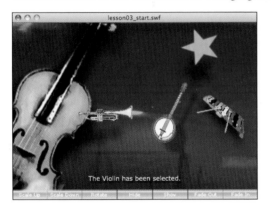

Creating animation using ActionScript tweens

Just as you can create animation using tweens on the Timeline, you can create tweens in ActionScript (for a review of creating tweens in the Timeline or an over-view of the tweening features in Flash CS5, see the Flash Help files or *Adobe Flash Classroom in a Book* by Adobe Press). As is often the case when comparing a task in ActionScript to a similar task performed in the Flash interface, the main benefit of creating tweens in code rather than on the Timeline is that the resulting anima-tion can be more versatile and more interactive. Using code also means that tweens can be created on a single frame of the Timeline, or even without any frames at all.

ActionScript tweens have a number of similarities to those created in the interface. In both cases, you are changing the properties of an object over a span of time. In both cases, you select the property that you want to change and then set initial and final values for that property's animation. Also in both cases, you have the option of setting the amount and type of easing that you want.

Easing classes in ActionScript 3.0

Easing is a technique for accelerating or decelerating the velocity of the start or end of an animation. In Flash CS5, easing can be controlled in the interface or with ActionScript. ActionScript provides quite a few built-in easing classes that create a wide variety of easing effects, including a `CustomEase` class that lets you create your own easing effects.

For more information, see the Flash CS5 ActionScript 3.0 language reference in the Flash Help files.

A reference to a new tween instance in ActionScript is typically stored in a variable. The syntax is similar to that for other variables you have created:

```
var tweenName:Tween = new Tween(objectToBeTweened,
¬"propertyToBeAnimated", EasingType, startingValue,
¬endingValue, time, trueForSeconds);
```

When a new tween variable is created in this way, all the parameters that control the tween are placed within parentheses and are separated by commas. The first parameter is the instance name of the object to be tweened. The second parameter indicates which property will be animated; this is referenced as a string and so is placed within quotation marks. The property names are the same as the ones you have already been working with. The third parameter is the easing type, which can control the way the animation begins or ends. The next two parameters are the numeric values for the tweened property at the start and end of the animation. Next is the length of time that it will take for the animation to change from the first property value to the second. By default, the length of time is set in frames, but if the optional final parameter is set to `true`, then the time of the tween is instead set in seconds.

For example, if you have a movie clip onstage with an instance name of `rocket` and you want to send it from the top of the Stage (y = 0) to the bottom of the Stage (y = 400) over a 5-second period, you can create a tween like this:

```
var rocketTween:Tween = new Tween(rocket, "y", None.easeOut, 0,
¬400, 5, true)
```

The only nonintuitive parameter is the third one, for the easing type. You can look up all the possibilities for the easing types in Flash Help. For now, we'll try a couple of examples by updating a few of our button functions.

Adding ActionScript tweens

The functions that you created to change the instrument properties are not very dynamic. Replace some of these property changes with tweens to make them more interesting.

1   In the Actions panel, with Frame 1 of the `actions` layer selected, scroll down to find the function you created called `fadeOut`. It should now read:

```
function fadeOut(e:MouseEvent):void {
 instrument.alpha = .5
}
```

2   Change the code in the `fadeOut` function to read:

```
function fadeOut(e:MouseEvent):void {
 var tweenFadeOut:Tween = new Tween(instrument, "alpha", None.
 ¬easeOut, 1, 0, 3, true);
}
```

● **Note:** You use the keyword `new` in ActionScript whenever you want to create a new instance of an ActionScript class. You will be learning a lot more about ActionScript classes and creating new instances in the coming lessons.

Now the `fadeOut` function will gradually fade the selected instrument from completely opaque (1) to completely transparent (0) over 3 seconds. There is no easing added in the third parameter of this tween.

Importing the Tween class and easing classes

As you saw earlier with the `MovieClip` class, Flash automatically created an `import` statement for the `Tween` class when you created the variable `tweenFadeOut` as an instance of the `Tween` class. This statement has been added to the top of your code below the `import` statement for the `MoveClip` class.

However, for the code that you just wrote to work, an additional `import` statement needs to be added for the easing classes. Since you did not explicitly create an instance of the `Easing` class, Flash did not create an `import` statement for you, but `easing` is a parameter of the `Tween` class, so it still needs to be imported.

You will learn much more about class files and importing starting in Lesson 4. For now we will add code to import the easing classes.

● **Note:** From this point on in the lessons the only import statements that will be addressed will be the ones that are required in order to make the lessons work. Flash may automatically generate other import statements that you may want to take note of, but they will not be included in the code for the lessons.

1   Select Frame 1 of the Timeline and make the Actions panel visible. If your Flash Preferences are set to the defaults, these two lines should appear at the top of the Actions panel:

```
import flash.display.MovieClip;
import fl.transitions.Tween;
```

The second of these lines is required for the lesson project to work, so if Flash did not autoinsert this code, you should add it yourself to the first line of the Actions panel.

2   Below these `import` statements add the `import` statement for the easing classes:

```
import fl.transitions.easing.*;
```

There are multiple easing classes, so rather than import them individually, we use the asterisk wildcard symbol (*) to import them all. Now the easing classes are available for use in this file.

Next you will add tweens to some of the other functions.

3   Locate the function called fadeIn. It should read:

```
function fadeIn(e:MouseEvent):void {
 instrument.alpha = 1
}
```

4   Modify this function to perform a tween by updating the code to read:

```
function fadeIn(e:MouseEvent):void {
 var tweenFadeIn:Tween = new Tween(instrument, "alpha",
 ¬None.easeIn, 0, 1, 3, true);
}
```

The new tween fades the selected instrument from 0 to 1 over 3 seconds.

5   Locate the rotate function, which should read:

```
function rotate(e:MouseEvent):void {
 instrument.rotation += 5;
 }
```

6   Change this function by replacing the change to the rotation property with a tween:

```
function rotate(e:MouseEvent):void {
 var spin:Tween = new Tween(instrument, "rotation",
 ¬Elastic.easeOut, 0, 360, 5, true);
}
```

The spin tween animates the selected instrument in one complete rotation over 5 seconds. Notice that the easing type is now set to Elastic. This will create a bouncing, rubbery effect to the tween.

7   Save and test the movie. Select different instruments and try out the updated versions of your buttons. You should now have an application that includes quite a lot of interactive animation.

Here is the completed code for this lesson:

```
import flash.display.MovieClip;
import fl.transitions.Tween;
import fl.transitions.easing.*;
star_mc.addEventListener(MouseEvent.CLICK,rotateStar);
function rotateStar(e:MouseEvent):void {
  star_mc.rotation += 5;
}
addEventListener(Event.ENTER_FRAME, starMove);
function starMove(e:Event):void {
```

```actionscript
  if (star_mc.x < stage.stageWidth) {
   star_mc.x += 2;
  } else {
   star_mc.x = 0;
  }
}
var instrument:MovieClip = banjo;
instrument_txt.text = "The Banjo has been selected.";
violin.addEventListener(MouseEvent.CLICK,onViolin);
banjo.addEventListener(MouseEvent.CLICK,onBanjo);
trumpet.addEventListener(MouseEvent.CLICK,onTrumpet);
glock.addEventListener(MouseEvent.CLICK,onGlock);
function onViolin(e:MouseEvent):void {
 instrument = violin;
 instrument_txt.text = "The Violin has been selected.";
}
function onTrumpet(e:MouseEvent):void {
 instrument = trumpet;
 instrument_txt.text = "The Trumpet has been selected.";
}
function onBanjo(e:MouseEvent):void {
 instrument = banjo;
 instrument_txt.text = "The Banjo has been selected.";
}
function onGlock(e:MouseEvent):void {
 instrument = glock;
 instrument_txt.text = "The Glockenspiel has been selected.";
}
grow_btn.addEventListener(MouseEvent.CLICK, grow);
shrink_btn.addEventListener(MouseEvent.CLICK, shrink);
rotate_btn.addEventListener(MouseEvent.CLICK, rotate);
hide_btn.addEventListener(MouseEvent.CLICK, hideClip);
show_btn.addEventListener(MouseEvent.CLICK, showClip);
fadeOut_btn.addEventListener(MouseEvent.CLICK, fadeOut);
fadeIn_btn.addEventListener(MouseEvent.CLICK, fadeIn);
function grow(e:MouseEvent):void {
 instrument.scaleX += .1;
 instrument.scaleY += .1;
}
function shrink(e:MouseEvent):void {
 instrument.scaleX -= .1
 instrument.scaleY -= .1;
}
function rotate(e:MouseEvent):void {
 var spin:Tween = new Tween(instrument, "rotation",
 ¬Elastic.easeOut, 0, 360, 5, true);
```

(code continues on next page)

```
}
function hideClip(e:MouseEvent):void {
 instrument.visible = false;
}
function showClip(e:MouseEvent):void {
 instrument.visible = true;
}
function fadeOut(e:MouseEvent):void {
 var tweenFadeOut:Tween = new Tween(instrument, "alpha",
 ¬None.easeOut, 1, 0, 3, true);
}
function fadeIn(e:MouseEvent):void {
 var tweenFadeIn:Tween = new Tween(instrument, "alpha",
 ¬None.easeIn, instrument.alpha, 1, 3, true);
}
```

● **Note:** It is not at all uncommon—even for experienced programmers—for things to not work the first time you test them. If you test your movie and something isn't working, check the feedback in the Output panel. Often, the errors listed in the Output panel can be the result of a single spelling mistake early in the code. If the error messages include line numbers, compare those lines carefully to the example code (line number visibility in the Actions panel can be turned on or off in the Actions panel preferences). Again, remember to look at color-coding, capitalization, and spelling. More often than not, the errors are small spelling or capitalization mistakes rather than major syntax errors. You can compare your code with the completed version of the lesson file found in Lessons > Lesson03 > Complete > lesson03_complete.fla.

Some suggestions to try on your own

You now have a large repertoire of techniques to play with. You can probably come up with endless variations on the techniques in this lesson to experiment with. Here are a few suggestions to get you started:

- Look in the Flash Help files and experiment with some of the other properties available for a movie clip.

- Try displaying the changing values of an animating property in a text field.

- Try creating a MovieClip instance that bounces off two or even four sides of the Stage.

- Try creating tweens for some other movie clip properties.

- Look in the Flash Help files and experiment with some of the other easing types.

- Create additional custom code snippets for other types of tweens and property changes you may wish to reuse.

You should be starting to get comfortable with the basics of animating with ActionScript. In the next lesson, you will learn to create ActionScript in an external ActionScript file. This technique is the foundation of object-oriented programming and will open many more possibilities for the creation of rich interactive applications.

Adding a custom code snippet
to create a tween

You have seen the usefulness of code snippets in the previous lessons. If you look at the code snippets that ship with Flash CS5, you will notice that there are a number in the animation folder that modify and animate the properties of a selected object. You may want to create a new file and experiment with some of these snippets.

No code snippets are supplied, however, for creating an ActionScript tween.

If you find yourself repeating chunks of code over and over, then adding your own custom code snippets can save a lot of time as you work. Practice this technique by turning one of the tweens that you just created into a custom code snippet.

1   With the Actions panel and the Code Snippets panel both visible, locate and select the line of code in the Actions panel that reads:

```
var tweenfadeOut:Tween = new Tween(instrument, "alpha",
¬None.easeOut, 1, 0, 3, true);
```

2   With this code selected, choose Create New Code Snippet from the pop-up menu in the upper-right corner of the Code Snippets panel.

3   In the dialog box that appears, give your custom code snippet the title **fadeOut Tween**.

4   Add a tooltip description to indicate the snippet's function, such as "Creates a Tween that fades an object from opaque to transparent over 3 seconds."

5   Click the Auto-fill button to add the selected code to your custom code snippet.

6   Click OK to create the code snippet.

The first time that you create a custom code snippet, a new folder is automatically created called Custom in the Code Snippets panel. The code snippet you just created is now available from this Custom folder and can be used like any other code snippet.

Review questions

1 Name four movie clip properties that can be controlled with ActionScript.

2 What is an event in ActionScript that you could use to have code repeat at the current frame rate?

3 What is the syntax in ActionScript 3.0 to indicate what type of data will be stored in a variable?

4 What keyword is used to create a new instance of an ActionScript class?

5 Which ActionScript classes need to be imported in order to create an Actionscript tween?

6 When creating an instance of the Tween class, what are the parameters (values within the parentheses that are used to determine how the tween behaves)?

Review answers

1 There are many movie clip properties that can be controlled with ActionScript, including:

- rotation
- x (horizontal position)
- y (vertical position)
- alpha (transparency)
- scaleX (horizontal size)
- scaleY (vertical size)

For a full list of movie clip properties, see the ActionScript 3.0 language reference in the Flash Help files.

2 The ENTER_FRAME event is used in ActionScript 3.0 to make code repeat at the current frame rate. For example, to make a movie clip named logo_mc rotate five degrees on every frame, you could write:

```
addEventListener(Event.ENTER_FRAME,rotateLogo);
function rotateLogo(e:Event):void {
 logo_mc.rotation += 5;
}
```

3 When a variable is created, the type of data it will store is indicated by typing a colon after the variable name followed by the data type. For example, to indicate that a variable named `totalPrice` will contain the data type Number, you could write:

```
var totalPrice:Number;
```

4 To create a new instance of an ActionScript class, you use the keyword new. For example, to create a new instance of the Sound class, you could write:

```
var song:Sound = new Sound();
```

The Sound class is covered in Lesson 9, "Controlling Sound with ActionScript."

5 The Tween class and at least one of the easing classes need to be imported in order create an ActionScript tween. The Tween class would be imported with this statement:

```
import fl.transitions.Tween;
```

Rather than import the easing classes one at at time you could use a wildcard (*) character to import them all in a single statement with this line:

```
import fl.transitions.easing.*;
```

6 There are six required parameters for an instance of the Tween class. The first parameter indicates the object that will have the tween applied to it. The second parameter indicates the property of that object that will be animated. The third parameter indicates the type of easing used. The fourth parameter is the starting value of the property to be animated, and the fifth parameter is the ending value to which that property will animate. The sixth parameter is the length of time over which the tween will take place. By default, the sixth parameter is measured in frames, but if an optional seventh parameter is set to `true`, then the sixth parameter is measured in seconds.

In this example, an instance of the Tween class named `spin` is set to animate the rotation of an object named `instrument`. The type of easing is `Elastic.easeout`, and the object will animate from 0 degrees to 360 degrees over the course of 5 seconds.

```
var spin:Tween = new Tween(instrument, "rotation",
¬Elastic.easeOut, 0, 360, 5, true);
```

4 CREATING ACTIONSCRIPT IN EXTERNAL FILES

Lesson overview

In this lesson, you will learn to do the following:

- Create an ActionScript file using the tools in Flash CS5.

- Create an ActionScript class that extends the MovieClip class.

- Create a constructor function.

- Define parameters for class methods.

- Use ActionScript code to create vector graphics.

- Use code to create instances of a custom class file in the Flash Timeline.

- Use the MOUSE_MOVE event.

- Turn off an event listener.

- Generate random color.

This lesson will take approximately 2 hours.

External ActionScript files can be convenient for reusing code, or they can be the foundation for large applications that use object-oriented programming (OOP) practices.

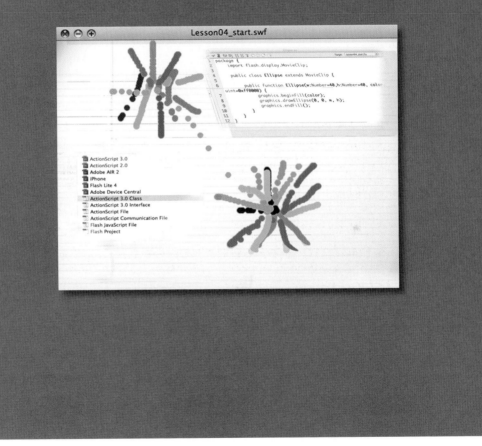

Each mouse movement in the Lesson 4 project produces a trail of ellipses with a different random color.

Up until this point, all the lessons have created ActionScript in frames of the Flash Timeline. This is a very useful way to work, and many Flash developers create all their projects exclusively using Timeline code. For simpler projects, this approach has the benefit of keeping all the graphics and media in the same file as the ActionScript. However, for Flash projects that are more complex, it is often cumbersome to have hundreds or even thousands of lines of code in the Timeline.

The alternative is to store the ActionScript for a project in one or more external files that contain only code. These ActionScript files can then be integrated with graphics, animation, and other Flash content to create the final project. External ActionScript files are really just plain text files saved with the .as file extension.

There are many benefits to developing larger projects in this manner. Most important, this approach allows you to divide the functionality of your applications into reusable chunks of code.

One common characteristic of a successful ActionScript file is that it's written to be as versatile as possible. For example, suppose you create an ActionScript file called Scoring.as that contains code to keep track of a user's score. By writing the code so that some of its properties can be individually modified, you can use the code in a game in which the user gets 10 points for shooting space aliens and needs 1000 points to win, or in a history quiz in which the user gets 1 point for each correct answer and proceeds to the next lesson when the score reaches 20 points.

In this lesson, you will get some experience creating an external ActionScript file designed to generate a simple graphic. You will then use this external .as file in a very simple Flash painting application as a source of generated brushstrokes.

Creating an ActionScript file

As mentioned, an ActionScript file is just a plain text file. Therefore, ActionScript files can be created with any software that can create text files, including TextEdit on the Mac and Notepad in Windows. Of course, it is preferable to create ActionScript files in tools that offer features like color-coding and error checking. Adobe tools like Flash Professional CS5, Flash Builder, and Dreamweaver offer full support for creation of ActionScript files, as do a number of third-party tools, some of which are free. So you have a lot of options, and over time you'll find the ones that are right for you. In this lesson, you will create an ActionScript file right in Flash CS5.

Creating an ActionScript class in Flash

In this lesson, you will use the tools in Flash CS5 to create a new ActionScript class file. When you create an external class file, you can place code in this file that can be used by other Flash projects.

In fact, you can think of the ActionScript 3.0 language as a large collection of classes that together offer the wide range of functionality available in the language.

If you have worked in Flash at all, then you have already worked with classes. For example, the `MovieClip` class is a built-in ActionScript class that describes the functionality that is unique to movie clips in Flash. In the previous lesson, you were able to manipulate many movie clip properties such as `rotation` and `alpha`, because the `MovieClip` class references code that describes those properties. Similarly, there are built-in ActionScript classes for working with text, sound, video, and other features available in the Flash platform.

When you create a movie clip in Flash, you are actually creating an instance of the `MovieClip` class. When you work with a text field, you are using an instance of the `TextField` class; with video, you use the `Video` class, and so on.

The functions that are contained in an ActionScript class file are referred to as *methods* of that class, and the variables that are in a class file are referred to as *properties* of the class.

By creating custom ActionScript classes, as you will do in this lesson, you are expanding the collection of classes that are available to you in your Flash projects. And many beginners find that once they become comfortable with the way classes work in ActionScript 3.0, then the entire language begins to make a lot more sense.

In previous versions of Flash, to create a new ActionScript class you had to create the new class from scratch, creating a blank ActionScript file and typing all of the code. In Flash CS5, you now have the option of creating a new ActionScript 3.0 Class file. This approach creates an ActionScript file with the basic code structure for an ActionScript class already added for you. You will do this now.

1 In Flash, choose File > New.

2 On the General tab of the New Document dialog box, choose ActionScript 3.0 Class and then click OK.

You will be presented with a dialog box offering you the choice of using Flash Professional to create your new ActionScript file, or launching Flash Builder (if it is installed on your machine) and creating the ActionScript class file in Flash Builder. There are a number of benefits to working in Flash Builder, especially when debugging, testing, and profiling complex applications, but for these lessons we will work exclusively in Flash Professional CS5.

3 Choose Flash Professional in the dialog box.

4 In the Class Name field, type **Ellipse** and click OK to close the dialog box.

A new ActionScript file is created with basic code for a class named Ellipse.

5 Choose File > Save, and name your new file **Ellipse.as**.

6 Save the new file in the Lesson04 > Start folder of your lessons folder.

The name of the class created in an ActionScript file must match the name of the file. Thus, in this case, the class is named Ellipse, and you saved the file as Ellipse.as. This name structure is what allows class files to be referenced by other files.

Basic structure of an ActionScript 3.0 Class file

In your new Ellipse.as file, look at the basic structure common to most .as class files. This is the code that was created by Flash in your new Ellipse class:

```
package  {

  public class Ellipse {

  public function Ellipse() {
   // constructor code
  }

  }

}
```

All ActionScript class files begin with the package keyword. You can think of the package as describing the path to your ActionScript file. For example, if the Ellipse.as file was inside a folder named scripts, and the scripts folder was in a folder named com, then the first line of code in the file would read:

```
package com.scripts {
```

For simplicity, in this example you will keep all of the Flash files and ActionScript files for the lesson together in the same directory. When this is the case, then no path needs to be described after the package keyword. However, the package reference still needs to be there. The right brace at the end of the code closes the package tag. All the code for the Ellipse class will go in between the package braces.

After the opening `package` tag is the code that creates a new ActionScript class named `Ellipse`. All the code for this class will go between this line and the second from the last right brace:

```
public class Ellipse{
```

1 Change this line so that it reads:

```
public class Ellipse extends MovieClip {
```

When one class extends another class, the new class has all the capabilities of the original parent class in addition to whatever new capabilities are added in the new class file.

In this case, the purpose of the `Ellipse` class will be to draw a simple ellipse. Here the keyword `extends` makes the `Ellipse` class a descendent, or child, of the `MovieClip` class. This allows instances of the `Ellipse` class to do all the things that can be done with movie clips, such as have their position, scale, and rotation set.

To make the `MovieClip` class available to your new `Ellipse` class, you need to write code that imports the `MovieClip` class into your file.

2 Place the following line between the opening `package` tag and the line that creates the public class `Ellipse`:

```
import flash.display.MovieClip;
```

The file so far should read:

```
package {

  import flash.display.MovieClip;

  public class Ellipse extends MovieClip {

  public function Ellipse() {
    // constructor code
  }
  }
  }
```

The final bit of code that was created when you created the new class file is a function named `Ellipse()`:

```
public function Ellipse() {
  // constructor code
}
```

Although a class file will often contain many functions, each class must have one function that has the same name as the class file. This is called the constructor function, and because it is mandatory, it is created automatically in Flash CS5 when you create a new class file. The constructor function is automatically called every time an instance of the class is created. You will put this into practice soon.

About access modifiers

There is another term in the line that creates the Ellipse class that you may not have encountered before:

```
public class Ellipse extends MovieClip {
```

The term *public* is what is known as an *access modifier*. By setting the class to public, you are indicating that this class can be accessed from any other file.

There are three other access modifiers:

- private: Methods and properties that are labeled private are available only from within the class file.

- protected: Methods and properties that are labeled protected are available only from within the class file and its descendents.

- internal: Methods and properties that are labeled internal are available from within the class file and to all other files within the same package.

For simplicity's sake, these lessons will mostly use only the public and private modifiers, but in other class files, you may see the other access modifiers used on methods (functions) and properties (variables) within the class. As you get more comfortable with ActionScript, it is a good idea to make a deeper study of how to use these modifiers in your applications. For more information, see the ActionScript 3.0 Help files or Colin Moock's excellent book, *Essential ActionScript 3.0*, from O'Reilly Media.

As mentioned, it is not uncommon for a class file to contain many functions, but because the function you're creating here is a simple function that will perform only one task, you will put all of the code for this class file in the Ellipse() constructor function.

3 Modify the Ellipse() function so that it reads:

```
public function Ellipse(w:Number=40,h:Number=40,
¬color:Number=0xff0000) {
  graphics.beginFill(color);
  graphics.drawEllipse(0, 0, w, h);
  graphics.endFill();
 }
```

Notice the three parameters you've added between the parentheses of the Ellipse() function. These will be used to set the width, height, and color of a new ellipse that will be created when the Ellipse() function is called. The parameters for width (w) and height (h) are given default values of 40, and the color parameter is given a default value of red.

The three lines of code inside the brackets of the Ellipse() function are used to create an ellipse. These lines call methods that are part of the extensive and powerful ActionScript toolset for creating and manipulating vector graphics. In the `Ellipse()` function, the first of these lines indicates that the vector graphics that are about to be created will have a specific fill color:

```
graphics.beginFill(color);
```

The `color` parameter determines the color of the ellipse. Remember that this parameter was set to a default of red when you created the function, but can be overridden when called.

The second line of code draws an ellipse using a built-in function called `drawEllipse()`.

```
graphics.drawEllipse(0, 0, w, h);
```

This function, or *method*, takes four parameters. The first two parameters set the position of the ellipse, in this case to 0 horizontally and 0 vertically (the upper-left corner). The next two use the w and h parameters of the `Ellipse()` function to set the width and height of the ellipse.

Required versus optional parameters

If a function has parameters that are given default values, as in the example in step 3, then when the function is called, references to those parameters do not need to be included. These are called *optional* parameters. If references to these parameters are included with new values, they will override the default values. You will see this in action soon.

If a function has parameters that are not given initial values, you need to assign these values when calling the function. These are called *required* parameters.

The third line inside the `Ellipse()` function ends the fill and completes the drawing:

```
graphics.endFill();
```

4 Save your file. Your entire `Ellipse` class file should now read:

```
package {
    import flash.display.MovieClip;

    public class Ellipse extends MovieClip {

        public function Ellipse(w:Number=40,h:Number=40, color:Number=0xff0000) {
            graphics.beginFill(color);
            graphics.drawEllipse(0, 0, w, h);
            graphics.endFill();
        }

    }
}
```

You'll soon get to test your handiwork.

ActionScript 3.0 and hexadecimal color

ActionScript 3.0 can describe colors in a variety of ways, but the most common is as numeric hexadecimal values. This system is very easy once you are used to it. The characters "0x" before a color description tell ActionScript that a hexadecimal value is to follow. Then a six-digit number describes the amount of red, green, and blue in the color. (Optionally, an eight-digit number can be used; in addition to the color values, it would include transparency information.)

If you have worked with hexadecimal colors in web design, you know that each digit can range from 0 to 15, with the letters A, B, C, D, E, and F representing the numbers 10, 11, 12, 13, 14, and 15, respectively. In this example, the color red is described as 0xFF0000, which has the greatest possible amount of red (FF) and no green (00) or blue (00). The hexadecimal color 0x0000FF would be a color with no red (00) or green (00) and the full amount of blue (FF).

To find the hexadecimal value of a specific color in Flash, you can open the Color panel (Window > Color). You can select a color in a variety of ways in this panel. The hexadecimal value of the selected color will be displayed in the lower right of the panel. If you are using a value from the Color panel in your ActionScript, replace the initial pound symbol (#) shown in the color panel with "0x" before typing the hexadecimal value in your code.

For more information about hexadecimal colors, see Flash Help or any basic web design book.

Creating instances of a class file in Flash

Without further ado, let's put your new class file to work.

1 Open the lesson04_start.fla file from the Lessons > Lesson04 > Start folder. This should be the same location where your ActionScript file is saved.

   Notice that this file is simply made up of a background layer with a full-screen bitmap image and an empty actions layer with no code added (yet).

2 With Frame 1 of the actions layer selected, open the Actions panel and select the first line, where you'll begin adding code.

3 To create a single instance of your Ellipse class, add the following code:

   ```
   var ellipse:Ellipse = new Ellipse();
   ```

4 To add the ellipse to the Stage, on a new line type the following code:

   ```
   addChild(ellipse);
   ```

Using the keyword new to create instances

To create a new instance from any ActionScript class, you use the keyword new. This is consistent across the entire ActionScript 3.0 language, whether you are creating instances of built-in classes as in:

```
var myClip:MovieClip = new MovieClip();
```

and:

```
var userForm:TextField = new TextField();
```

or, as in this lesson, you are creating a new instance of a custom class as in:

```
var ellipse:Ellipse = new Ellipse();
```

Many newcomers to ActionScript find that this consistency makes ActionScript much easier than they expected once they get comfortable with learning the foundations of the language.

About addChild() and the display list

In the background of every Flash file, every visual object that is onstage is tracked in what is called the *display list*. This is true whether a visual object was placed onstage using the tools in the Flash interface, imported to the stage as an external file, or created from scratch using ActionScript.

All visual objects in a Flash project, including movie clips, shapes, buttons, text fields, bitmaps, and video, are considered *display objects* and are added to the display list when they are made viewable.

When a visual object is created with ActionScript, it may exist in code, but that does not mean that it will automatically be visible onstage. To place something in the display list, and therefore onstage, you call the method addChild(). A common mistake for ActionScript beginners is to forget to use addChild() and then wonder why the expected graphics do not appear onstage. You will be delving deeper into display objects and the display list in later lessons.

5 Save and test your movie. You should see a single red ellipse in the upper-left corner of the Stage.

A single red ellipse is not too exciting, so next you will add a few things to make more interesting use of the Ellipse class.

First, instead of having a single instance of the Ellipse generated automatically, you will let the user generate multiple instances, creating a new instance whenever the mouse is moved.

6 Select all the existing code in the Actions panel and cut it to the clipboard.

7 On the first line of the now empty Actions panel, add an event listener for an event called MOUSE_MOVE:

```
stage.addEventListener(MouseEvent.MOUSE_MOVE, makeShapes);
```

This event takes place whenever the user moves the mouse. This movement will call a function called makeShapes().

8 On a new line, create the makeShapes() function:

```
function makeShapes(e:MouseEvent):void {
}
```

9 Paste the code from the clipboard in between the curly braces of the makeShapes() function so that the function now reads:

```
function makeShapes(e:MouseEvent):void {
  var ellipse:Ellipse = new Ellipse();
  addChild(ellipse);
}
```

If you tested your movie now, every time the mouse was moved, a new ellipse would be added to the stage—but they would all be in the exact same spot in the upper left. As with the parent MovieClip class, each Ellipse class instance has an X and Y property with a default location of 0,0. To give each new ellipse a unique location, you will set each new ellipse to be placed at the current mouse location using the mouseX and mouseY properties.

10 Add two new lines to the makeShapes() function so that it now reads:

```
function makeShapes(e:MouseEvent):void {
  var ellipse:Ellipse = new Ellipse();
  addChild(ellipse);
  ellipse.x = mouseX;
  ellipse.y = mouseY;
}
```

11 Save and test your movie. Move the mouse around. A trail of red circles should be created that follow your mouse path. Congratulations, you have created a virtual paintbrush that uses big red ellipses (which are circles because the w and h parameter default values were set equal). More important, you have succeeded in creating and using a custom ActionScript class in a Flash file!

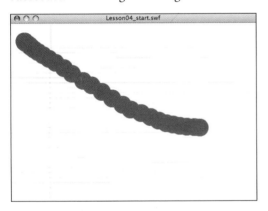

12 Close the lesson04_start.swf file to exit the testing environment.

Overriding the parameters of each ellipse instance

At this point, your Flash file is creating nothing but big red ellipses from your class file—but remember, they are big and red because those are the defaults you placed in the constructor function. Each time a new ellipse is created, those defaults can be overridden by passing new parameters. Let's change the parameters to create smaller green ellipses.

1 In the makeShapes() function, change the line of code that currently reads:

```
var ellipse:Ellipse = new Ellipse();
```

so that it reads:

```
var ellipse:Ellipse = new Ellipse(10, 10, 0x00FF00);
```

2 Save and test your movie.

Now, moving the mouse should produce a trail of 10-pixel-by-10-pixel green circles. If you want, you can experiment by trying different sizes and colors and test the results.

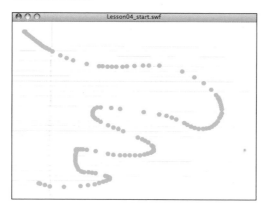

Turning the makeShapes() function on and off

Even software that does nothing but paint green trails should give users control over when they paint. So far, you have added event listeners using the addEventListener() method; you can also remove a listener using a similar method called removeEventListener(). Here, you'll alter your code so that the listener for mouse movement is added when the user clicks onstage and removed when the mouse is released.

1 In the Actions panel, click to place the mouse pointer before the first line of code and press the Enter (Windows) or Return (Mac) key a few times to insert a few lines of space before the beginning of the code.

2 On the first line of the Actions panel, above the existing code, add two new addEventListener() methods to listen for the MOUSE_UP and MOUSE_DOWN events by typing the following code:

```
stage.addEventListener(MouseEvent.MOUSE_DOWN, startDrawing);
stage.addEventListener(MouseEvent.MOUSE_UP, stopDrawing);
```

The MOUSE_DOWN event will call a function named startDrawing(), and the MOUSE_UP event will call a function named stopDrawing(), so next add those two new functions.

3 On the lines below the event listeners, add this code:

```
function startDrawing(e:MouseEvent):void {
}
function stopDrawing(e:MouseEvent):void {
}
```

4 Next, find and select the line in your code that reads:

```
stage.addEventListener(MouseEvent.MOUSE_MOVE, makeShapes);
```

5 Cut this line of code (Edit > Cut) to place it on the clipboard.

6 Place the mouse pointer between the curly braces of the new startDrawing() function and paste the code from the clipboard. The function should now read:

```
function startDrawing(e:MouseEvent):void {
  stage.addEventListener(MouseEvent.MOUSE_MOVE, makeShapes);
}
```

7 Place the mouse pointer between the curly braces of the stopDrawing() function and paste the same code from the clipboard.

8 In your newly pasted code in the stopDrawing() function, change addEventListener to removeEventListener. The function should now read:

```
function stopDrawing(e:MouseEvent):void {
  stage.removeEventListener(MouseEvent.MOUSE_MOVE, makeShapes);
}
```

The result of these changes is that the function that draws the ellipses when the mouse moves will occur only when the user clicks the mouse and will stop occurring when the mouse is released.

9 Save and test your movie. Click the Stage and move the mouse. Ellipses should be created that follow the mouse. Release the mouse, and the ellipses should stop being generated.

Randomizing the color of the ellipses

To generate a random number in ActionScript 3.0, you use the random method of the Math class. The syntax for that is:

```
Math.random();
```

This code will return a random number between 0 and 1, usually with multiple decimal places. To control the range that Math.random generates, you perform some math on the resulting random number. For example, if you want to generate a random number between 0 and 50, you multiply the Math.random result by 50:

```
Math.random() * 50;
```

If you want to generate a random number from among the full range of possible hexadecimal colors, you write:

```
Math.random() * 0xFFFFFF;
```

Now you'll use this technique to add random colors to the ellipses.

Note: An asterisk is the ActionScript character for the multiplication operation.

1 Add a variable to your file to store a numeric color value: At the top of the Actions panel, above the existing code, add a new line and create a new variable with this code:

```
var color:Number;
```

2 Locate the `startDrawing()` function and add to the code so that it now reads:

```
function startDrawing(e:MouseEvent):void {
 stage.addEventListener(MouseEvent.MOUSE_MOVE, makeShapes);
 color = Math.random() * 0xFFFFFF;
}
```

Now each time the user clicks to begin drawing, a new random color will be chosen.

To assign that color to the ellipses, you will use the new `color` variable as the parameter that is passed to the `Ellipse()` constructor function.

3 Locate the `makeShapes()` function and change the line that currently reads:

```
var ellipse:Ellipse = new Ellipse(10,10,0x00FF00);
```

so that it reads:

```
var ellipse:Ellipse = new Ellipse(10,10,color);
```

4 Save and test your movie. Each mouse movement produces a trail of ellipses with a different random color.

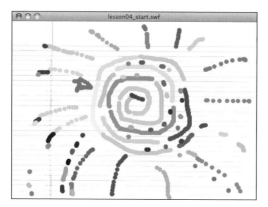

The completed code in Flash should now read:

```
var color:Number;
stage.addEventListener(MouseEvent.MOUSE_DOWN, startDrawing);
stage.addEventListener(MouseEvent.MOUSE_UP, stopDrawing);
function startDrawing(e:MouseEvent):void {
 stage.addEventListener(MouseEvent.MOUSE_MOVE, makeShapes);
 color = Math.random() * 0xFFFFFF;
}
function stopDrawing(e:MouseEvent):void {
 stage.removeEventListener(MouseEvent.MOUSE_MOVE, makeShapes);
```

```
}
function makeShapes(e:MouseEvent):void {
 var ellipse:Ellipse = new Ellipse(10, 10, color);
 addChild(ellipse);
 ellipse.x = mouseX;
 ellipse.y = mouseY;
}
```

By learning to create external ActionScript files and integrate them into your Flash projects, you can begin to make your rich interactive applications much more modular. It can take some time to get comfortable with this way of working, but the efforts will be very rewarding.

In the coming lessons, you will get more practice working with ActionScript classes.

Give your brain a rest between each lesson, and go back to earlier lessons for review as many times as you need to. You may be surprised how much more sense ActionScript concepts make after you are exposed to them a few times.

Some suggestions to try on your own

There are many, many ways to enhance the application you created in this lesson using techniques that we have already covered.

The Lesson04 folder has an Addendum folder containing a tutorial that goes through the steps of creating a class that is a simple variation of the Ellipse class, but that creates rectangles instead of ellipses. Use the Lesson 4 addendum file "Creating Animation with ActionScript—Addendum," in the Lesson04 > Addendum folder, to create the second class file, and then try experimenting with some of the following techniques:

- Change your Flash file so that mouse movements paint rectangles instead of ellipses.

- Create buttons that allow users to switch between painting ellipses and painting rectangles.

- Create buttons that let users set the size of the shapes that they paint.

- Create buttons that let users choose the color they paint.

- Look in the Flash Help files and explore some of the other possible shapes you can create with the drawing capabilities in ActionScript. See if you can create additional ActionScript files that create new shapes and then incorporate them into your Flash file.

You will learn more about generating visual elements with ActionScript in upcoming lessons. In the next lesson, you will learn to import external content into a Flash application at runtime using ActionScript and Flash components.

Review questions

1 When creating an ActionScript class file, how should the file be named?

2 How does the constructor function in an ActionScript class file need to be named?

3 Define an ActionScript method and an ActionScript property.

4 What is the difference between a required parameter and an optional parameter in an ActionScript method?

5 How do you create an instance of an external class in ActionScript?

6 How is a display object added to the display list in ActionScript?

7 What is one way to generate a random color in ActionScript?

Review answers

1 An ActionScript class file must have the same name as the class that it contains, followed by the suffix .as. For example, if a file contains an ActionScript class called `ScoringSystem`, then the filename needs to be ScoringSystem.as.

2 The constructor function in an ActionScript class file is the function in that file with the same name as the class. For example, in a class named `ScoringSystem`, the constructor function would look like this:

```
public function ScoringSystem(parameters){
//code that does something goes here
}
```

3 A method in ActionScript 3.0 is a function that is contained in a class. A property in ActionScript 3.0 is a variable contained in a class.

4 When a function is created in an ActionScript class file, it can be given any number of parameters. If those parameters are given initial default values when they are created, then they are considered optional parameters, and it is not necessary to pass parameters to the function when calling it. If a parameter does not have a default value, then a value must be passed when the function is called, and these are required parameters. For example, in the following example, the `finalScore` parameter has no initial value, so it is a required parameter. However, the `startingScore` parameter has an initial value of 0, so it is an optional parameter.

```
public function ScoringSystem(finalScore:Number,
¬startingScore:Number = 0,){
 //code that does something goes here
}
```

5   To create an instance of an external class in ActionScript, you can use the keyword new
     followed by the class name. For example, to create a new instance of the Rocket class
     in a variable named rocket1, you can write:

```
var rocket1:Rocket = new Rocket();
```

6   To add an object to the display list with ActionScript and make it appear onstage, you
     use the addChild() method. For example, to add an instance named rocket1 to the
     Flash Stage, you can write:

```
addChild(rocket1);
```

     or

```
stage.addChild(rocket1);
```

7   You can generate a random color value by calling the Math.random() method and
     multiplying the result by the full range of hexadecimal colors, as in:

```
var color:Number = Math.random() * 0xFFFFFF;
```

5 USING ACTIONSCRIPT AND COMPONENTS TO LOAD CONTENT

Lesson overview

In this lesson, you will learn to do the following:

- Work with Flash CS5 User Interface components.

- Create an instance of the List component and customize its parameters.

- Trigger an ActionScript event listener when the selected item in a List component instance changes.

- Use the UILoader component to control SWF file and bitmap image loading and display.

- Change the source file of the UILoader component with ActionScript.

- Work with the URLLoader class to load text data from an external file into a Flash movie.

- Add an event listener to respond to the successful completion of a data load operation.

- Set the properties of a text field with ActionScript.

- Use the UIScrollBar component to create a scrolling text field.

This lesson will take approximately 2.5 hours.

If you have been proceeding through the lessons sequentially, you now have a collection of ActionScript 3.0 techniques in your repertoire to add functionality to your Flash files. Most large Flash projects, however, are not made up of just a single Flash file, but instead consist of a number of SWF files plus supporting content and data that is loaded at runtime.

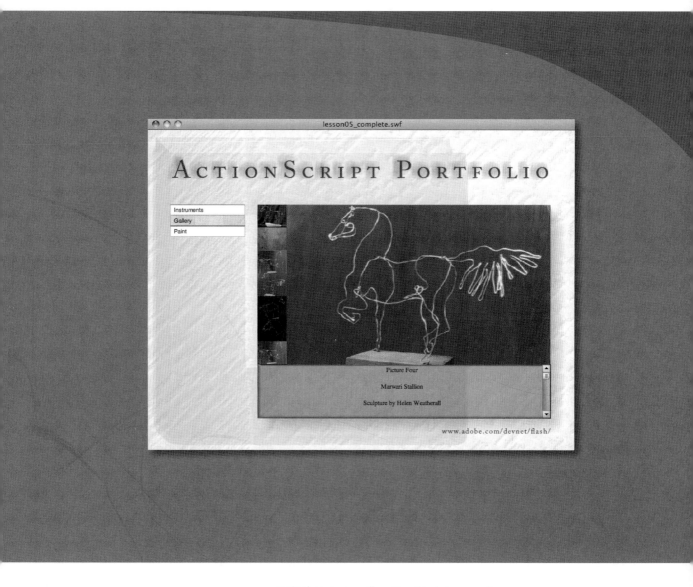

In this lesson, you will create a simple image gallery
and integrate it into a larger Flash project.

Since one of the main goals of this lesson is to integrate multiple files into a single Flash project, the materials for this lesson are more varied than in previous lessons.

Take a minute to examine the contents of the Lessons > Lesson05 folder. This folder contains an Images folder with JPG files and a Text folder with plain text files, all of which you will load into your Flash project using ActionScript.

The Start folder has a lesson05_start.fla file that you will work with in this lesson. It also has an instruments.swf file and a paint.swf file. These files are completed versions of the Lesson 3 and Lesson 4 projects, respectively. You will begin the lesson by learning to load these two SWF files into the lesson05_start.fla file using instances of the List and UILoader components. After that, you will create a new gallery file that lets the user select from a list of thumbnails to display larger loaded images. Each image will have a text caption. The captions will each be loaded from separate text files. The finished gallery file will then be added to the list of files that can be loaded into the lesson05_start.fla file.

Creating a List component instance and setting its parameters

The List component that ships with Flash CS5 makes it easy to create lists of objects for users to choose from. The List component has parameters that can be set in the Flash interface or in ActionScript for adding labels and associating data with the items in the list. The component also has built-in events that occur automatically when the user makes a selection from the list.

Begin the lesson by opening the lesson05_start.fla file in the Lessons > Lesson05 > Start folder. In this lesson, you will begin to create working interface elements for the project.

1   In the Timeline, above the text layer, add a new layer and name it **components**.

2   Open the Components panel (Window > Components).

3   In the Components panel, open the User Interface group and choose the List component.

4   With Frame 1 of the new components layer selected, drag an instance of the List component to the Stage. You will use this component to create a list of files that the user can select and load into this project.

5   With the Properties panel visible (Window > Properties), select the new List component instance onstage.

6   In the Properties panel, name the List instance **loadList**.

7 Also in the Properties panel, set the X property for `loadList` to **30** (X = 30) and the Y property to **150** (Y = 150).

8 Set the width and height properties of `loadList` as follows: W = **140** and H = **60**.

9 With the List component still selected onstage, go to the Component Parameters section of the Properties panel. Select the `dataProvider` parameter, and then click the pencil icon that appears to the right of the parameter.

● **Note:** A copy of the List component with some color adjustments to match the interface has been added to the library of the Lesson05_start.fla file. When you drag the List component from the Components panel to the Stage, a dialog box will ask you if you wish to use or replace the component in the library. Choose Use Existing Component.

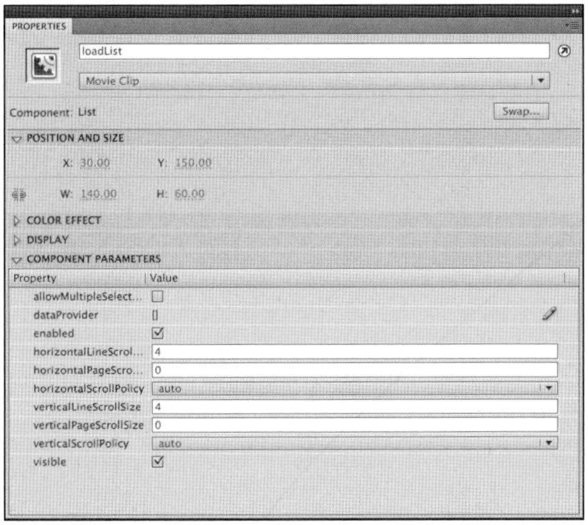

The Values dialog box opens. You use this dialog box to populate the list with labels and data values.

10 Add three items to the list by clicking the Plus button (+) three times.

11 Select the `label` parameter of the first item, and in the field on the right, type **Instruments**.

This will be the label for the first item in the list.

12 Select the `data` parameter for the first item, and give it the value **instruments.swf**.

You will use the data associated with each item in the list to store the name of the file that you want to load when that item in the list is selected.

13 Give the second item the label **Paint** and the data value **paint.swf**.

You will add code to the file so that selecting this item in the list loads a finished version of the painting application that was created in Lesson 4, "Creating ActionScript in External Files."

14 Give the third item in the list the label **Gallery** and the data value **gallery.swf**.

You will create the gallery file later in this lesson.

15 Click OK to exit the Values dialog box.

Adding an instance of the UILoader component

Later in this lesson, you will learn to load content into Flash using just ActionScript. But if you want to load SWF, JPG, PNG, or GIF files, then using the UILoader component can save you several steps. Here you will use the UILoader component to load SWF files into the lesson05_start.fla file. Later in your project, you will use the same component to load JPG images into a gallery file. Finally, you will load text into the gallery file using ActionScript only, since text files cannot be loaded with the UILoader component.

You'll start by adding an instance of the UILoader to the Stage.

1 With Frame 1 of the `components` layer selected and the Components panel visible, select the UILoader component from the User Interface folder.

2 Drag an instance of the UILoader component to the Stage.

3 With the UILoader instance selected onstage, in the Properties panel name the instance **loadWindow**.

4 Also in the Properties panel, set the following values for the `loadWindow` instance: X = **205**, Y = **140**, W = **550**, and H = **400**.

You will be loading a series of SWF files that have a Stage size of 550 × 400 pixels into this UILoader.

Adding a CHANGE event listener to the List component

When the user selects an item in an instance of the List component, an event named CHANGE automatically fires. You respond to the CHANGE event with ActionScript very similarly to the way you have responded to other events in earlier lessons.

1 With the Actions panel visible (Window > Actions), on the Timeline select Frame 1 of the actions layer.

2 Insert the following code at the top of the Actions panel:

```
loadList.addEventListener(Event.CHANGE, loadFile);
function loadFile(e:Event):void {
}
```

This syntax should be starting to look familiar to you. The listener for the CHANGE event is added in the same way that listeners were added for mouse events and frame events in earlier lessons.

Your loadFile() function will be called whenever the user makes a selection from the list.

Next, you will add code so that each selection from the list loads a different SWF file into the UILoader instance.

Loading SWF files into a UILoader component

You can load any SWF, JPG, PNG, or GIF file into the UILoader component with ActionScript by setting the source property of the UILoader. The basic syntax is:

```
UILoaderInstanceName.source = "Path file to be loaded goes here";
```

For example, if you want to load the instruments.swf file into the loadWindow component instance, you enter this code:

```
loadWindow.source = "instruments.swf";
```

In this exercise, you want to write a single function that determines which file to load by using the data that you stored in each item of the list. Remember setting the dataProvider parameters a little while ago? You will use those parameters each time the user selects an item from the list. For example, if the user selects the item labeled Paint in the list, then the paint.swf file will be loaded into the UILoader instance, because paint.swf is what you set as data for that particular item.

1 In the `loadFile()` function that you just created, add code between the curly braces so that the function now reads:

```
function loadFile(e:Event):void {
 loadWindow.source = e.target.selectedItem.data;
}
```

The term *target* in this case (`e.target`) refers to the list, the `selectedItem` property is the item that the user chose from the list, and the `data` property is the data that you added to that particular item in the list.

Your completed code in Frame 1 should look like this:

2 Save and test the movie.

3 In the testing environment, select the Paint item in the list. The paint.swf file will seamlessly load into the interface with its full functionality.

4 Select the Instruments item in the list. The instruments.swf file will load.

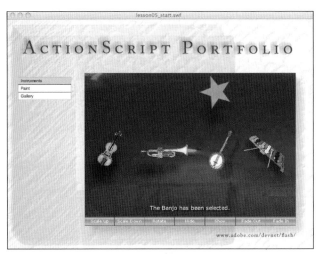

5 Select the Gallery item in the list. This will cause an error, because the gallery. swf file has not yet been created. You will create that file next.

In Lesson 11, "Using ActionScript to Control Video," you will learn how to respond to error events at runtime so that the user does not have a confusing experience if a problem occurs when a file should be loading.

6 Close the Lesson05_start.swf file to leave the testing environment and return to the authoring environment.

Creating the gallery file

Now you will create the gallery file that you referred to in the List component. This file will let the user select from a set of thumbnails to load and display JPG images in a UILoader instance. When a thumbnail image is clicked, text from an external text file that describes the selected image will also load. The text will be displayed in a text field on the Flash Stage.

The starting point for this file is provided for you as gallery.fla in the Lesson05 > Start folder. You will add quite a bit of ActionScript to this file to create its functionality, but first you will take a look at the content already in the file.

Examining the gallery.fla file

The basic layout and graphics for the gallery file have been prepared for you. You will add ActionScript to the file to control the loading of text and images.

1 From the Lessons > Lesson05 > Start folder, open the gallery.fla file.

There are four layers on the Timeline and three items on the Stage. There are no actions yet. You will add code to the `actions` layer soon. The `loader` layer contains an instance of the UILoader component.

2 With the Properties panel visible, select the UILoader component instance. It has been given the instance name `ldr`.

3 In the `text` layer, select the text field. It has been given the instance name `info`.

4 In the `thumbs` layer, select the movie clip that contains a series of thumbnail images. You will see in the Properties panel that it has been given the instance name `thumbs_mc`.

5 Double-click the `thumbs_mc` movie clip.

The seven thumbnails are each individual buttons. If you select these buttons, you'll see that they have the instance names `btn1` through `btn7`. Because these buttons are inside a movie clip named `thumbs_mc`, you describe the path from the main Timeline to these buttons in ActionScript as thumbs_mc.btn1, thumbs_mc.btn2, and so on.

6 Go back to the main Timeline by choosing Edit > Edit Document.

Adding event listeners to the thumbnails

In earlier lessons, you used the `addEventListener()` method to create buttons that respond to user clicks. Now you will do the same for the seven buttons in the `thumbs_mc` clip. In this situation, however, you will need to indicate the path for each of the buttons so that your ActionScript targets objects that are within the `thumbs_mc` clip.

1 With Frame 1 of the actions layer selected and the Actions panel visible, place the insertion point in the first line of the Actions panel.

2 Keeping in mind the path to the seven thumbnail buttons, add the following code to create an addEventListener() method for each button:

```
thumbs_mc.btn1.addEventListener(MouseEvent.CLICK, ldr1);
thumbs_mc.btn2.addEventListener(MouseEvent.CLICK, ldr2);
thumbs_mc.btn3.addEventListener(MouseEvent.CLICK, ldr3);
thumbs_mc.btn4.addEventListener(MouseEvent.CLICK, ldr4);
thumbs_mc.btn5.addEventListener(MouseEvent.CLICK, ldr5);
thumbs_mc.btn6.addEventListener(MouseEvent.CLICK, ldr6);
thumbs_mc.btn7.addEventListener(MouseEvent.CLICK, ldr7);
```

The buttons will now call functions named ldr1, ldr2, and so on. Next, you will create these functions.

3 In a line below the addEventListener() calls, create the ldr1() function to respond to the first button:

```
function ldr1(e:Event):void {
 ldr.source = "../images/image1.jpg";
}
```

When the first button is clicked, it will load an image called image1.jpg into the UILoader instance onstage. Notice the syntax for describing the path to the JPG file. The characters "../" tell ActionScript to go up one level from the location of the current Flash file and then to look in a folder named images for a file named image1.jpg. If this method of describing a path is unfamiliar to you, compare the syntax to the location of the files in the Lessons > Lesson05 folder.

4 Add one more line to this function so that it reads:

```
function ldr1(e:Event):void {
 ldr.source = "../images/image1.jpg";
 textLoad("../text/picture1.txt", 0xFFE59A);
}
```

When each button is clicked, it will load an image into the UILoader. The line you just added calls a function named textLoad() that will load text files into the text field onstage. This function does not exist yet; if you test the movie before you create the function, you will get an error message.

Notice that the call to the textLoad() function includes two parameters. The first one passes the path to a text file. The second passes a numeric color value that will be used to set the background color of the text field. You will create the textLoad() function soon, but first you'll add the functions for the remaining buttons.

5 Create functions similar to the `ldr1()` function for the other six buttons.

Note that in earlier lessons, each `addEventListener()` method you created was followed by its corresponding function. In this exercise, all the `addEventListener()` calls are grouped together, followed by all the functions. The order in which you arrange the listeners is up to you.

Your Actions panel should look like this:

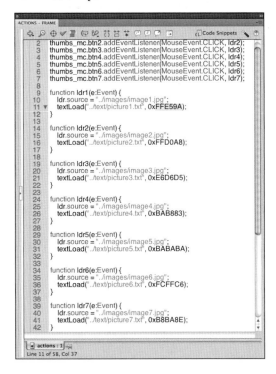

Loading text from an external file

Now you will create the code to load a different text file into the info text field for each button. The UILoader component that you have been using to load SWF and image files makes use of an ActionScript class called the `Loader`. Because the UILoader component was used, you didn't need to write ActionScript to load any files—the component took care of this process in the background. To load text or data into Flash, you use a class called `URLLoader`. Because you will not be using a component to help with the loading of the text, you will write ActionScript to create an instance of the `URLLoader` class to load text.

1 In the Actions panel, below the existing code, add a new `URLLoader` instance:

```
var loader:URLLoader = new URLLoader();
```

Next, you will create the `textLoad()` function to load text from an external file. This is the function that the button listeners that you created earlier refer to.

2 Add the following code below the code in the Actions panel:

```
function textLoad(file:String, color:uint):void {
 loader.load(new URLRequest(file));
 info.backgroundColor = color;
}
```

● **Note:** You will learn much more about formatting text fields with ActionScript in Lesson 8, "Controlling Text in ActionScript 3.0."

The textLoad() function is called when any one of the seven thumbnail buttons is clicked. If you review the button functions, you'll see that when the textLoad() function is called two parameters are sent: file and color. The file parameter is a string that describes a path to a text file, and the color parameter is a numeric color value that will be used to set the background color of the info text field onstage.

When the textLoad() function is called, it loads the text file into Flash and changes the color of the text field, but the text will not yet be displayed. To display the text, you need to set the data that has been loaded so that it is the text property of the text field.

Before you display data that is loaded from the external text files, however, you always should confirm that the data that you asked to load has actually arrived. For this, you use the COMPLETE event.

Using the COMPLETE event to confirm the loading of external text before displaying the text

The COMPLETE event uses a listener, just like the other events you have used. Add the COMPLETE event to listen for the successful loading of the requested data before the data is displayed.

1 Below the existing code in the Actions panel, add the following line:

```
loader.addEventListener(Event.COMPLETE, displayText);
```

2 Add the following lines to display the text:

```
function displayText(e:Event):void {
 info.text = loader.data;
}
```

When the loader object successfully completes the loading of one of the text files, it will display the text from that file in the info text field instance.

Confirming the loading of external content

You could have just one line of code to display the text you loaded into the loader object in the text field named info. That line would read:

```
info.text = loader.data;
```

Intuitively, you might have been inclined to add this line to the textLoad() function, like this, for example:

```
function textLoad(file:String, color:uint) {
  loader.load(new URLRequest(file));
  info.backgroundColor = color;
  info.text = loader.data;
}
```

However, while this code would work reliably locally, it would likely cause problems when the loaded text files are downloaded from a server. Remember that each line of ActionScript is usually executed in a small fraction of a second. If on one line of code you instruct Flash Player to load a text file from a server, and a few lines later you give instructions to display the text, the odds are good that there will not have been enough time to download the text file needed for display. This will cause a runtime error.

Whenever you use ActionScript to load content from a remote location, it's good practice to confirm that the load has completed before you use the loaded content.

Fortunately, as you have seen, ActionScript makes doing so relatively easy, because the Loader class and the URLLoader class each have a built-in COMPLETE event, which automatically fires when a request for loaded content is completed successfully.

The completed code for this file should look like this:

```
thumbs_mc.btn1.addEventListener(MouseEvent.CLICK, ldr1);
thumbs_mc.btn2.addEventListener(MouseEvent.CLICK, ldr2);
thumbs_mc.btn3.addEventListener(MouseEvent.CLICK, ldr3);
thumbs_mc.btn4.addEventListener(MouseEvent.CLICK, ldr4);
thumbs_mc.btn5.addEventListener(MouseEvent.CLICK, ldr5);
thumbs_mc.btn6.addEventListener(MouseEvent.CLICK, ldr6);
thumbs_mc.btn7.addEventListener(MouseEvent.CLICK, ldr7);

function ldr1(e:Event) {
  ldr.source = "../images/image1.jpg";
```

(code continues on next page)

```
    textLoad("../text/picture1.txt", 0xFFE59A);
  }

  function ldr2(e:Event) {
    ldr.source = "../images/image2.jpg";
    textLoad("../text/picture2.txt", 0xFFD0A8);
  }

  function ldr3(e:Event) {
    ldr.source = "../images/image3.jpg";
    textLoad("../text/picture3.txt", 0xE6D6D5);
  }

  function ldr4(e:Event) {
    ldr.source = "../images/image4.jpg";
    textLoad("../text/picture4.txt", 0xBAB883);
  }

  function ldr5(e:Event) {
    ldr.source = "../images/image5.jpg";
    textLoad("../text/picture5.txt", 0xBABABA);
  }

  function ldr6(e:Event) {
    ldr.source = "../images/image6.jpg";
    textLoad("../text/picture6.txt", 0xFCFFC6);
  }

  function ldr7(e:Event) {
    ldr.source = "../images/image7.jpg";
    textLoad("../text/picture7.txt", 0xB8BA8E);
  }

  var loader:URLLoader = new URLLoader();

  function textLoad(file:String, color:uint):void {
    loader.load(new URLRequest(file));
    info.backgroundColor = color;
  }

  loader.addEventListener(Event.COMPLETE, displayText);

  function displayText(e:Event):void {
    info.text = loader.data;
  }
```

Adding a scroll bar to the text field

The text files that you will be loading contain more text than will fit visibly in the onstage text field. Fortunately, a built-in component called UIScrollBar lets you easily create a working scroll bar for that field.

Scrolling text is an important feature in many interfaces when space is limited. Because the info text field onstage is not large enough to display all the text in the text files that may be loaded into it, you will create a scroll bar for that field.

1 Select the info text field onstage.

2 Open the Text menu and ensure that the text field has been set to Scrollable.

3 With the Components panel open (Window > Components), select the UIScrollBar component from the list of User Interface components.

4 Drag a UIScrollBar instance to the Stage so that it lines up with the upper-right corner of the info text field.

Depending on your "Snapping" settings (View > Snapping) you may need to use your arrow keys or type numeric settings in the Property inspector to place the UIScrollBar exactly where you wish.

5 With the new UIScrollBar instance selected onstage, make the Property inspector visible (Window > Properties).

6 In the component parameters section of the Property inspector, locate the `scrollTargetName` property. Flash CS5 will automatically associate an instance of the UIScrollBar with an abutting text field. Confirm that `scrollTargetName` is set to `info;` if it is not, then type **info** in the field for this property.

7 Save and test the movie. When you click any of the thumbnail buttons, a new image loads and appears in the UILoader, and text appears in the info field, with its background color changed. A working scroll bar is available for the text field.

8 Save this file and return to the lesson05_start.fla file.

9 Test the lesson05_start.fla file. Pressing the Gallery item in the list now opens your new gallery file in the file's UILoader instance. The gallery's buttons should still perform their functions in the movie's interface.

Some suggestions to try on your own

Experimenting on your own will help you solidify your knowledge of the techniques in this lesson. Here are a few suggestions to get you started:

- Create a new Flash movie, and add another item to the list in lesson05_start.fla to load your new movie.

- Replace the JPG files in the gallery.fla file with your own JPG files. Try getting files to load from a different path.

- Experiment with some of the other User Interface components that ship with Flash CS5. Refer to Flash Help for information about their parameters.

In the next lesson, you will learn how to create preloaders to monitor the loading progress of your Flash files.

Review questions

1 Name the file types that you can load into a Flash project with the UILoader component.

2 Name an event that is available for the List component that can respond when the user makes a selection from a List instance.

3 Name an event associated with the URLLoader class that you can use to confirm that data has finished loading.

Review answers

1 The UILoader component can be used to load SWF, JPG, PNG, and GIF files into a Flash file.

2 You can use the CHANGE event to keep track of when a user makes a new selection from a List component instance.

3 You can use the COMPLETE event to confirm the successful loading of data into a URLLoader instance.

6 CREATING PRELOADERS IN ACTIONSCRIPT 3.0

Lesson overview

In this lesson, you will learn to do the following:

- Check your Flash files to determine whether you need to use a preloader.

- Use the testing and simulation tools in Flash to experience your projects at different connection speeds.

- Use the PROGRESS event and methods of the UILoader class to track the progress of loading media.

- Use the ProgressBar component to give the user feedback on loading media.

- Calculate the percentage of requested content that has loaded, and display that percentage in a text field for the user.

- Use the COMPLETE event to hide the preloader and display content when it is completely loaded.

- Use the percentage of a file that is loaded to trigger the playback of frames in a movie clip.

 This lesson will take approximately 2.5 hours.

In this lesson you will learn to monitor and give your users feedback on the progress of loading content.

The lessons so far have supplied you with enough ActionScript to add quite a bit of functionality to your Flash projects, and the lesson files you have completed should all work seamlessly on your local machine. However, a large percentage of Flash projects are intended as online applications. When you are creating a Flash project for the web, you must take into account the important fact that all the content in your project must be downloaded to your end users' machines before they can view it. The term *preloader* is frequently used to describe the techniques used to track the loading of content into Flash Player, give the user any needed feedback on that loading, and respond to the results of the loading.

Nearly everyone who has surfed the web has encountered preloaders. You meet the classic example of a preloader when you load content into a web page: While the content is loading, a progress bar appears and expands gradually to the right as a text message tells you what percentage of the content has loaded. When the content is fully loaded, both the progress bar and text disappear and are replaced by the loaded content. In this lesson, you will create this archetypal preloader.

While creating a basic preloader may not be the most intriguing use of ActionScript, knowledge of how to ensure that your user has a good experience downloading your content is a critical part of good Flash development. As you become more comfortable with the concepts of preloaders, you will be able to implement creative variations on the techniques that serve the purpose of a preloader but offer the user something more interesting to do than watch the movement of a progress bar. The final steps in the lesson will show you some possibilities for alternative preloading techniques.

The file for this lesson is called lesson06_start.fla and can be found in the Lessons folder (Lessons > Lesson06 > Start > lesson06_start.fla). It is the completed file from Lesson 5, "Using ActionScript and Components to Load Content." Up until this point, we have not done much to prepare this file for successful web streaming. Now we'll look at some of the tools in Flash that will help you see how this file will perform online.

Tools in the testing environment

Flash ships with a number of extremely helpful tools for troubleshooting potential problems in your projects and testing your projects' performance under various user conditions. Each time you test a Flash web-based project by choosing Control > Test Movie, you are taken to the testing environment in Flash. In this testing environment, the Flash menu system changes, offering a number of useful features that help ensure that your Flash projects will perform as desired. Two important features in the testing environment are Bandwidth Profiler and Simulate Download. You may already be using these tools in Flash; if not, you are about to discover how to use them to help create a good user experience.

Bandwidth Profiler

The Bandwidth Profiler tool offers visual feedback helpful for estimating the download times for the content of your Flash projects. It works in conjunction with the Download Settings menu to compare the size of the content in the frames of your Flash files with the time needed to download this content at the estimated connection speed of your audience. Since the Lesson 2 project made use of the Flash Timeline, you will use the completed file from that lesson with the Bandwidth Profiler tool.

1   Open the Lesson02_complete.fla file (Lessons > Lesson02 > Complete > lesson02_complete.fla).

2   Test the file (Control > Test Movie).

   The feedback visible in the Bandwidth Profiler tool, as well as that offered by some of the other testing tools, is based on what you tell Flash is the minimum connection speed of your intended audience. For this lesson, we will assume that all users have at least a 32 kilobytes-per-second (KB/s) connection. However, this connection speed will not necessarily be the speed used by a given audience; in real projects, be sure to discuss the intended audience with the team or the client.

3   While still in the testing environment, choose View > Download Settings > DSL (32.6 KB/s).

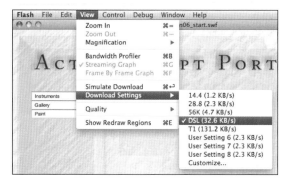

   Now the testing tools will give you feedback on how your movie will perform at this data rate.

4 Choose View > Bandwidth Profiler.

The Bandwidth Profiler tool contains a lot of useful information. Let's focus on the main streaming graph in the right part of the Bandwidth Profiler screen. The Timeline in this graph represents the main Timeline of the Flash file that you are testing. The movie we are working with is set to a frame rate of 15 fps. This means each frame in the graph represents 1/15 of a second.

If a SWF file is streaming from the web, the content in each frame of the Flash Timeline is downloaded sequentially, starting with Frame 1. If the content in a frame is not fully downloaded when Flash Player reaches that frame, then the entire movie freezes until the frame's content is fully loaded; playback then resumes. Obviously, having frames that are not fully loaded when the viewer needs to see them is a situation to be avoided.

The Bandwidth Profiler tool gives visual feedback that clearly shows where potential problems may lie. The red line across the graph represents the data rate that you have set for your download setting, and the vertical bars represent frames of content that need to be downloaded. When the bars are on or below the red line, the frames they represent have content whose total size will download in real time under typical circumstances at your selected download setting. Bars that extend above the line represent frames whose total content is too large to download in real time.

In this file, Frame 1 is the only frame that is significantly above the line. As the streaming graph shows, Frame 1 needs to download approximately 64 KB of content before it can play, and that will take more than the 1/15 of a second it would take to play that frame. However, at our selected rate of 32 KB/s, the user would need to wait only approximately 2 seconds before the file would begin to play—and most users would not mind, or even notice, a wait of 2 seconds before a file begins. All of the other frames in the project have significantly less new content and would likely load in real time. If, however, you notice that the Bandwidth Profiler graph shows frames after Frame 1 that spike up significantly higher than the red line, then you will want to either modify that content to decrease the file size or use some type of preloading technique to account for the time needed to load that content. For Timeline-based projects, this graph is extremely helpful.

However, for projects like the one you completed in Lesson 5, in which the Timeline is not used extensively but content is loaded in at runtime, you are likely to have loading issues that are not made apparent in this graph. Fortunately, the Flash testing environment has tools for simulating the loading of files into a Flash project that can help in this situation. The Lesson06_start.fla file is the same as the completed file in Lesson 5. This is the file you will use to test the loading of content and to create a preloader when you need it.

5 Close the Lesson02_complete.fla file. You do not need to save any changes to this file.

Simulate Download

The purpose of this lesson is to create the feedback that will keep users aware of what is happening, so that they'll stay around long enough to view your content. But before we begin creating that feedback, let's look at the Simulate Download feature in the testing environment that allows you to experience the downloading of your Flash files as your users might. Simulate Download plays your file as if it were being downloaded at whatever connection speed was chosen in the Download Settings menu (View > Download Settings).

● **Note:** Remember that these settings are just approximations of average connections, and that every user's experience on the Internet can vary dramatically from moment to moment regardless of their typical connection speed. The values reported by all the testing tools should be seen as fairly conservative estimates under normal circumstances.

1 Open the Lesson06_start.fla file.

2 Test the file (Control > Test Movie).

3 In the View menu, deselect Bandwidth Profiler.

   The biggest problem with this file will occur when the user tries to load the external SWF files in the UILoader that you created in Lesson 5. These files are not huge—they range only from about 12 KB to about 70 KB—but they are large enough that your intended audience will not receive the files instantly. If members of your audience tried to view this file from the web in its current state, each time they selected a file to load from the menu, they would receive no feedback about the status of the load in progress.

4 While still in the testing environment, play your file (lesson06_start.fla) as if it were downloading from a typical DSL connection by choosing View > Simulate Download.

The Simulate Download command works in conjunction with the current download setting. The current test will run at 32.6 KB/s, since that's what you set in an earlier step.

The file should take a few seconds longer to start than in previous tests, but then it should play normally.

5   From the list on the left, choose Paint. The paint.swf file should load relatively quickly, because it's fairly small.

6   Choose either Gallery or Instruments from the list, and notice that the wait is much longer than for the Paint file. Most users would consider it unacceptable to have to wait this long for content, with no interim feedback letting them know that something is happening. You will add feedback that reports to the user what percent of the requested data is loaded.

7   Close the window containing the lesson06_start.swf file to leave the testing environment and return to the Flash authoring environment.

Creating a text field and progress bar to track loading

As mentioned earlier, the classic example of a preloader is a progress bar that shows both the loading progress and a text field displaying the percent of the loading that has taken place. Now you will begin to add those elements to the project.

1   Add a new layer to your Timeline above the existing components layer and name it **preloader content**. This is where you will place the progress bar and text field for your preloader.

● **Note:** TLF is the new default text engine in Flash CS5. You will learn more about the format and its capabilities in Lesson 8.

2   From the Tools panel, select the Text tool and create a new Text Layout Format (TLF) text field onstage.

3   In the Properties panel, give the new text field the instance name **prog_txt**.

4   Switch to the Selection tool and with the prog_txt field still selected in the Properties panel, under Position And Size, give the text field these settings: X = **30**, Y = **440**, W = **150**, H = **50**.

5 In the Characters settings in the Properties panel, choose any font family you like, a font size of 12, and a color that contrasts with the background. (In a coming lesson, you will learn to create and format text entirely with code.)

Next, you will add a ProgressBar component.

6 Open the Components panel (Window > Components), and from the User Interface components list, select the ProgressBar component.

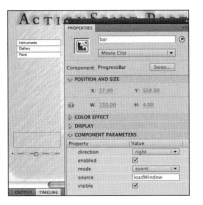

7 With the `preloader content` layer selected, drag an instance of the ProgressBar to the Stage and place it directly below the prog_txt field. If a dialog box appears saying A Component with This Name Already Exists in This Document, click Replace Existing Component and then OK.

8 With the new instance selected and the Properties panel visible, give your ProgressBar the instance name **bar**.

9 With the new ProgressBar instance still selected, in the Component Parameters section of the Properties panel, set the ProgressBar component's `source` parameter to `loadWindow`.

The `ProgressBar` instance will now be used to track the progress of files loading into the onstage `UILoader` instance.

Inserting ActionScript to track progress of the UILoader component

If you completed Lesson 5, you will remember using a UILoader component to load image and SWF files. The UILoader component has ActionScript events, properties, and methods that make it relatively easy for you to monitor the progress of files being loaded into it. The text field and ProgressBar instances that you just created will use these UILoader methods and properties to give accurate feedback to the user on loading progress.

1 With the Actions panel visible, select Frame 1 of the `actions` layer.

   Since the ProgressBar component you added does not need to be visible until the user chooses to load a file, we'll hide it by setting its `visible` property to `false`.

2 On a new line below the existing code, add the following:

   ```
   bar.visible = false;
   ```

   The Actions panel should now look like the following screen.

   You may remember from Lesson 5 that content is being loaded into a `UILoader` instance onstage that has an instance name of `loadWindow`. The loading takes place any time the user makes a selection from the onstage list component that has an instance name of `loadList`.

   The code on line 4 here (your line numbers may vary) uses the `source` property of the UILoader component to load each selected file. This technique works fine for choosing the file that will load into the UILoader component, but it does not offer many options for tracking the loading progress. The `load` method of the UILoader component provides an alternative way to load content into the component and offers much more control.

3 Change the line that now reads:

   ```
   loadWindow.source = e.target.selectedItem.data;
   ```

   so that it reads:

   ```
   loadWindow.load(new URLRequest(e.target.selectedItem.data));
   ```

If you tested the file now, the results would be exactly the same as before. Each selection from the list would load the file that was associated with that selection. However, now that the loading is being accomplished by the `load` method, you can access events that are associated with the loading.

Repeatedly while a requested file is loading, an event takes place called PROGRESS. Each time this event occurs, it reports the number of bytes of the file that have loaded. When the file has successfully finished loading, another event, named COMPLETE, automatically occurs. These are the events you will use for your preloader.

Adding event listeners for PROGRESS and COMPLETE

The process for adding event listeners for the PROGRESS and COMPLETE events is nearly identical to the process you followed to add event listeners for mouse and frame events in previous lessons. First you create addEventListener() methods for these two events, and then you write event-handling functions to respond when the events take place.

1 Make sure that the Actions panel is visible and that the actions layer is selected.

2 In the existing code, locate the loadFile() function. It should now read:

```
function loadFile(e:Event):void {
  loadWindow.load(new URLRequest(e.target.selectedItem.data));
}
```

3 In the body of the function, add two addEventListener() methods to the loadWindow component so that the function now reads:

```
function loadFile(e:Event):void {
  loadWindow.load(new URLRequest(e.target.selectedItem.data));
  loadWindow.addEventListener(ProgressEvent.PROGRESS,
  ¬progressHandler);
  loadWindow.addEventListener(Event.COMPLETE, completeHandler);
}
```

The PROGRESS event will fire repeatedly any time a file is loading into the UILoader component. When the PROGRESS event occurs, it will call a function named progressHandler(). You will create this function soon, and it will contain much of the preloader functionality.

The COMPLETE event will be triggered once each time a file has loaded into the UILoader component successfully. When the COMPLETE event occurs, it will call a function named completeHandler(). This function will be used to hide all the preloader elements and to remove the event listeners when they are no longer needed. You will create this function soon as well.

Creating the progressHandler() function

The progressHandler() function will repeat regularly while the requested file is loading (exactly how often will vary). This function will be used to monitor and report on the progress of the loading.

In the Actions panel, below the existing code, add the following function:

```
14   function progressHandler(e:ProgressEvent):void
15   {
16       bar.visible = true;
17       prog_txt.visible = true;
18       var percent:int = loadWindow.percentLoaded;
19       prog_txt.text = String(loadWindow.bytesLoaded) + " of " + String(loadWindow.bytesTotal) + " bytes" + "\n" + " (" + percent + "% loaded)";
20       bar.setProgress(e.bytesLoaded, e.bytesTotal);
21   }
```

Notice that the parameter for the progressHandler() function has the data type of ProgressEvent. The ProgressEvent event works very similarly to the events you have already used.

Lines 16 and 17 here (your line numbers may vary) set both the ProgressBar component and the text field you created to visible when the ProgressEvent event takes place.

Line 18 creates a new local variable called percent and stores the percentLoaded property of the UILoader component. This property should change every time the ProgressEvent event takes place. The percent variable keeps track of the percentage of the requested file that has been loaded. Notice that the data type of the percent variable is set to int. Previously, when you have stored a numeric value in a variable, you have set the data type to Number. The reason that int was chosen in this case is that unlike the Number data type, which can return any number including fractions, int will always return an integer—in this case, an integer between 0 and 100. Now your users will read that, say, 49 percent of the file has loaded, rather than 49.34572194858 percent.

Line 19 is where the text feedback is created for the user. First, two additional very useful properties of the UILoader class are used. The bytesLoaded property, not surprisingly, returns the number of bytes of the file loaded; equally intuitively, the bytesTotal property returns the total number of bytes for the entire file. These two properties are converted to strings so they can be added to a sentence that tells the user how many bytes of the total have loaded. The characters \n force a new line in the text field, and then the current value of the variable percent is displayed, along with some literal characters to make the line more readable.

Finally, line 20 uses the setProgress method of the ProgressBar component to provide graphical feedback of the loading progress. The setProgress method takes two parameters: The first value describes the progress that has been made so far: in this case, the number of bytes that are currently loaded. The second parameter is the maximum possible progress, which in this case is the total size (in bytes) of the loading file. As the value of bytesLoaded approaches that of bytesTotal, the progress bar expands to the right.

Before you test your movie, there is one more function to add for the COMPLETE event.

Adding the completeHandler() function

Now we'll add the function that will respond to the COMPLETE event.

1 Below the existing code in the Actions panel, add the following:

```
23  function completeHandler(event:Event):void
24  {
25      bar.visible = false;
26      prog_txt.visible = false;
27      loadWindow.removeEventListener(ProgressEvent.PROGRESS, progressHandler);
28      loadWindow.removeEventListener(Event.COMPLETE, completeHandler);
29  }
```

This code is a little simpler than that for the progressHandler() function.
Lines 25 and 26 hide both the progress bar and the text field that display the
loading progress. Remember that since the requested load is now completed,
these items are no longer necessary. The event listeners themselves are also no
longer needed, so lines 27 and 28 remove both the PROGRESS and COMPLETE
listeners. If the user decides to load a file later by selecting another item from
the list, the listeners will be added once again.

Your completed code should now look like this:

```
//import statements may appear here that were automatically
¬added by Flash

loadList.addEventListener(Event.CHANGE, loadFile);

function loadFile(e:Event):void
{
 loadWindow.load(new URLRequest(e.target.selectedItem.data));
 loadWindow.addEventListener(ProgressEvent.PROGRESS,
 ¬progressHandler);
 loadWindow.addEventListener(Event.COMPLETE, completeHandler);
}

bar.visible = false;

function progressHandler(e:ProgressEvent):void
{
 bar.visible = true;
 prog_txt.visible = true;
 var percent:int = loadWindow.percentLoaded;
 prog_txt.text = String(loadWindow.bytesLoaded) + " of " +
 ¬String(loadWindow.bytesTotal) + " bytes" + "\n" + "
 ¬(" + percent + "% loaded)";
```

(code continues on next page)

```
    bar.setProgress(e.bytesLoaded, e.bytesTotal);
}

function completeHandler(event:Event):void
{
bar.visible = false;
prog_txt.visible = false;
loadWindow.removeEventListener(ProgressEvent.PROGRESS,
¬progressHandler);
loadWindow.removeEventListener(Event.COMPLETE,
¬completeHandler);
}
```

2 Test your movie.

3 In the testing environment, choose View > Simulate Download.

4 From the list, choose Instruments. The progress bar and the text field should give accurate information about the loading of the file.

5 Try choosing the other two items in the list and watch their load progress. Notice that when the load is complete, the preloader items (the text field and the progress bar) disappear.

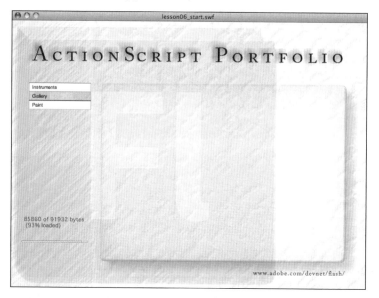

Controlling the frames of a movie clip to reflect loading progress

The ProgressBar component provides a very easy and useful way to give the user clear feedback on loading progress. Anyone who has used a computer will understand the purpose of the progress bar. However, it is not the most interesting thing to stare at for very long. Fortunately, the same techniques that you just used to track loading progress can be used in a wide variety of ways to give the user a more interesting waiting-period experience. For example, for users who have very slow connections and a lot of content to load, you may want to display new text in a text field every time a certain percentage of the content has loaded. With this technique, you can give users lots of instructional or entertaining information to read while they are waiting.

Another useful technique is to have the percentage of loaded content determine which frame of a movie clip onstage is displayed. The data rate of the download will determine the frame rate of the movie clip.

Let's add a movie clip to the project that is triggered by loading progress. You don't want to give the user a new, large movie clip to load, since the goal of this technique is just to maintain interest while other content is loading, so we will add a small clip that relies on some simple graphics and text.

1 Open the library, if it's not visible (Window > Library).

2 Locate the LoadClip symbol and double-click its icon to view its Timeline. Notice that the symbol's Timeline contains 100 frames.

You will write code that uses the UILoader loading percentage to determine which frame of this movie clip is displayed.

3 In the upper-left corner of the Stage, click the tab that says Scene 1 to return to the main Timeline.

4 With the preloader content layer selected, drag an instance of the LoadClip symbol to the Stage above your other preloader content.

5 With the LoadClip symbol selected, go to the Properties panel and give the symbol the instance name **loadAnimation**.

Adding ActionScript for the loadAnimation clip

If you tested the movie now, the loadAnimation clip would play continuously for the duration that it is on the Stage. By adding a few lines of code, you can make the loadAnimation clip appear only when new content is loading, and you can make it play once through as the load progresses.

1 With the Actions panel visible, select Frame 1 of the actions layer.

2 Directly below the loadFile() function, locate the line of code that reads:

```
bar.visible = false;
```

3 On a new line below this code, add code to stop the Timeline of the loadAnimation clip:

```
bar.visible = false;
loadAnimation.stop();
```

4 Add a line to make the loadAnimation clip invisible at the start of the movie:

```
bar.visible=false;
loadAnimation.stop();
loadAnimation.visible = false;
```

5 On the next line, give the animation a little transparency (which will not be noticed until the visible property is set to true):

```
bar.visible=false;
loadAnimation.stop();
loadAnimation.visible = false;
loadAnimation.alpha = .8;
```

You want the loadAnimation clip to appear while the progress of a loading file is being tracked. You will add some code to the existing progressHandler() function to accomplish this.

Currently, the function should read:

```
function progressHandler(e:ProgressEvent):void {
bar.visible = true;
prog_txt.visible = true;
var percent:int = loadWindow.percentLoaded;
```

```
prog_txt.text = String(loadWindow.bytesLoaded) + " of
¬" + String(loadWindow.bytesTotal) + " bytes" + "\n"+
¬" (" + percent + "% loaded) ";
bar.setProgress(e.bytesLoaded, e.bytesTotal);
}
```

6 Click at the end of the line that reads:

```
prog_txt.visible = true;
```

and press Enter/Return to add a new line.

7 On the new line, add this code to make the loadAnimation clip visible:

```
loadAnimation.visible = true;
```

Now add the code that ties the frames of the loadAnimation clip to the loading progress.

8 In the progressHandler function, locate the line that creates the percent variable:

```
var percent:int = loadWindow.percentLoaded;
```

9 On a new line below the percent variable, insert the following code:

```
loadAnimation.gotoAndStop(percent);
```

Recall that the variable percent represents the percentage of the file that is loaded.

By using a variable to stand in for the frame number, you can create a goto action whose frame changes as the variable value changes. In this case, as the percentage of the file loaded increases, the movie clip progressively plays through its frames. Each 1 percent of loading progress would advance the loadAnimation clip one frame.

The only remaining potential problem with this code is that it might send a request to navigate to Frame 0 when 0 percent of the file is loaded. To prevent this, we will use a Math class method named ceil, which rounds any number up to the nearest whole number.

10 Adjust the new line so that it reads:

```
loadAnimation.gotoAndStop(Math.ceil(percent));
```

The full function should now read:

```
function progressHandler(e:ProgressEvent):void {
 bar.visible = true;
 prog_txt.visible = true;
 loadAnimation.visible = true;
 var percent:int = loadWindow.percentLoaded;
```

(code continues on next page)

```
loadAnimation.gotoAndStop(Math.ceil(percent));
prog_txt.text = String(loadWindow.bytesLoaded) + " of
¬" + String(loadWindow.bytesTotal) + " bytes"+"\n" + "
¬(" + percent + "% loaded) ";
bar.setProgress(e.bytesLoaded, e.bytesTotal);
}
```

When the loading is complete, you want the animation to disappear with the rest of the preloader content.

11 Locate the `completeHandler()` function.

12 Add a line to set the `loadAnimation` clip's `visible` property to `false`. The completed function should now read:

```
function completeHandler(event:Event):void {
bar.visible = false;
prog_txt.visible = false;
loadAnimation.visible = false;
loadWindow.removeEventListener(ProgressEvent.PROGRESS,
¬progressHandler);
loadWindow.removeEventListener(Event.COMPLETE,
¬completeHandler);
}
```

The completed code should look like this:

```
loadList.addEventListener(Event.CHANGE, loadFile);
function loadFile(e:Event):void {
loadWindow.load(new URLRequest(e.target.selectedItem.data));
loadWindow.addEventListener(ProgressEvent.PROGRESS,
¬progressHandler);
loadWindow.addEventListener(Event.COMPLETE, completeHandler);
}
bar.visible = false;
loadAnimation.visible = false;
loadAnimation.stop();
loadAnimation.alpha = .8;
function progressHandler(e:ProgressEvent):void {
bar.visible = true;
prog_txt.visible = true;
loadAnimation.visible = true;
var percent:int = loadWindow.percentLoaded;
loadAnimation.gotoAndStop(Math.ceil(percent));
prog_txt.text = String(loadWindow.bytesLoaded) + " of
¬" + String(loadWindow.bytesTotal) + " bytes" + "\n"+"
¬(" + percent + "% loaded) ";
bar.setProgress(e.bytesLoaded, e.bytesTotal);
}
function completeHandler(event:Event):void {
```

```
bar.visible = false;
prog_txt.visible = false;
loadAnimation.visible = false;
loadWindow.removeEventListener(ProgressEvent.PROGRESS,
¬progressHandler);
loadWindow.removeEventListener(Event.COMPLETE,
completeHandler);
}
```

13 Test your movie: In the testing environment, choose View > Simulate Download.

14 From the file list, choose Gallery. You should still get the feedback about the loading progress, but in addition the animation should now appear and play exactly once through while the file is downloading. When the load is complete, the animation should disappear.

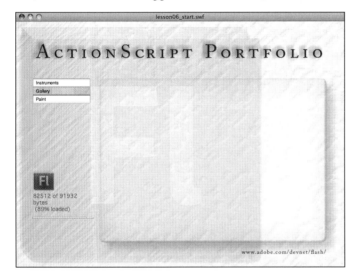

Remember, the loadAnimation clip could have any graphical content, and it would work the same way, offering many creative possibilities. Be sure, however, to monitor the file size of movie clips that you are using in this way. Making the content of a movie clip too large would defeat its purpose as a preloader.

The preloader techniques in this lesson were used for loading content into a UILoader component, but the same or similar techniques could be used for loading any media or data into Flash Player. They could also be used to monitor loading of the main movie.

Get in the habit of using preloaders whenever necessary, and search the Flash Help files and other Flash community resources for variations on the preloading techniques covered here.

As your projects get larger and more sophisticated, staying aware of the user's potential experience when streaming and loading your files becomes increasingly important. The creativity you apply to the otherwise mundane task of creating preloaders can become a significant and interesting feature of your Flash project's identity.

Some suggestions to try on your own

You now have a large and expanding repertoire of techniques to play with. You can probably come up with many variations on the techniques in this lesson. Here are a few suggestions to get you started:

- Create your own movie clip and use it as feedback for loading progress. Your work will be easier if the number of frames in your clip is a multiple of 100, so that the frames can easily be associated with the integer for the percentage of the file that has been loaded.

- Add a new item to the loadList component and use it to load a much larger file. Try to create preloader content that will hold the user's interest that much longer.

- Create a new text field and have the `text` property of the field change as the percentage of the file loaded increases. For example, you could use a conditional statement to make the text change every time the `percent` variable increases by 20. Tell a story that unfolds while a large file downloads.

- Go to the gallery file that you created in Lesson 5 and try to add a preloader for the images being loaded into the UILoader instance in that file.

Review questions

1   Name two features in the Flash testing environment that can help determine the user's experience when downloading your Flash projects.

2   What are the two ActionScript properties that keep track of the total number of bytes in a file and the current number of bytes loaded?

3   What are two events of the UILoader component class that can be used to track loading?

Review answers

1   In the Flash testing environment, you can use the Bandwidth Profiler tool (View > Bandwidth Profiler) to determine which frames will load in real time at a given data rate, and you can use Simulate Download (View > Simulate Download) to play a Flash project as if it were being downloaded over a connection with a specific bandwidth. Both of these tools test your project based on the download settings (View > Download Settings) chosen in the testing environment.

2   The UILoader PROGRESS event has two properties that can keep track of loading content. The number of bytes of requested content that have loaded can be retrieved as the bytesLoaded property, and the total number of bytes can be found with the bytesTotal property.

3   The PROGRESS event of the UILoader class takes place regularly while a file is being loaded into the component, and the COMPLETE event takes place when the file has successfully finished loading.

7 USING ARRAYS AND LOOPS IN ACTIONSCRIPT 3.0

Lesson overview

In this lesson, you will learn to do the following:

- Associate a movie clip symbol in the library with an ActionScript class.

- Create ActionScript arrays to store, manipulate, and reference lists of data from a single variable.

- Use methods of the `Array` class to store and remove references to `MovieClip` instances and their properties.

- Create `for` loops to control the repetition of ActionScript.

- Add `MovieClip` instances to the Stage from the library using ActionScript.

- Use ActionScript to drag and drop movie clips.

- Use the hitTestObject() method to detect when two movie clips are overlapping.

- Use a `for` loop to cycle through an array and check the properties of its elements.

- Create a simple game with scoring and outcome feedback given in text fields.

 This lesson will take approximately 3 hours.

This lesson introduces two very important ActionScript tools: the array and the `for` loop. These are common tools in many programming languages; once you have gained a level of comfort with them, you'll find that they make a great many tasks possible.

ActionScript that places library items onstage and
makes them interactive.

As with many other programming concepts, the syntax for implementing these techniques can initially be confusing. But rest assured that with a little experience you'll find the techniques actually very easy, and what seemed perplexing at first will soon seem straightforward and quickly become a useful part of your ActionScript repertoire.

In the exercise for this lesson, you'll learn to create a simple game that makes extensive use of arrays and `for` loops.

Examining the completed file

To get a sense of what you are building in this lesson, it may be helpful to view the completed version. You can do this by opening the Lessons > Lesson07 > Complete > lesson07_complete.fla file.

1   With the lesson07_complete.fla file open, choose Control > Test Movie to test the file as a SWF file.

2   Click the basket to move it around and attempt to catch as much fruit as you can.

   • If you catch 20 pieces of fruit before letting 20 pieces get past your basket, you will win the game.

   • If you let 20 pieces of fruit fall below Stage level, you will lose the game.

3   If you want, play the game multiple times. Close the lesson07_complete.swf file and retest the movie.

4   When you are finished, close the lesson07_complete.fla file.

Examining the starting file

To begin this project, open the Lessons > Lesson07 > Start > lesson07_start.fla file. The main Timeline of the lesson07_start.fla file has four layers. The bottom `background` layer contains a static background graphic created using Flash CS5 Professional's new and improved Deco tool. The `basket` layer contains an instance of a movie clip symbol that contains a graphic of a basket. This has been given the instance name of `basket_mc`. The `text` layer has two text fields with the instance names of `field1_txt` and `field2_txt`. The `actions` layer is empty. You will place all the code for this lesson in Frame 1 of this top layer. Before that, however, let's take a closer look at the movie clips that will be used in this project.

1   With the Properties panel visible, select the `basket_mc` movie clip in the `basket` layer.

2 Double-click the basket_mc clip on the Stage to view the clip's Timeline. Notice that the clip's Timeline has three layers and 20 frames. The basket layer contains the static image of the basket. The fruit layer has a new keyframe every five frames. The first frame of the fruit layer contains no content. Each subsequent keyframe in this layer contains increasing amounts of fruit.

3 The actions layer of the Basket clip has an action on the first frame. With the Actions panel visible, select Frame 1 of the clip's actions layer.

Notice that there is a stop() action on Frame 1. When the Flash project is played, this action will prevent the movie clip from going beyond its first frame. This means that at the beginning of the game, there will be no fruit in the basket. As your user collects fruit in the basket, ActionScript that you will create later in this lesson will send the user to the later frames in this Timeline to create the illusion that the basket is being filled with fruit.

4 In the upper-left corner above the Stage, click the tab labeled Scene 1 to return to the main Timeline. The remaining graphics and functionality for this project will be added using ActionScript in Frame 1 of the main Timeline.

Adding MovieClip instances to the Stage from the Flash Library

One of the great benefits of Flash is that it gives you a strong set of design tools that you can control with a powerful programming language. One excellent use of this combination of design and programming tools in Flash is to create graphics and animations in movie clip symbols that can be stored in the Flash Library and added to or removed from the Stage at runtime using ActionScript.

Setting the linkage properties of a movie clip

If you plan to place instances of a movie clip from the library onto the Stage using ActionScript, you first need to set the linkage properties of that clip in the library.

The library is a convenient tool for storing and managing multiple elements. Objects in the library that are not placed onstage at authoring time are not, by default, included in published SWF files (which is generally a good thing, since including them would make SWF files unnecessarily large).

When an object is added to the Flash Stage from the library, it is automatically identified for inclusion in the compiled .swf file. However, when a movie clip in the library is not placed onstage in the Flash interface but is instead added to the Stage at runtime with ActionScript, it needs to be explicitly set to be included in the .swf file. This is accomplished in the clip's linkage settings, which can be found in the Symbol Properties dialog box for each movie clip symbol in the library.

You will set these properties for the movie clips in the library that contain images of fruit so that you can place instances of these clips onstage and control them with ActionScript.

1   Open the library for the lesson07_start.fla file (Window > Library).

2   In the Library panel, select the Apple movie clip symbol.

3   With the Apple clip selected, choose Properties from the menu found in the upper-right corner of the Library panel.

4   If you don't see the Linkage section of the Symbol Properties dialog box, click the Advanced button in the bottom-left corner.

5   In the Linkage section, select the Export For ActionScript check box.

6   Leave the Class field and all other settings as they are, and click OK.

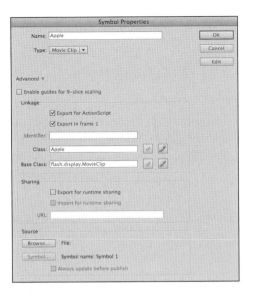

About the base class and inheritance

Notice in the Symbol Properties dialog box that the new Apple class will have a base class of flash.display.MovieClip. This is another way of saying that the Apple class extends the MovieClip class, so that in addition to performing the functions of its own particular class, the Apple class will be able to do anything that the MovieClip class can do and can function as a movie clip. Inheritance is a large part of object-oriented programming (OOP), and you will see a number of ways to take advantage of inheritance in coming lessons.

7 A dialog box will likely appear that indicates that a definition for the class cannot be found. This is normal and is telling you that Flash is creating a new class for your movie clip. Click OK, and Flash will create a new Apple class.

8 Repeat steps 2 through 7 for the Banana, Orange, Pear, and Strawberry movie clip symbols.

When Export for ActionScript is selected as it is here, a new ActionScript class is created that references this movie clip. The name in the Class field defaults to the same name as the symbol (in this case, Apple, Banana, and so on). Of course, you have the option of changing the class name, but for this lesson, the defaults are fine.

Now that all of the fruit movie clips are available for ActionScript control, you will write ActionScript to add instances of them to the Stage.

Adding a new instance of the Apple class to the Stage

You will soon create many instances of all of the various fruit movie clips to the Stage using arrays and for loops, but first, just so you can see how easy it is to place a MovieClass instance on the Stage from the library, you will practice by adding a single Apple class instance to the Stage.

1 With the Actions panel visible and Frame 1 of the actions layer selected, add the following code to the top of the Actions panel:

```
var testApple:Apple = new Apple();
addChild(testApple);
```

This creates a variable named testApple that stores a new instance of the Apple class and adds it to the Stage.

2 Test your movie. A single instance of the Apple class should appear at the upper-left corner of the Stage.

Your goal for this game, however, is not to generate a single Apple instance, but to create multiple random fruits. To do that, you will use a for loop. So delete the code you just wrote.

3 With the Actions panel visible and Frame 1 of the actions layer selected, select and delete all of the code that is there.

Now, starting with an empty Actions panel, you will begin to create the code to build the actual game.

Adding the initial variables

You will begin by adding to your game code a few variables that will be used to reference the information the game needs. To create the functionality that you saw in the completed game, you will need a list of all the fruit movie clips and another list of all the fruit instances that are currently onstage. These two lists will be stored as arrays.

Also, to keep track of the user's score, you will need to keep track of the number of fruits that the user has caught in the basket and the number of fruits that the user has let fall. In the coming tasks, you will create four new variables to store all of this numeric data, starting with the two that will contain arrays.

Introducing the array

An *array* is a Flash data type that allows a list of values to be stored in a single variable. Methods and properties of the `Array` class let you add to and remove elements from an array, sort the contents of an array alphabetically or numerically, and keep track of the number of items that are in an array at any given time. You can store lists of objects with multiple properties, and even store lists of lists.

There are infinite uses for `Array` objects in a Flash project: An array can store a list of high scorers in a game, a list of contacts for an address book, a list of products that have been bought at an e-commerce site, and countless other lists. As mentioned, in this project you will use one array to store a list of all the fruit movie clips and a second array to store a list of the fruit instances that are currently onstage.

You create an array as you do any other variable. Here's the basic syntax:

```
var listOfThings:Array = new Array();
```

When you create a new array, you can populate it with a list of elements, or you can create it as an empty array and add elements to it later. You will name the array for storing the list of all fruit `fruitArray`. It will be populated when you create it. The list of fruit instances currently onstage will be called `fruitsOnstage`. It will start out empty and be populated as fruit is added to and removed from the Stage.

You will start by creating the new arrays.

1 With Frame 1 of the `actions` layer selected, add a new `Array` instance:

```
var fruitArray:Array = new Array(Apple,Strawberry,Pear,Banana,
¬Orange);
```

2 On the next line in the Actions panel, add the following code to create the second array:

```
var fruitsOnstage:Array = new Array();
```

Keeping track of arrays

A location in an array is referred to numerically by its *index* value, and items in the array are referred to as *elements*. The first element in an array has the index number 0, the second element has the index number 1, the third element has the index number 2, and so on.

You created `fruitArray` with five elements:

```
var fruitArray:Array = new Array(Apple,Strawberry,Pear,
¬ Banana,Orange);
```

Another way to say that `fruitArray` has five elements is to say that it has a length of 5.

In ActionScript, when you want to refer to a specific element in an array, you use the array's instance name followed by square brackets that contain the element's index number. For example, to refer to the third fruit in `fruitArray`, you would write:

```
fruitArray[2];
```

In this example, `fruitArray[2]` would equal Pear. Remember that elements in an array are counted starting at 0, not 1.

Adding variables to track the user's score

As mentioned, you will also need variables to keep track of the number of fruits the user has collected and the number the user has lost. You will add those now.

1 With Frame 1 of the `actions` layer selected, add two new variables on lines below your existing code:

```
var fruitsCollected:int = 0;
var fruitsLost:int = 0;
```

Both of these variables start with an initial value of 0. Later you will add code that will change the value of these variables as the user plays the game.

The next task is to create a script that will place 20 instances of the various fruit clips at random locations above the Stage and give them random speeds at which to fall. To accomplish this, you will use a `for` loop.

Generating multiple instances with a for loop

There are a number of ways to make ActionScript repeat code a specific number of times. Probably the most convenient and commonly used means is the `for` loop. The basic syntax of a `for` loop looks like this:

```
for(var i:int = 0; i < someCondition; i++) {
  repeatSomething();
}
```

The code starts with the keyword `for`, which is followed by statements within parentheses; the first statement within the parentheses creates a variable with an initial numeric value, the second statement sets a condition that will be checked each time the code loops, and the third statement increases or decreases the variable from the first statement each time the loop is repeated. Code between the curly braces is executed each time the loop repeats until the condition in the second statement is no longer true.

Seeing how for loops work

For the game, you will create a `for` loop that repeats 20 times, adding a new fruit instance each time. But first try a simpler example of a `for` loop, to see how `for` loops work.

1 To display the numbers 0 through 19 in the Output panel, add a `for` loop below the existing code in the timeline:

```
for(var i:int = 0; i < 20; i++) {
  trace(i);
}
```

2 Test the movie. The `for` loop should execute the code in between the braces 20 times, and display the numbers 0 though 19 in the Output panel.

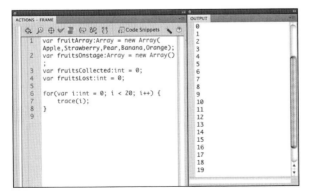

3 Close the lesson07start.swf file to leave the testing environment.

About trace statements

The trace statement in this example is a very useful technique in ActionScript, providing you feedback on your projects and helping you troubleshoot problems.

The basic syntax for a trace statement is trace(). Whatever is between the parentheses is evaluated and displayed in the Output panel when the code executes. You use trace statements primarily for feedback while developing, and not in your finished application. You can turn off trace statements before you publish your finished applications by selecting the Omit Trace Actions option on the Flash tab in the Publish Settings dialog box (File > Publish Settings).

Creating a for loop

For the game you are creating, instead of displaying numbers in the Output panel, you want the for loop to create 20 elements at random from the fruitArray array you created and place instances of the movie clips with those names onstage.

1 Between the curly braces of the for statement you wrote in the previous task, change the code so that it reads:

```
for (var i:int = 0; i < 20; i++) {
var pickFruit = fruitArray[int(Math.random() * fruitArray.
¬length)];
var fruit:MovieClip = new pickFruit();
addChild(fruit);
}
```

Each time the for loop repeats, it will select a different random fruit from the list. Remember that to refer to an element in an array, you use the instance name of the array followed by the element's index number between square brackets. By referring to fruitArray[int(Math.random() * fruitArray.length)], you will reference a random element from the items in fruitArray each time the for loop repeats. These references will be temporarily stored in a local variable named pickFruit, in the line that reads:

```
var fruit:MovieClip = new pickFruit();
```

The variable fruit is used to store the randomly selected item from fruitArray as a MovieClip instance. This instance is then placed onstage using addChild(fruit);.

If you tested the file now, all 20 randomly selected fruits would appear onstage, but they would all appear at the default location in the upper-left corner (0,0). Instead, each time a fruit instance is created, you want it to appear in its own separate position.

2 Change the `for` statement so that it reads:

```
for (var i:int = 0; i < 20; i++) {
var pickFruit = fruitArray[int(Math.random() * 5)];
var fruit:MovieClip = new pickFruit();
addChild(fruit);
fruit.x = Math.random() * stage.stageWidth;
fruit.y = Math.random() * -500;

}
```

Each fruit is given a random horizontal location somewhere within the bounds of the Stage (`fruit.x = Math.random() * stage.stageWidth;`) and a vertical position somewhere randomly within the 500 pixels above the Stage. Using these initial properties, your fruits are positioned and ready to begin falling from above the Stage.

To determine how fast each individual fruit moves when you animate the fruit later in this lesson, you will give each fruit a speed property with a random value.

3 Below the line that reads:

```
fruit.y = Math.random() * -500;
```

add the following code:

```
fruit.speed = Math.random() * 15 + 5;
```

This will give each piece of fruit a random speed property that ranges from 5 to 20. You will soon use this value to make each piece of fruit fall at its assigned speed.

About dynamic classes and creating MovieClip properties

The speed property that you just added to each fruit instance is not a built-in property of the MovieClip class; it was created for this project, to specifically serve the needs of the project. Properties, as well as functions, can be dynamically created and added to instances of the MovieClip class (and other classes that extend it, such as the Apple class). You can do this because the MovieClip class is what is known as a *dynamic class*. In a dynamic class, if you refer to a property that doesn't exist in that class, the property will be created automatically. With a nondynamic class, if you try to refer to a property that doesn't exist in the class, you will get an error message.

The two most commonly used dynamic classes in ActionScript 3.0 are the MovieClip class and the Object class. In general, you should assume that most other built-in classes are not dynamic.

If the concept of dynamic classes is not clear right now, you can come back and reread this section after you have a little more experience with ActionScript.

Adding items dynamically to an array with push()

To be able to keep track of and manipulate each fruit that is added to the Stage, you need to add it to the fruitsOnstage array. To add an element to an array, you use the push() method of the Array class. When data is pushed into an array, it is stored at the first open index location in the array.

In our example, each time the for loop repeats and fruit is created with initial properties, that fruit needs to be pushed into the fruitsOnstage array.

1 Add the following code above the closing curly brace of the for loop:

```
fruitsOnstage.push(fruit);
```

2 Review your code. The full for loop should now read:

```
for (var i:int = 0; i<20; i++) {
 var pickFruit = fruitArray[int(Math.random() * 5)];
 var fruit:MovieClip = new pickFruit();
 addChild(fruit);
 fruit.x = Math.random() * stage.stageWidth;
 fruit.y = Math.random() * -500;
 fruit.speed = Math.random() * 15 + 5;
 fruitsOnstage.push(fruit);
}
```

If you tested the movie at this point, all 20 fruits would be added to the display list, but most of them would not be visible in the Stage area because you have deliberately added them above the Stage so that they can fall into view. Before you make them fall, you will give the user the capability to catch them by giving the user interactive control over the basket_mc clip using the drag-and-drop functionality built into ActionScript.

Generating drag-and-drop functionality

You can easily turn movie clips into draggable objects in ActionScript using two built-in methods called startDrag() and stopDrag(). You will use these methods to give your user drag-and-drop control of the basket_mc clip.

Using the startDrag() and stopDrag() methods

You can call the startDrag() method to make any MovieClip instance (or sprite) draggable and the stopDrag() method to make it no longer draggable. For instance, you may want to make an object draggable when the user presses the mouse button on it, and to make the dragging stop when the mouse button is released. This behavior is what most people think of as dragging and dropping an object. You will add event listeners for the MOUSE_DOWN and MOUSE_UP events to add this functionality to the basket_mc clip.

Add the event listeners to your code that will be used to add drag-and-drop functionality to the basket.

1 Below the existing code in the Actions panel, add the following code:

```
basket_mc.addEventListener(MouseEvent.MOUSE_DOWN, dragBasket);
stage.addEventListener(MouseEvent.MOUSE_UP, dragStop);

function dragBasket(e:Event):void {
 basket_mc.startDrag();
}

function dragStop(e:Event):void {
 basket_mc.stopDrag();
}
```

Notice that instead of using the CLICK event as you have done in the past, you use the MOUSE_DOWN and MOUSE_UP events so that you can respond separately to each part of the click. This approach allows you to make basket_mc draggable when the user presses the mouse button, and to stop the dragging when the user releases the mouse button.

Also notice that whereas you added the MOUSE_DOWN event to basket_mc to make it draggable, you added the MOUSE_UP event to the Stage to stop the dragging. If instead you had added the MOUSE_UP event to the basket_mc clip, if the user drags the basket very quickly, the user sometimes may not be over the basket when the user releases the mouse, causing a problem. Experiment if you like by changing the word stage in the code you just wrote to basket_mc and see if you can spot the problem. You should see that for your users, it is better to apply the MOUSE_UP listener to the Stage.

2 Test your movie. Click the basket. You should be able to drag it around the entire Stage area. Release the mouse button, and the basket should stay where you dragged it.

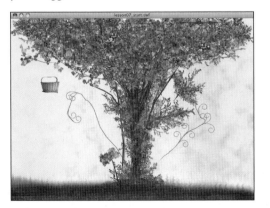

3 Close the lesson07_start.swf file to return to the authoring environment.

Some things to know about the startDrag() method

Although you won't need them in this lesson, the startDrag() method has two useful optional parameters. The first parameter, lockCenter, which defaults to false, specifies whether the registration point of the draggable object snaps to the center of the cursor position (true), or drags from the point where the user first clicked (false). The second optional parameter, bounds, can be used to indicate a rectangular area that will constrain the draggable range of the object.

Only one object at a time in any given file can be made draggable using startDrag(); and if you call startDrag() on a second object while something is draggable, the first object will stop dragging.

If you need to create the effect of multiple objects being dragged, you can set objects to match the position of the mouse cursor instead of or in addition to using the startDrag() method. For more information about this technique, see Flash Help.

Creating the game play in an ENTER_FRAME listener

Once the game is actually running, you want fruit to be constantly falling while the user tries to catch it. At the same time, you want to constantly keep track of the number of fruits that have been caught and missed. You will add all of this functionality in a single function that will repeat on every frame, using an ENTER_FRAME listener.

1 With Frame 1 still selected in your Timeline, add the following code on lines below your existing code:

```
stage.addEventListener(Event.ENTER_FRAME, catchFruit);

function catchFruit(e:Event):void {
}
```

Within the ENTER_FRAME function that you just created, you want to move every fruit that is onstage down by adding its speed property to its current y value. To do this for each fruit in every frame, you will create another for loop that will cycle though all of the items in the fruitsOnstage array.

2 Between the curly braces of the catchFruit() function, add the following code:

```
for (var i:int = fruitsOnstage.length-1; i > -1; i--) {
 var currentFruit:MovieClip = fruitsOnstage[i];
 currentFruit.y +=  currentFruit.speed;
}
```

Notice that in the previous `for` loop that you wrote, the first statement within the parentheses set the variable i to 0 and the last statement increased the value until the middle condition was met. This is a very common way to use a `for` loop. This time, however, the initial value of the i variable is set to 1 less than the total number of items in the `fruitsOnstage` array (`fruitsOnstage.length-1`), and the third statement subtracts from that value until i equals 0. You will see the logic behind this approach soon when you add code to remove items from the array using the `splice()` method.

In the `for` loop you just wrote, you cycled through each fruit in the `fruitsOnstage` array and changed the y value of each fruit in succession. The `for` loop was made to work on a different fruit each time by using the variable i to access sequential elements in the array:

```
var currentFruit:MovieClip = fruitsOnstage[i];
```

You will frequently find that the easiest way to modify the behavior of the code in a `for` loop is to work with the variable whose value changes each time the loop repeats. In our example file, that variable is i and its value decreases by 1 on each repeat. You will access the final element in the `fruitsOnstage` array on the first loop, and each incremental loop will work back until the first element in the array is accessed.

3   Test the movie. You should now have 20 random pieces of fruit falling from the sky until they disappear below the Stage. At this point, there is no way to stop their fall, but you will soon change this.

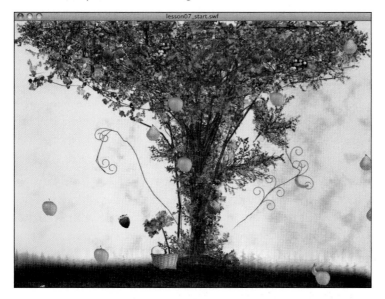

4   Close the lesson07_start.swf file to return to the authoring environment.

Keeping track of the movie clips that leave the Stage

As things now stand, each time a piece of fruit leaves the bottom of the Stage, it is gone forever. This is bad for two reasons: It makes the game short and not very satisfying, and even though those pieces of fruit are no longer visible or useful, they are still using a lot of processor cycles as they move farther and farther below the viewable area.

One way to solve this problem is to remove any fruit clips that go below the Stage and then generate new clips at the top of the Stage. However, a more efficient way to achieve the same effect is to take any clip that has left the bottom of the Stage and shuttle it back to the top using ActionScript. To the user, clips moved in this way will appear to be new objects, but in terms of performance you will be working with just the same 20 clips over and over.

1 Locate the line in your code that reads:

```
currentFruit.y += currentFruit.speed;
```

and below this line, add the following code:

```
if (currentFruit.y > stage.stageHeight - currentFruit.height) {
  currentFruit.y = 0 - currentFruit.height;
}
```

Now each time a fruit has moved entirely off the bottom of the Stage, it is placed directly above the Stage to fall again. The reason that the `currentFruit` height is subtracted from the top and bottom of the Stage in this code is because a movie clip's position is measured from its registration point, which for the fruit clips is in their upper-left corner. By subtracting the clip's height, we are assured that the clip is entirely below the Stage before we place it entirely above the Stage.

The conditional statement that you just wrote checks to see when a fruit object has left the Stage. This is the event that will cause the user to lose points in the game, so this is a good time to add to the value of the `fruitsLost` variable and to update one of the text fields onstage to inform the user that a piece of fruit has been lost.

2 In the conditional statement you just created, below the line that reads:

```
currentFruit.y = 0 - currentFruit.height;
```

add the following code:

```
fruitsLost++;
field2_txt.text = "Total Fruit Lost: " + fruitsLost;
```

Now the full `catchFruit()` function should read:

```
function catchFruit(e:Event):void {
 for (var i:int = fruitsOnstage.length-1; i > -1; i--) {
  var currentFruit:MovieClip = fruitsOnstage[i];
```

```
    currentFruit.y +=  currentFruit.speed;
    if(currentFruit.y > stage.stageHeight-currentFruit.height){
      currentFruit.y = 0 - currentFruit.height;
      fruitsLost++;
      field2_txt.text = "Total Fruit Lost: " + fruitsLost;
      }
    }
  }
```

3 Test the movie.

At this point you have reached the nadir of fun as far as the game play goes, but you are making a lot of progress with your ActionScript. The fruit should fall in an eternal fruit shower, and the text field should show an ever-increasing loss of fruit. Now is the time to give the user some way of collecting the fruit in the basket.

4 Close the lesson07_start.swf file to return to the authoring environment.

Using hitTestObject() to check for collisions

The key interactivity in this game is the user's catching pieces of fruit in the basket. So far you have added code that allows the user to move the basket and code that makes the fruit fall, so now all you need to do is detect when fruit has made contact with the basket.

You will do this using a method called hitTestObject(), which checks to see if the boundary of one displayed object is intersecting the boundary of another displayed object. Often this type of collision detection is performed within a conditional statement, like this:

```
if (object1.hitTestObject(object2)) {
 doSomething();
}
```

You will add a statement like this in the `for` loop that is moving the fruit so that, in each frame, each fruit will be checked to see if it has made contact with the basket.

1 In the `catchFruit()` function, locate the conditional statement that reads:

```
if (currentFruit.y > stage.stageHeight - currentFruit.height) {
 currentFruit.y = 0 - currentFruit.height;
 fruitsLost++;
 field2_txt.text = "Total Fruit Lost: " + fruitsLost;
}
```

2 On the line below this code (and above the final two closing braces), add another conditional statement to perform collision testing with the following code:

```
if (currentFruit.hitTestObject(basket_mc)) {
 fruitsCollected++;
 removeChild(currentFruit);
 field1_txt.text = "Total Fruit Collected: " +
 ¬fruitsCollected;
 fruitsOnstage.splice(i,1);
}
```

Remember that the code that you just created is still within the for loop, so it will run once for each object in the `fruitsOnstage` array.

Each time this statement runs, it will check to see whether the fruit being checked is in contact with the basket, and if it is, the code will increment the `fruitsCollected` variable. It will also remove the fruit from the Stage so it will no longer continue falling. This will partially create the illusion that the caught fruit has landed in the basket. We will enhance this illusion soon.

After this, the text field named `field1_txt` is updated to show the total number of fruits that have been collected based on the new value of the `fruitsCollected` variable.

Last, a method of the Array class called `splice()` is used.

```
fruitsOnstage.splice(i,1);
```

This method is used to remove elements from an array. The first parameter of the `splice()` method indicates at what point in the array elements should start to be removed; by using the value of `i` here, you are telling ActionScript to begin removing from the element that is currently being checked. The second parameter indicates the number of elements that should be removed. By setting that parameter to 1, you ensure that only one element is removed: in this case, the element that has hit the basket.

3 Test your movie.

You now have a game that can be played. As the fruits fall, you can move the basket around to collect them. The ones that you catch are removed from the Stage, and the total number caught is reflected in the upper text field. The ones you missed are recycled and continue to fall until they are caught. This behavior will continue until you have caught all 20 of the original fruits, at which point there is no more fruit to catch.

4 Close the lesson07_start.swf file to leave the testing environment.

Your catchFruit() function should now read:

```
function catchFruit(e:Event):void {

 for (var i:int = fruitsOnstage.length-1; i > -1; i--) {
  var currentFruit:MovieClip = fruitsOnstage[i];
  currentFruit.y +=  currentFruit.speed;
  if (currentFruit.y > stage.stageHeight - currentFruit.
  ¬height) {
   currentFruit.y = 0 - currentFruit.height;
   fruitsLost++;
   field2_txt.text = "Total Fruit Lost: " + fruitsLost;
  }

  if (currentFruit.hitTestObject(basket_mc)) {
   fruitsCollected++;
   removeChild(currentFruit);
   field1_txt.text = "Total Fruit Collected: " +
   ¬fruitsCollected;
   fruitsOnstage.splice(i,1);
  }
 }
}
```

About splicing elements from an array

When you remove elements from an array using the `splice()` method, all of the elements to the right of the removed elements are shifted over to fill the index values of the elements that were removed. For instance, here you have an array with five elements:

```
fruitArray = new Array(Apple,Strawberry,Pear,Banana,Orange);
```

Assume that beginning at index number 2, you remove two items:

```
fruitArray.splice(2,2);
```

The fruit elements that would be removed would be Pear and Banana (remember that array index numbers count from 0), and Orange would then be shifted into index number 2. Now trace `fruitArray` after this slice:

```
trace(fruitArray);
```

The Output panel would read:

```
Apple,Strawberry,Orange
```

Recall that the `for` loop that is used to cycle through the fruits in the `fruitsOnstage` array is keeping track of the number of loops by counting backwards instead of forwards. This approach was used to take into account the splicing that is taking place each time a fruit makes contact with the basket. The value of `i` from the `for` loop is used to indicate which item in the array is spliced. If the items in the array were shifting to the left while `i` was counting up, then all of the items would not be accounted for in the `for` loop. By looping through the array backwards, this potential problem is eliminated. Don't worry if this process is not entirely clear to you. It often takes a little experience to understand all the steps for eliminating a potential problem, but each time you are exposed to solutions like this, you can add them to your mental notes for future reference.

You can have a working game. However, it is still missing one feature—an outcome—so within the `catchFruit()` function, you will add two more conditional statements: one that will let users know that they have won the game when they have caught all 20 pieces of fruit, and one that will give them the sad news that they have lost when they have missed 20 pieces of fruit. If either of these conditions is true, the game will end, so the catchFruit() function will be turned off with either outcome. First you will add the conditional statement that checks for a winning outcome.

Adding conditional statements to determine the game's outcome

In the code that you have written so far, fruits are removed from the `fruitsOnstage` array whenever they make contact with the basket. Therefore, if there are no elements left in the `fruitsOnstage` array, you know that the user has caught all 20 fruits in the basket and you can declare the user the winner.

1 Above the final closing brace of the `catchFruit()` function, add the following code:

```
if (fruitsOnstage.length <= 0) {
  field1_txt.text = "You Win! You have collected enough fruit
  ¬ for dinner.";
  field2_txt.text = "";
  stage.removeEventListener(Event.ENTER_FRAME, catchFruit);
 }
```

This conditional statement checks to see whether there are any items in the `fruitsOnstage` array. If there are none, then the upper text field on the Stage lets the user know that the user has won the game, and the lower text field is cleared. The ENTER_FRAME event is then removed so that the `catchFruit()` function stops being called. In a more complex game, you might at this point give the user the option of replaying the game or advancing to the next level.

Now add a second conditional statement to check for a loss. Since the `fruitsLost` variable is keeping track of the number of fruit that have fallen below the Stage, you can use its value to check whether more than 20 fruits—and the game—have been lost.

2 Below the code you just wrote and above the closing brace of the `catchFruit()` function, add the following code:

```
if (fruitsLost >= 20) {
  field1_txt.text = "Sorry, you lose. You have lost too much
  ¬ fruit!";
  field2_txt.text = "";
  stage.removeEventListener(Event.ENTER_FRAME, catchFruit);
 }
```

Like the previous conditional statement that you wrote, this one updates the text fields to let the user know the outcome and removes the event listener. When the user wins, it is because the user has collected all the fruit so there is no fruit still onstage at that point. However, if the user loses, multiple fruits may still be in play. If you tested the movie and let yourself lose, you would see this.

To remove all of the remaining fruit from the Stage in case of a loss, you will add one more `for` loop inside the conditional statement you just wrote.

3 Add code to the conditional statement that you just created so that it reads:

```
if (fruitsLost >= 20) {
field1_txt.text = "Sorry, you lose. You have lost too much
¬fruit!";
  field2_txt.text = "";
  stage.removeEventListener(Event.ENTER_FRAME, catchFruit);
  for (var j:int = fruitsOnstage.length-1; j > -1; j--) {
   currentFruit = fruitsOnstage[j];
   removeChild(currentFruit);
   fruitsOnstage.splice(j,1);
  }
}
```

The code you just added should start to seem familiar. The only difference between this and the other for loops that you have added is that the variable is named j. This is because the name i has been used within the catchFruit() function already. Because you are again using this loop to splice items out of the fruitsOnstage array, this loop also counts backwards as it cycles through that array. Any fruits remaining in this array after the user has lost the game will now be removed from the Stage and from the array.

4 Test the movie.

If you collect 20 fruits in your basket before losing 20, you should get winning feedback in the text field. If you lose 20 fruits below the Stage, you should get losing feedback and the remaining fruit should disappear. The functionality of the game is complete.

To make the play more realistic, you will add one final step to make it appear that fruits are being gathered in the basket as they are caught.

5 Close the lesson07_start.swf file to return to the authoring environment.

Giving visual feedback by navigating to MovieClip frames

If you recall, the Basket movie clip symbol has a series of frames with graphics showing increasing amounts of fruit in the basket. You will now add code to sequentially navigate to those frames as the user collects more fruit. First reacquaint yourself with the frames in the Basket movie clip.

1 In the Library panel, double-click the Basket movie clip.

2 Notice that the graphics in Frame 1 show an empty basket onstage. The first frame of the Actions layer has a stop() method. This means that the basket instance onstage will appear empty until ActionScript is used to send it to this Timeline's later frames.

3 Scrub across the Timeline and notice that every frame shows increasing amounts of fruit in the basket. This is because in the fruit layer a new keyframe is added every five frames with additional fruit clips onstage.

4 From the Edit menu, choose Edit Document to leave the Timeline of the Basket clip and return to Scene 1.

You will now add ActionScript that advances the frames of the basket_mc instance as the user collects fruit.

5 In the main Timeline, select Frame 1 of the Actions layer to return to the code you have written for this file.

6 In the catchFruit() function, locate the code that reads:

```
if (currentFruit.hitTestObject(basket_mc)) {
    fruitsCollected++;
    removeChild(currentFruit);
    fruitsOnstage.splice(i,1);
    field1_txt.text = "Total Fruit Collected: " +
    ¬fruitsCollected;
  }
 }
```

Recall that this is the code that checks whether a piece of fruit has made contact with the basket_mc and then responds. This is where you will add a long conditional statement that advances through the frames of the Basket movie clip as more and more fruit is collected (as tracked in the variable fruitsCollected).

7 Modify the conditional statement in step 6 so that it reads:

```
if (currentFruit.hitTestObject(basket_mc)) {
    fruitsCollected++;
    removeChild(currentFruit);
    fruitsOnstage.splice(i,1);
    field1_txt.text = "Total Fruit Collected: " +
    ¬fruitsCollected;
    if (fruitsCollected >= 20) {
      basket_mc.gotoAndStop(20);
    } else if (fruitsCollected > 15) {
      basket_mc.gotoAndStop(15);
    } else if (fruitsCollected > 10) {
      basket_mc.gotoAndStop(10);
    } else if (fruitsCollected > 5) {
      basket_mc.gotoAndStop(5);
    }
}
```

● **Note:** After an `if` conditional statement checks for and responds to an initial condition, you can check for other conditions by adding `else if` statements at the end of the conditional statement, as in:

```
if (this == true) {
  doSomething();
} else if (anotherThis == true) {
  doSomethingElse();
}
```

You can add as many `else if` statements as you wish.

In the code you just added, the first condition checks to see if 20 fruits have been collected; if so, the `basket_mc` clip is sent to its twentieth frame and displays a full basket. A series of `else if` statements after this check for lesser quantities of fruit, working back in multiples of five and navigating to the other frames in the Basket clip that have keyframes.

8 Test the movie. Notice now that as you catch increasing amounts of fruit in your basket, the basket appears to gradually fill up.

One of the really satisfying things about working with Flash and ActionScript is the power of connecting graphics and animation in movie clips with interactive responses created with code.

The full code for Frame 1 of this file should read:

```
var fruitArray:Array = new Array(Apple,Strawberry,Pear,Banana,
¬Orange);
var fruitsOnstage:Array = new Array();
var fruitsCollected:int = 0;
var fruitsLost:int = 0;

for (var i:int = 0; i<20; i++) {
 var pickFruit = fruitArray[int(Math.random() * fruitArray.
 ¬length)];
 var fruit:MovieClip = new pickFruit();
 addChild(fruit);
 fruit.x = Math.random() * stage.stageWidth;
 fruit.y = Math.random() * -500;
 fruit.speed = Math.random() * 15 + 5;
 fruitsOnstage.push(fruit);
}

basket_mc.addEventListener(MouseEvent.MOUSE_DOWN, dragBasket);
stage.addEventListener(MouseEvent.MOUSE_UP, dragStop);


function dragBasket(e:Event):void {
 basket_mc.startDrag();
}

function dragStop(e:Event):void {
```

(code continues on next page)

```
    basket_mc.stopDrag();
}

stage.addEventListener(Event.ENTER_FRAME, catchFruit);

function catchFruit(e:Event):void {

 for (var i:int = fruitsOnstage.length-1; i > -1; i--) {
  var currentFruit:MovieClip = fruitsOnstage[i];
  currentFruit.y +=  currentFruit.speed;
  if (currentFruit.y > stage.stageHeight - currentFruit.
  ¬height) {
   currentFruit.y = 0 - currentFruit.height;
   fruitsLost++;
   field2_txt.text = "Total Fruit Lost: " + fruitsLost;
  }

  if (currentFruit.hitTestObject(basket_mc)) {
   fruitsCollected++;
   removeChild(currentFruit);
   fruitsOnstage.splice(i,1);
   field1_txt.text = "Total Fruit Collected: " +
   ¬fruitsCollected;
   if (fruitsCollected >= 20) {
    basket_mc.gotoAndStop(20);
   } else if (fruitsCollected > 15) {
    basket_mc.gotoAndStop(15);
   } else if (fruitsCollected > 10) {
    basket_mc.gotoAndStop(10);
   } else if (fruitsCollected > 5) {
    basket_mc.gotoAndStop(5);
   }
  }
 }

 if (fruitsOnstage.length <= 0) {
  field1_txt.text = "You Win! You have collected enough fruit
  ¬for dinner.";
  field2_txt.text = "";
  stage.removeEventListener(Event.ENTER_FRAME, catchFruit);
 }
 if (fruitsLost >= 20) {
  field1_txt.text = "Sorry, you lose. You have lost too much
  ¬fruit!";
  field2_txt.text = "";
  stage.removeEventListener(Event.ENTER_FRAME, catchFruit);
  for (var j:int = fruitsOnstage.length-1; j > -1; j--) {
```

```
      currentFruit = fruitsOnstage[j];
      removeChild(currentFruit);
      fruitsOnstage.splice(j,1);
    }
  }


  }
```

If you have problems with your code, review any error messages in the Output or Compiler Errors panels. Especially keep track of the number and placement of curly braces, as this lesson has numerous conditional statements and `for` loops inside of functions. Go through the steps in the lesson as many times as you need to, and remember that you can compare your file to the completed version of the file found at Lessons > Lesson07 > Complete > lesson07_complete.fla.

If you have succeeded in getting your game to work, congratulations! Although this is a relatively simple game, it contains numerous techniques used to create many types of games, and you now have the foundation that will allow you to take on more advanced ActionScript challenges.

Some suggestions to try on your own

If you have successfully completed this lesson and are comfortable with the materials covered so far, you can consider yourself a serious student of ActionScript with some formidable capabilities already in your toolkit. This might be a good time to reward yourself with a break before proceeding. Go for a walk in a beautiful place, watch a movie, do something fun with people you like—get away from the computer for awhile.

After that, you may want to try a few techniques for review before proceeding to the next lesson:

- Add an item to the List component in the completed file from Lesson 6, "Creating Preloaders in ActionScript 3.0." Use the list to load your finished file from this lesson into the UILoader component in that file.

- In this lesson's file, create a button that allows the user to replay the game. This will involve creating a function that resets the initial values of the `fruitsCollected`, `fruitsLost`, and `fruitsOnstage` variables and re-executing the `for` loop that initially places the fruits onstage.

- Add graphics in movie clips that are triggered when the user wins or loses the game.

- Create additional levels of the game that work with larger numbers of items to be caught or faster-moving items.

- Create a new movie clip on the Stage that the user needs to avoid. Using `hitTestObject()`, write ActionScript that takes away points when the user touches this new clip.

Review questions

1 What needs to be done to a movie clip symbol in the library before it can be controlled from ActionScript?

2 What is the basic syntax to use a for loop in ActionScript 3.0?

3 In an if conditional statement, what is the syntax to add more conditions?

4 What method is used to check whether one display object is intersecting another display object?

5 Name an ActionScript class that can be used to store a list of objects.

6 What method can be used to add a new element to the next available location in an Array instance?

7 In ActionScript, how might you identify the first element in an array named cars?

Review answers

1 To indicate that a symbol from the library can be controlled with ActionScript, you need to set its linkage properties to Export For ActionScript.

2 The basic syntax to use a for loop is:

```
for (var i:int = 0; i< someNumber; i++) {
  doSomething();
}
```

3 To check for more than one condition in an if statement, you can use the syntax else if with additional conditions after the closing brace of the first condition, as in this example:

```
if (a == true) {
  doSomething();
} else if (b == true) {
  doSomethingElse();
}
```

4 The `hitTestObject()` method is used to determine if the bounding box of one object is intersecting with another. For example, to see whether a `MovieClip` instance named `ship1` had contact with a `MovieClip` instance named `baseStation`, you could write:

```
if(ship1.hitTestObject(baseStation){
doSomething();
}
```

5 `Array` is a class that can be used to store a list of objects. An instance of an array can be created and stored in a variable like any other ActionScript data type, as in this example:

```
var employeeList:Array = new Array();
```

6 The `push()` method of the `Array` class can be used to add a new element to the next available location in an array, as in this example:

```
employeeList.push("John Smith");
```

7 Keeping in mind that the elements in an array are counted beginning with 0, the first element in an array named `cars` can be identified as `cars[0]`.

8 CREATING AND FORMATTING TEXT WITH ACTIONSCRIPT

Lesson overview

In this lesson, you will learn to do the following:

- Create a text field with ActionScript using the new `TLFTextField` class.

- Set `TLFTextField` properties with ActionScript.

- Use methods and events of the `URLLoader` class to load text into a `TLFTextField` instance.

- Use the `TextFormat` class to control the color, font, and size of a `TLFTextField` instance.

- Load a `MovieClip` asset from the library at runtime that contains multiple user interface components that allow the user to format text.

- Create an event listener for a keyboard event to show and hide the loaded movie clip.

- Create a UIScrollBar instance using ActionScript.

- Use ActionScript to hide and show a text field scroll bar as needed.

 This lesson will take approximately 2.5 hours.

One of the most exciting new features in Flash CS5 is the powerful text engine that uses Adobe's Text Layout Format (TLF). The TLF format is the default text engine in Flash, and it offers a lot of new capabilities for working with Flash in the authoring environment. For instance, it provides the capability to work with more than 30 writing systems, including Arabic, Hebrew, Chinese, Korean, and Japanese.

In this lesson, you will use ActionScript to create and format a TLFTextField instance.

Text in Flash can now be threaded or automatically flow from one text box to the next. You can add multicolumn text and control the use of kerning, ligatures, typographic case, digit width, and discretionary hyphens.

Of course, as with all other features in the Flash interface, TLF text can be completely controlled with ActionScript. In fact, the entire TLF API is built on an open source text engine also created by Adobe that gives advanced programmers powerful tools for working with text. There are also a number of ActionScript classes with methods and properties for easily creating and formatting TLF text fields. This lesson just scratches the surface of the possibilities for using ActionScript and the TLF format, but this will be enough to give you some powerful capabilities for dynamically creating and formatting text fields.

Examining the completed file

To get an idea of what you will be doing in this lesson, look at the completed version of the lesson project.

1   Open Lessons > Lesson08 > Complete > lesson08_complete.fla.

2   Test the movie (Control > Test Movie > In Flash Professional).

3   Press the letter F on your keyboard; a formatting panel appears. Press F again and it disappears.

4   Press F again to make the formatting panel visible once more and notice that it can be dragged around the Stage.

5   Using the tools in the formatting panel, change the font, color, and size of the text.

6   Click the up arrow next to the control that sets the number of columns, and notice that the columns in the text field automatically update.

7   Notice as you change the font formatting that when the text exceeds the white area of the Stage, a scroll bar automatically appears. When the text again fits in the white area, the scroll bar disappears.

8   Close the lesson08_complete.swf file to leave the testing environment.

9   Close the lesson08_complete.fla file.

Examining the starting file

You will start by examining the starting file for this lesson.

1 Open the starting file for this lesson: Lessons > Lesson 08 > Start folder > lesson08_start.fla.

Notice that there is nothing on the Stage or in the main Timeline. The text field for this lesson will be created with code, and the text it contains will be loaded using ActionScript. The only prebuilt graphical item that will be used for this lesson is a movie clip in the library that contains the text formatting panel that you saw in the completed file.

2 If the Library panel is not visible, open it (Window > Library).

The items in the library for this file are the pieces that make up the movie clip called Formatter. These pieces include a background JPEG image and a number of user interface (UI) components. Notice that the Linkage property for the Formatter clip has been set and has an ID of Formatter. In Lesson 7, "Using Arrays and Loops in ActionScript 3.0," you set this property yourself so that new instances of the pieces of the fruit could be created using ActionScript. Here it has been done for you.

3 Double-click the icon for the Formatter movie clip in the library to view its contents.

Notice that this clip has two layers: one with a background image and one with instances of the UI components. It also has a few read-only text fields that describe how the layers will be used.

4 If it is not already visible, open the Property inspector and then select the List component onstage in the Choose Font section.

Tip: The List component was used extensively in Lessons 5 and 6, where you can review its use.

Notice that this List component has been given an instance name of `fontList` and that it has been given five labels that correspond to common font names. You will soon write ActionScript that will set the text in a text field to the font that is selected from this list.

5   Select the color chip under Color.

This is an instance of a component called ColorPicker. Notice in the Property inspector that it has been given the instance name `colorPicker`. This component is used to select a color from a provided palette and is familiar to most computer users. You will add ActionScript so that users can use this component instance to choose the color of the text in a text field.

6   Select the component to the right of Size.

This is an instance of a component called NumericStepper. The user can click the up and down arrows to select a number. The initial number that is selected and the available range that can be chosen are properties that can be set in the Property inspector.

7 With the NumericStepper component still selected, in the Property inspector notice that this component has been given the instance name `fontSizer`.

8 In the Component Parameters section of the Property inspector, notice that the range of numbers available for the `fontSizer` instance is set to a minimum of 1 and a maximum of 24. The initial value is set to 12, and it is set to change its value in increments of 2 when it is clicked.

You will use ActionScript to let the user set the font size of a text field with this NumericStepper instance.

9 Below the NumericStepper component that will be used for font size is another one that will be used to set the number of columns in a text field. Select this component, and in the Property inspector notice that this component has been given the instance name `columnNum`. In the Component Parameters section you will see that this instance has been given a range from 1 to 10, with an initial value of 1.

You will write ActionScript that makes the number that is chosen with this instance determine the number of columns in a text field.

10 From the Edit menu, choose Edit Document to close the Formatter component and return to the main Timeline. Now you will begin adding the ActionScript for this lesson, starting with the code to create a TLF text field.

Creating a TLF text field with ActionScript

In previous versions of Flash, you could create a new text field with ActionScript 3.0 by creating a new instance of the class named TextField. This class is still available in Flash CS5; however, a new class named TLFTextField has been added to the language and offers a number of advanced options for working with text. This is the class you will use to create the text field for this lesson. The first step will be to import the TLFTextField class.

1 Select Frame 1 of the actions layer and open the Actions panel if it is not visible already.

2 On the first line of the Actions panel, type the `import` statement for the `TLFTextField` class:

```
import fl.text.TLFTextField;
```

Later in this lesson you will be using the `UIScrollBar` class, which also requires an import statement, so add that now as well.

3 Below the line you just typed, add this line:

```
import fl.controls.UIScrollBar;
```

Flash CS5 may automatically add other import statements as you work, but the two statements you just created are the only ones that are required for this project to work when the code is written in the Flash Timeline.

Next you will create a new instance of the `TLFTextField` class.

4 Below the code you already typed, add the following line:

```
var t:TLFTextField = new TLFTextField();
```

Tip: For a full list of the available properties for the `TLFTextField` class, see the Flash CS5 ActionScript 3.0 reference.

The `TLFTextField` class has a large number of properties that can be set in ActionScript in the same way that you have set properties for other classes in previous lessons. You will set a few of those properties now.

5 To the code you have already typed, add the following lines:

```
t.width = 500;
t.height = 600;
t.background = true;
t.paddingTop = 20;
t.paddingLeft = 20;
t.paddingRight = 20;
```

Most of these properties are intuitive. The width of the text field is set to 500 pixels, the height to 600 pixels. The background of the text field is set to visible, which will create an opaque white background behind any text added to this field. The three padding properties will create 20 pixels of space around the top, left, and right of the text field when text is displayed in it. You will soon load some text from an external file into this field, but first you will place the field onto the Stage using `addChild()`.

6 Below the existing code, add this line:

```
addChild(t);
```

7 Test the movie. An empty white 500 × 600–pixel text field will appear onstage.

You will not be able to see the results of the padding properties until some text is added to the Stage, so close the lesson08_start.swf file and return to the authoring environment, where you will use the `URLLoader` class to load text into this field.

Loading an external text file into a TLF text field

In Lesson 5, "Using ActionScript and Components to Load Content," you loaded text into a text field that was created on the Stage in Flash using the URLLoader class. The process for loading a text file into a dynamically generated text field is exactly the same.

1. On the line below the existing code in the Actions panel, add a new instance of the URLLoader class:

```
var textLoad:URLLoader = new URLLoader();
```

   Remember that before you display any data that is loaded into a Flash project, you should make sure that the data has successfully loaded. As you did in Lesson 5, "Using ActionScript and Components to Load Content," you will add an event listener for the URLLoader COMPLETE event that will respond when the requested data has successfully loaded.

2. On the next line in the Actions panel, add this code:

```
textLoad.addEventListener(Event.COMPLETE, textLoaded);
```

   Now that you are listening for anything that is loaded, you can call the load() method to load a text file that is included in the lesson08 > Start folder.

3. Below the line you just typed, add this code:

```
textLoad.load(new URLRequest("sample.txt"));
```

   When the sample.txt file has completed loading, the event listener you add will call a function named textLoaded() that you will create now.

4. On the next line in the Actions panel, add the shell for the textLoaded() function:

```
function textLoaded(e:Event):void
{

}
```

   The textLoaded() function will store the text data from the loaded file as a string and set that string as the text property of the text field named t.

5. Add code to the textLoaded() function so that it reads as shown here:

```
function textLoaded(e:Event):void
{
 var txt:String = URLLoader(e.target).data as String;
 t.text = txt;
}
```

6 Test the movie. The text from the external file should appear in the text field. Notice that there are 20 pixels of white space around the text field on the top, left, and right sides.

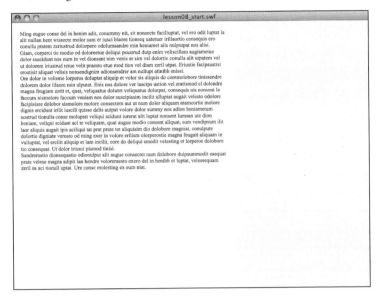

7 Close the lesson08_start.swf file to return to the authoring environment.

Using the TextFormat class

As mentioned, the TLFTextField class offers many methods and properties for controlling the appearance of text with ActionScript. In addition, ActionScript has many other classes that offer precise control over the text in your projects.

One of the easiest classes to work with for formatting a text field is the TextFormat class. You can simply create an instance of the TextFormat class, set a few properties, and assign the instance to a text field. You will use an instance of the TextFormat class to set the font, color, and size of the TLFTextField instance that you created. You will do this now by creating a new TextFormat instance.

1 It makes sense to place the code that creates the TextFormat instance near the code in the Actions panel that creates the TLFTextField instance, so locate this line:

```
var t:TLFTextField = new TLFTextField();
```

Then, on the line below this code, create a TextFormat instance:

```
var tf:TextFormat = new TextFormat();
```

Since you cannot apply formatting to text that isn't loaded, you will add code to set properties for font, size, and color within the textLoaded() function.

2 Locate the `textLoaded()` function and on the line above its closing brace add the following code:

```
tf.color = 0x003300;
tf.font = "Arial";
tf.size = 14;
```

3 On a line below the code you just added, set the `TextFormat` property of the `TLFTextField` instance by adding this code:

```
t.setTextFormat(tf);
```

4 Test your movie.

The text field should now display Arial 14-point dark green text. Soon you will give your user control over these and other properties.

5 Close the lesson08_start.swf file to return to the authoring environment.

Giving the user a custom panel to format text

▶ Tip: If you need to review the process of adding clips from the library to the Stage using ActionScript, see Lesson 7.

One of the benefits of controlling the appearance of text with ActionScript is that you can give your user tools to format text at runtime. At the start of this lesson you examined a movie clip in the library that included a number of UI components. You will now add an instance of that movie clip to the project and add ActionScript to allow it to control the appearance of the text field. You will also add ActionScript to allow the user to show and hide this panel with a keyboard shortcut and drag it around the Stage. The movie clip in the library has already been set to export for ActionScript and has been given the Linkage identifier Formatter. You will start by creating an instance of the Formatter clip.

1 On a new line below all of the existing code in the Actions panel, add this line:

```
var formatClip:Formatter = new Formatter();
```

If you wanted to place the Formatter clip onstage automatically, you would simply write addChild(formatClip). In this lesson, however, you will flex your ActionScript skills by letting the user show and hide this panel using a keyboard shortcut. Typically, computer applications use a single keyboard shortcut to toggle the showing and hiding of interface elements. To create toggle functionality like this, you will write ActionScript to keep track of whether the panel is shown or hidden. You can then write a conditional statement to see whether the appropriate key has been pressed and, within this conditional statement, you can write another conditional statement to determine whether the panel is hidden or shown.

First create a new variable that will be used to keep track of whether the Formatter panel is visible.

2 On the line in the Actions panel below the existing code, add the following:

```
var showFormat:Boolean = true;
```

The Boolean data type is used when a variable is going to store only one of two possibilities: true or false. In this case, the value of showFormat will be toggled between true and false as the panel is added and removed. Because the panel should be added the first time the user presses the required keyboard shortcut, the initial value of this variable is set to true. In the next task, you will create the KeyboardEvent listener that will contain the functionality to make this keyboard shortcut work.

Toggling the Formatter panel with a keyboard shortcut

An event listener for a keyboard event works the same way as the other event listeners that you have already used. You can use the addEventListener() method to listen for either a KEY_DOWN event or a KEY_UP event and respond with a function. Now that you have worked with a number of different types of events, the process should be familiar to you. A keyboard event will respond when any key is pressed, so if you want to respond to specific keys, you write a conditional statement inside the event-handling function that checks to see whether those keys were pressed.

To listen for the user's key press, add an event listener to the Stage.

1 In the Actions panel of the lesson08_start.fla file, add this line below all of the existing code:

```
stage.addEventListener(KeyboardEvent.KEY_DOWN, showFormatter);
```

2 On a line below this code, create the shell for the showFormatter() function:

```
function showFormatter(e:KeyboardEvent):void
{

}
```

Keyboard events and key codes

When a keyboard event is dispatched, it passes in its keyCode property. Each key on a standard keyboard has a unique key code. Within a KeyboardEvent listener you can check to see which key has been pressed by checking the keyCode value.

To try this, add the following code to a new Flash ActionScript 3.0 file:

```
stage.addEventListener(KeyboardEvent.KEY_DOWN, keyCheck);
function keyCheck(e:KeyboardEvent):void
{
  trace("Key number " + e.keyCode + " was pressed");
}
```

Test the movie. Press random keys, and the output pane will display the keyCode property for each key you press. Notice that the F key has a keyCode value of 70. This is the key you will use in this lesson to toggle the Formatter panel.

In addition to the numeric key codes, ActionScript 3.0 has added constants to represent some of the keyboard shortcuts commonly used in games. These include values for the arrow keys (Keyboard.UP, Keyboard.LEFT, keyboard.DOWN, and keyboard.RIGHT) and the spacebar (keyboard.SPACE).

Try these by modifying the keyCheck() function you just wrote as follows:

```
function keyCheck(e:KeyboardEvent):void
{
  if(e.keyCode == Keyboard.RIGHT){
    trace("The Right Arrow key was pressed");
  } else {
  trace("Key number " + e.keyCode + " was pressed");
  }
}
```

Now when you test the movie, you will still see the key code for most of the keys in the output pane, but pressing the right arrow will trace "The Right Arrow key was pressed."

When you are done testing, close this file and return to the lesson08_start.fla file.

You can now make the user's keyboard an integral part of the interactivity in your Flash projects. For more information about keyboard control, see the ActionScript 3.0 Language Reference.

3 Within the curly braces of the showFormatter() function, add a conditional statement that checks to see whether the F key has been pressed. Remember that the letter F has a key code of 70. The function should now read as follows:

```
function showFormatter(e:KeyboardEvent):void
{
 if (e.keyCode == 70)
 {

 }
}
```

The Boolean variable showFormat you created will be used to determine whether to show or hide the formatClip panel. If showFormat is true, the panel will be shown, and if it is false the panel will be hidden. Each time the showFormatter() function is called, the showFormat variable will be set to its opposite. Since the showFormat variable is initially set to true, the first time the function is called it will reveal the formatClip panel and set the showFormat variable to false.

To make this happen within the conditional statement that checks the keyCode property, add another conditional statement to check the value of the showFormat variable and add the formatClip instance to the Stage. At the same time, give formatClip an x position that aligns with the right side of the text field.

4 Add code to the showFormatter() function so that it reads as follows:

```
function showFormatter(e:KeyboardEvent):void
{
 if (e.keyCode == 70)
 {
   if (showFormat)
   {
     addChild(formatClip);
     formatClip.x = t.width;
     showFormat = false;
   }
 }
}
```

Next you will add an else statement to the conditional statement. When the value of showFormat is false, the formatClip panel should be removed from the Stage and the showFormat variable should be set to true again.

Working with values that evaluate to true

Notice that in step 4 you typed

```
if (showFormat)
```

instead of

```
if (showFormat==true)
```

Since the value of showFormat is true, both of these statements have the same meaning and would cause the conditional statement to run.

5 Add code to the showFormatter() function so that it reads as follows:

```
function showFormatter(e:KeyboardEvent):void
{
 if (e.keyCode == 70)
 {
  if (showFormat)
  {
   addChild(formatClip);
   formatClip.x = t.width;
   showFormat = false;
  }
  else
  {
   removeChild(formatClip);
   showFormat = true;
  }
 }
}
```

6 Test the movie. Press the F key on the keyboard. The formatClip panel should appear to the right of the text field. Press F again, and the panel will disappear.

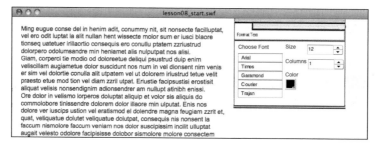

7 Close the lesson08_start.swf file to return to the Flash authoring environment.

Making the formatting panel draggable

A common feature of interface elements like the formatting panel you added to this project is their ability to be dragged. In Lesson 7, you saw how to make a movie clip draggable.

To make the formatClip panel draggable, you will add a MOUSE_DOWN event listener when the panel is shown and remove the listener when the panel is hidden.

1   Within the showFormatter() function, add a MOUSE_DOWN listener within the second if statement; within the else statement, remove the same listener. The completed function should look like this:

```
function showFormatter(e:KeyboardEvent):void
{
 if (e.keyCode == 70)
 {
  if (showFormat)
  {
   addChild(formatClip);
   formatClip.x = t.width;
   formatClip.addEventListener(MouseEvent.MOUSE_DOWN, drag);
   showFormat = false;
  }
  else
  {
   formatClip.removeEventListener(MouseEvent.MOUSE_DOWN, drag);
   removeChild(formatClip);
   showFormat = true;
  }
 }
}
```

Next add the drag() function that will make the panel draggable.

2   Below all of the existing code, add this new function:

```
function drag(e:Event):void
{
 formatClip.startDrag();
 formatClip.addEventListener(MouseEvent.MOUSE_UP, noDrag);

}
```

Notice that this function adds a listener that will run when the mouse button is released. This listener will be used to stop that panel from being dragged.

3 Add the `noDrag()` function below the code you just added.

```
function noDrag(e:Event):void
{
 formatClip.stopDrag();
}
```

4 Test the movie. Press the F key to reveal the panel and now use the mouse to drag the panel around the Stage. When you release the panel, it stays where it was dragged.

You now have a very handy panel that does nothing at all. You will fix that in the next task. The next ActionScript you write will control the formatting of the text field using the components within this panel.

Controlling text formatting using components and ActionScript

You will create an event listener for each of the four components in `formatClip` to format the font, size, and color of the text in the text field as well as the number of columns in the field.

1 Below all of the code in the project, create `addEventListener()` methods that listen for CHANGE events on each of the components in `formatClip`:

```
formatClip.fontList.addEventListener(Event.CHANGE, setFont);
formatClip.fontSizer.addEventListener(Event.CHANGE, setFontSize);
formatClip.colorPicker.addEventListener(Event.CHANGE, setColor);
formatClip.columnNum.addEventListener(Event.CHANGE, setColumns);
```

Now you will add the functions that format the text. Each of the first three functions will set a property of the `textFormat` instance you created, called `tf`, and then reapply `textFormat` to the `t` text field.

The `font` property will be determined when a change is made to the selected item in the FontList component. The text size will be determined by the value chosen in the `fontSizer` instance of the NumericStepper component, and the text color will be determined by the color selected in the `colorPicker` instance.

2 Below the `addEventListener()` methods you just added, write the following three functions:

```
function setFont(e:Event):void
{
 tf.font = e.target.selectedItem.label;
 t.setTextFormat(tf);
}

function setFontSize(e:Event):void
{
```

```
 tf.size = e.target.value;
 t.setTextFormat(tf);
}

function setColor(e:Event):void
{
 tf.color = e.target.selectedColor;
 t.setTextFormat(tf);
}
```

In each of these functions, `e.target` represents the component that has had a change made to it. The user's selection is set as the value of a `TextFormat` property.

For the `setColumns()` function, which will be called when a change is made to the fourth component, you will set a property of the new `TLFTextField` class that allows you to add columns to a text field. When the `columnCount` property of a `TLFTextField` instance changes, any text in that field will rewrap to flow across the new columns.

3 Add the `setColumns()` function below your existing code:

```
function setColumns(e:Event):void
{
 t.columnCount = e.target.value;
}
```

4 Test the movie. Press the F key to display the `formatClip` panel. Choose a font from the list and notice that the font in the text field changes. Pick a new color from the color picker, and the text in the field changes to the selected color. Click to set the column number to 2 or more, and try increasing the font size.

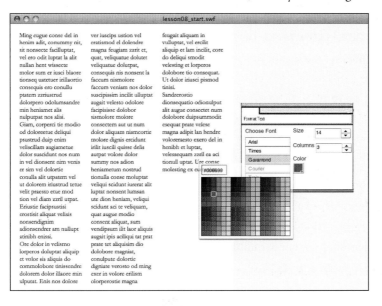

If you have been successful with the code up to this point, you should now have a working formatting panel. One issue you may have noticed as you change settings is that if the text is too large to fit into the text field with the current settings, part of the text is not viewable. To solve this problem, you will add a scroll bar to the text field using ActionScript and add code so that the scroll bar appears and disappears automatically as needed.

5 Close the lesson08_start.swf file to return to the authoring environment

Creating a scroll bar using ActionScript

In Lesson 5, you added an instance of the UIScrollBar component and set some of its properties in the Flash authoring environment to create a scroll bar for a text field. In this lesson you will use the same UIScrollBar component, but you will add it, set its properties, and remove it dynamically with ActionScript.

If you have made it this far, you probably can guess how to write the code that will create an ActionScript instance of the UIScrollBar component.

1 Below all of the code in the Actions panel, type the following:

```
var scroller:UIScrollBar = new UIScrollBar();
```

2 On all of the UI components in Flash CS5, a move() method is available that allows you to pass x and y values to a component to position it. Call this method for the new scroller instance on a new line:

```
scroller.move(t.x + t.width, t.y );
```

The first parameter of the move() method sets the x position of scroller so that it lines up with the right side of the text field, and the second parameter sets the y value of scroller to match the text field.

3 On a new line, set the height of scroller so that it matches the height of the text field:

```
scroller.height = t.height;
```

4 To tell an instance of the UIScrollBar component which text field it should control, you set its scrollTarget property. Do this on the next available line:

```
scroller.scrollTarget = t;
```

5 On a new line, add scroller to the Stage:

```
addChild(scroller);
```

6 On the next line, set the initial visible property of scroller to false so that the scroll bar does not appear until needed:

```
scroller.visible = false;
```

Showing and hiding the scroll bar

Now you will write a function that shows and hides the scroll bar based on the amount of text in the text field. Since the content of the text field in this project changes only based on settings that are made in formatClip, you will use an event listener to check the content of the text field to determine whether a scroll bar is needed each time the user clicks the formatClip panel.

1   Below the existing code in the Actions panel, add an event listener for formatClip:

```
formatClip.addEventListener(MouseEvent.CLICK, setScrollbar);
```

2   The scroll bar will be needed when the height of the text in the text field exceeds the height of the field itself. Create this functionality by adding the following function below the rest of the code in the Actions panel:

```
function setScrollbar(e:Event):void
{
 if (t.textHeight > scroller.height)
 {
  scroller.visible = true;
 }
 else
 {
  scroller.visible = false;
 }
}
```

Before you test your movie, add one final line to the setScrollbar() function. The scrollV property of a TextField or TLFTextField instance determines which line of text will be the first to appear in the field. By setting this property to a value of 1 when the setScrollbar() function is called, you can make sure that when text is reformatted, the text is reset to the top of the page.

3   Above the final closing brace of the setScrollbar() function, add this line:

```
t.scrollV = 1;
```

4   Test the movie. Try increasing the size of the text until it no longer all fits in the field, and notice that the scroll bar appears. Reduce the size of the text, and notice that the scroll bar disappears. Notice that the text field always starts at the top of the page when you reset it.

To get a clearer sense of what the scrollV property does, go back to your code and comment out or remove the last line you added and then test the movie again. You will see how much better the user's experience will be with this property set.

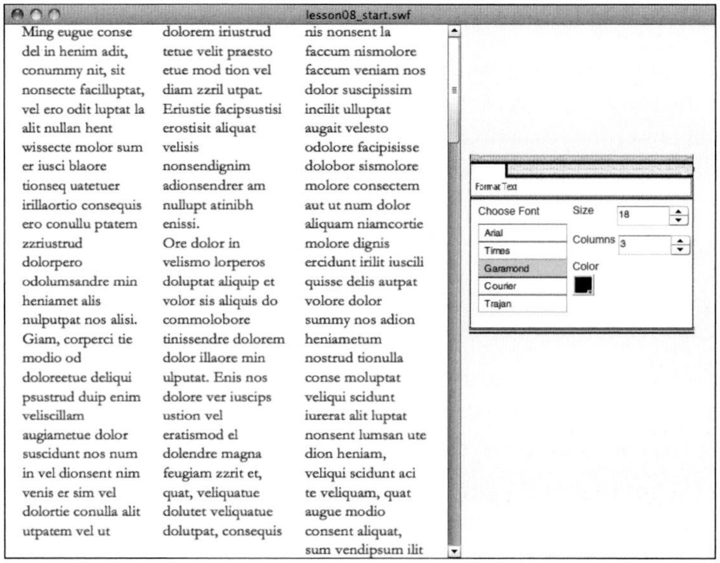

Here is the complete code you created for this lesson:

```
import fl.text.TLFTextField;
import fl.controls.UIScrollBar;

var t:TLFTextField = new TLFTextField();
var tf:TextFormat = new TextFormat();

t.width = 500;
t.height = 600;
t.background = true;
t.paddingTop = 20;
t.paddingLeft = 20;
t.paddingRight = 20;

addChild(t);

var textLoad:URLLoader = new URLLoader();
textLoad.addEventListener(Event.COMPLETE, textLoaded);
textLoad.load(new URLRequest("sample.txt"));

function textLoaded(e:Event):void
{
 var txt:String = URLLoader(e.target).data as String;
 t.text = txt;
 tf.color = 0x336633;
 tf.font = "Arial";
 tf.size = 14;
 t.setTextFormat(tf);
```

```
}

var formatClip:Formatter = new Formatter();
var showFormat:Boolean = true;

stage.addEventListener(KeyboardEvent.KEY_DOWN, showFormatter);

function showFormatter(e:KeyboardEvent):void
{
 if (e.keyCode == 70)
 {
  if (showFormat)
  {
   addChild(formatClip);
   formatClip.x = t.width;
   formatClip.addEventListener(MouseEvent.MOUSE_DOWN, drag);
   showFormat = false;
  }
  else
  {
   formatClip.removeEventListener(MouseEvent.MOUSE_DOWN, drag);
   removeChild(formatClip);
   showFormat = true;
  }
 }
}

function drag(e:Event):void
{
 formatClip.startDrag();
 formatClip.addEventListener(MouseEvent.MOUSE_UP, noDrag);
}

function noDrag(e:Event):void
{
 formatClip.stopDrag();
}

formatClip.fontList.addEventListener(Event.CHANGE, setFont);
formatClip.fontSizer.addEventListener(Event.CHANGE, setFontSize);
formatClip.colorPicker.addEventListener(Event.CHANGE, setColor);
formatClip.columnNum.addEventListener(Event.CHANGE, setColumns);


function setFont(e:Event):void
```

(code continues on next page)

```
{
 tf.font = e.target.selectedItem.label;
 t.setTextFormat(tf);
}

function setFontSize(e:Event):void
{
 tf.size = e.target.value;
 t.setTextFormat(tf);
}

function setColor(e:Event):void
{
 tf.color = e.target.selectedColor;
 t.setTextFormat(tf);
}

function setColumns(e:Event):void
{
 t.columnCount = e.target.value;
}

var scroller:UIScrollBar = new UIScrollBar();
scroller.move(t.x + t.width, t.y );
scroller.height = t.height;
scroller.scrollTarget = t;
addChild(scroller);
scroller.visible = false;

formatClip.addEventListener(MouseEvent.CLICK, setScrollbar);

function setScrollbar(e:Event):void
{
 if (t.textHeight > scroller.height)
 {
  scroller.visible = true;
 }
 else
 {
  scroller.visible = false;
 }
 t.scrollV = 1;
}
```

Bear in mind that what you did here demonstrates just a tiny fraction of the functionality that is available for working with text in ActionScript and that entire volumes could be dedicated to additional capabilities. What you learned in this lesson should give you plenty of tools to work with as well as a good launching point for your continued exploration of the many ActionScript classes, methods, and properties connected with text.

Some suggestions to try on your own

A deeper study of the two text classes covered in this lesson, the `TLFTextField` and `TextFormat` classes, would reveal many other useful capabilities. In addition, many other classes associated with text in general and TLF text specifically can be found in the Flash Help files. Particularly useful is the `TextFlow` class. Flash also supports the use of HTML tags and Cascading Style Sheets (CSS) for formatting text. Also, an understanding of XML, which is introduced in Chapters 10 and 11, can be helpful when loading text content into Flash projects.

Here are a few suggestions you may want to try right away with this lesson's project:

- Add a few more components to an expanded formatting panel and use them to modify additional `TLFTextField` and `TextFormat` properties.

- Create multiple panels and give each panel a set of related features such as font formatting and page layout.

- Create a list or menu to load additional text files.

- Complete the project in Lesson 13 and then add printing capabilities to this project.

- Complete the project in Lesson 14 and turn this project into an AIR application that can save a copy of the text field as a file to the user's machine.

- Explore the `TextFlow` class and other TLF features for controlling the flow of text; then add fields to the project and load a single text file across multiple fields.

Review questions

1 Name three properties of the TLFTextField class.

2 Name three properties of the TextFormat class.

3 What two values can be stored in a variable with a data type of Boolean?

4 How can you use ActionScript to determine which key was pressed on the keyboard?

Review answers

1 The TLFTextField class has many properties, including the following that were used in this lesson: text, width, height, background, paddingTop, paddingLeft, paddingRight, and columnCount.

2 Among the many properties of the TextFormat class are the following that were used in this lesson: font, color, and size.

3 A Boolean data type can store one of two values: true or false.

4 One way to use ActionScript to determine which key has been pressed is to create a KeyboardEvent listener and then use the keyCode property of that event, as in this example:

```
stage.addEventListener(KeyboardEvent.KEY_DOWN, keyCheck);
function keyCheck(e:KeyboardEvent):void
{
 trace("Key number " + e.keyCode + " was pressed");
}
```

9 CONTROLLING SOUND WITH ACTIONSCRIPT

Lesson overview

In this lesson, you will learn to do the following:

- Create instances of the Sound, SoundChannel, and SoundTransform classes.

- Control the loading and playback of external MP3 files.

- Use the SoundTransform class to control the volume and panning of sounds.

- Use the Slider component to control the properties of the SoundTransform class.

- Use an array to store a playlist of MP3 files.

- Use methods of the TextField class to add characters to, and remove characters from, text strings.

- Use the ID3 tags of an MP3 file to access information about the file.

This lesson will take approximately 2.5 hours.

Sound is one of the most effective tools for evoking strong responses from your audience. By making the audio in your Flash projects interactive using ActionScript, you can use sounds to significantly enhance the user's experience. Whether employing simple sound effects that occur as the user interacts with an interface, or a full interactive soundscape in a game, you can use ActionScript 3.0 to immerse your users in a responsive aural environment.

```
72    snd = new Sound();
73    snd.load(new URLRequest(currSong));
74
75    channel = new SoundChannel  ;
76    trans = new SoundTransform(currVol,currPan);
77    channel = snd.play();
78    channel.soundTransform = trans;
79    panSlide.visible = true;
80    volSlide.visible = true;
81    //currVolume and pan values are used here for displ
82
83    volLabel.text = "Current Volume " + int(currVol * 1
84    panLabel.text = "Current Pan " + int(currPan * 100)
85
86    //listens for arrival of ID3 tags
87    snd.addEventListener(Event.ID3, id3Handler);
88 }
89
90 //triggered when id3 tags are available
91 //sets info text field to display current song informat
92 function id3Handler(event:Event):void {
93    var id3:ID3Info = snd.id3;
94    if (id3.songName != null) {
95        songTitle.text = id3.songName + "\n";
96        info.text="Artist: \n"+id3.artist+"\n \n";
97        info.appendText("Album: \n" + id3.album);
98        info.appendText("\n\n" + "Available at: \n" + "passionrecords \n.com");
99    }
100 }
101
102
```

lesson09__start.swf

TapTouch

TapTouch	Shelter
Sparkles On Her Dress	Healing Invitation
Looking Up	Faster

Current Volume 50

Current Pan 0

Artist:
Jonathan Keezing

Album:
Tap Touch

Available at:
**passionrecords
.com**

A simple Flash music player controlled by
ActionScript.

In this lesson, you will use ActionScript to create a simple music player. You will add basic sound control to your ActionScript repertoire and gain familiarity with a number of sound-related ActionScript techniques.

A number of ActionScript classes work with sound. This lesson focuses on three of them: the Sound, SoundChannel, and SoundTransform classes. These three classes work together to give you control over individual sound files. A fourth class, not covered in this lesson, is the SoundMixer class; it is used to control multiple channels of sound simultaneously.

Examining the completed file

To get an idea of what you will be doing in this lesson, take a look at the completed version: go to Lessons > Lesson09 > Complete > lesson09_complete.fla. The file uses six MP3 music files, which are in the Lesson09 > MP3 folder. Open lesson09_complete.fla and test it (Control > Test Movie) to see the results of this lesson. When clicked, each of the six jukebox titles plays a different song by loading it at runtime from the MP3 folder. When a song is loaded, information about that song is displayed.

You will add additional features to this music player project in Lesson 10, "Working with an XML Playlist."

Examining the starting file

The starting file for this lesson—lesson09_start.fla—can be found in the Lessons > Lesson 09 > Start folder. Open this file to begin the lesson.

1 With the Flash timeline visible, notice that there are three layers with content. The background layer is a full-screen static graphic. The song buttons layer contains six MovieClip instances that will be used to select and play six different songs. There is also a layer with text fields that you will control with ActionScript later in the lesson.

2 If it is not already visible, open the Properties panel, and, one at a time, select the six movie clips onstage that look like graphics of classic jukebox elements. Notice that they have instance names of *song1* through *song6*. These clips will be used to let users select the songs they want to play. You will add ActionScript to give these song clips functionality.

3 Double-click any of the song clips onstage to view that symbol's Timeline. You will see that inside each clip is a text field with the instance name `title`. These text fields will display the titles of the songs in the music player.

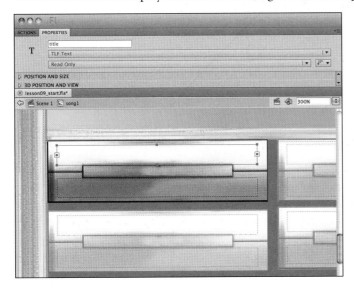

4 Click the Scene 1 tab in the upper left of the Stage to return to the main Timeline.

5 On the main Timeline, the text fields layer has four text fields: one at the top of the Stage, one at the lower right, and two at the lower left. With the Properties panel still visible, select these fields one at a time. Notice that the top field has an instance name of songTitle, the right field has an instance name of info, and the two fields at the lower left are named volLabel and panLabel. You will control the contents of all these fields with ActionScript.

Adding sliders to the project

The only graphical content items for this project not already placed onstage are the sliders that you will use to give users control over the volume and panning of the songs. These sliders will be instances of a User Interface component called Slider that ships with Flash CS5.

1 With Frame 1 of the sliders layer selected, open the Components panel (Window > Components) and, from the directory of User Interface components, locate the Slider component.

2 Drag two instances of the Slider component to the Stage: one to the right of the panLabel text field, and one to the right of the volLabel text field.

3 With the Properties panel visible, select the Slider instance to the right of the volLabel text field. Give this slider the instance name **volSlide**.

4 Select the slider to the right of the panLabel text field. Give this slider the instance name **panSlide**.

Next you will set the starting settings for the two Slider instances in the Properties panel.

5 With volSlide selected, make the Component Parameters section of the Properties Panel visible (Window > Properties).

6 Specify the initial settings for the volSlide instance as shown in the image here. The volume slider will have a range from 0 to 1 and an initial value of 0.5 (50%).

7 Select the `panSlide` instance and, in the Properties panel, give it the settings shown here.

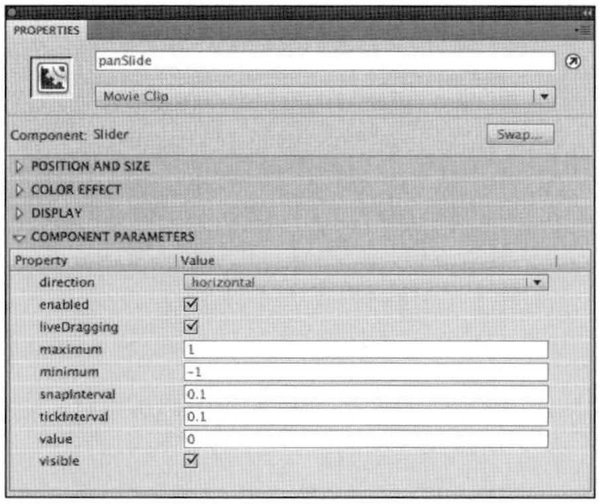

These settings give the slider a range between the left and right speaker and set the initial value to the center of the stereo field.

All the remaining additions to this project will be implemented with ActionScript. In this lesson, the ActionScript to control the project will all be added in Frame 1 of the Timeline's `actions` layer.

8 With Frame 1 of the `actions` layer selected, open the Actions panel if it is not already visible.

The first code in the file will import the `SliderEvent` class.

You will use several ActionScript classes in this project, but only one of them needs to be imported into the file. This is a class called `SliderEvent` that is used when the user adjusts the volume and panning using the sliders. Later in the lesson, you'll program the sliders to control the volume and panning of sound.

9 With Frame 1 of the `actions` layer selected, add the following code on the first line in the Actions panel:

```
import fl.events.SliderEvent;
```

Remember that depending on your preference settings, Flash CS5 may automatically add other import statements, but this is the only one required to make the code in this lesson work.

With the sliders prepared, the graphics for this file are all set and you are ready to begin coding the sound controls. The first step will be to create variables to store references to the three classes that you will use to work with sound: `Sound`, `SoundChannel`, and `SoundTransform`.

About import statements

For classes whose package description begins with the word "flash," importing that class before using it in the Flash Timeline is optional. Other classes need to be imported. By default, Flash CS5 will write many of the import statements for you as you create instances of objects of specific data types, but as you have seen, not all import statements that your projects will need are automatically created.

If you are not sure which classes need to be imported into a Flash project, which classes are optional, or what the path is for a class, you can find out in Flash Help. Look in the "ActionScript 3.0 Reference for the Adobe Flash Platform," where you will see a menu of all the classes in Flash. This is a great resource for researching an ActionScript class and learning about its methods, properties, and events.

When you select a class from the menu on the left, the top of the reference page for that class will show a reference to that class's package. In the image here, you can see the reference for the SliderEvent class. Notice that its package is listed as fl.events.

In an import statement for this class, you would use the package path followed by a dot and the class name:

```
import fl.events.SliderEvent;
```

Most of the built-in classes in ActionScript 3.0 have a path description that begins with the word "flash," as in:

```
import flash.media.Sound
```

When importing a class for your own custom classes, you may want to consider the option of setting the class paths associated with your Flash project. You can use the Publish settings (File > Publish Settings) to set class paths for a single Flash file, or you can globally set class paths for all your Flash projects using the Flash Preferences (Edit > Preferences in Windows, or File > Preferences on Mac OS). For more information about setting class paths, see Flash Help.

Remember, when you are writing code in external ActionScript files, you must import every class you reference.

The Sound, SoundChannel, and SoundTransform classes

As stated earlier, ActionScript 3.0 contains a number of classes that control sound. These classes often work together on the same sound file to load the sound into the project and determine how and when the sound plays. In this project, you will use an instance of each of three classes to control your sounds.

Here's a brief overview of how these three classes work together:

The Sound class is used mainly to load sounds into a Flash project and play them. You can also use the Sound class to read text data that is stored in MP3 files, as you will see in this lesson. (The Sound class also provides the capability to generate sounds from scratch, but we will not cover that feature in this lesson.)

The SoundChannel class is used to stop playback of individual sounds as well as to monitor the volume and panning of sound. When a sound is played in a Flash project, it is automatically assigned to a SoundChannel object, but to access the methods and properties of the SoundChannel class, you need to explicitly create a SoundChannel instance.

You can create instances of the SoundChannel class and assign specific sounds to a specific SoundChannel instance. A Flash project can have many separate sounds, all playing in their own SoundChannel instances simultaneously. Each SoundChannel instance can be controlled individually. The SoundChannel class works with the SoundTransform class, which is used to control the volume and panning of sounds.

Creating Sound, SoundChannel, and SoundTransform instances

You will create an instance of the Sound class that loads and plays songs that the user selects. You will associate the Sound instance with an instance of the SoundChannel class, and then associate the SoundChannel instance with a SoundTransform instance so that the user will be able to adjust the volume and panning in the songs.

Start by creating three variables to store the instances of these three classes.

1   In the Actions panel, below the line that reads:

    ```
    import fl.events.SliderEvent;
    ```

    add the following code:

    ```
    var snd:Sound;
    var channel:SoundChannel;
    var trans:SoundTransform;
    ```

The variable named snd has a data type of Sound, the variable named channel has a data type of SoundChannel, and the trans variable has a data type of SoundTransform. These variables have no initial values but will soon contain instances of their respective classes.

Adding comments to your files

While you are writing code, it may seem perfectly clear to you what you are trying to create, but often when you come back to a file later (sometimes much later!), it is less obvious what your thought process was at the time.

Adding comments in your ActionScript to explain key points of the code can be extremely helpful to you when you later have to recall the development process. Clear comments can also be very useful when a team is working together on a project or when you are sharing your code with others.

You designate a single-line comment in ActionScript with two forward slashes, as in:

```
// this code doesn't do anything but provides useful information
```

For multiline comments, you surround the comment with the tags /* and */, as in:

```
/* this line and the
lines below this
are all
commented out
until the asterisk-end
characters */
```

It's a good idea to get in the habit of generously adding comments to your ActionScript files. As you progress through the lessons, add whatever comments you think might be helpful to you when you go back to review them later or want to apply the techniques you learn in the lesson to your own projects.

For example, when you're reviewing this lesson in the future, you may be grateful that you added a comment like this before the code you added to create class instances:

```
//these variables will store instances of sound-related classes
var snd:Sound;
var channel:SoundChannel;
var trans:SoundTransform;
```

If you look at the code in the lesson09_complete.fla file, you will see a number of comments that help clarify the ActionScript.

Adding more variables

In this project, you'll also use variables to keep track of the currently selected song as well as the current volume and pan settings. So while you are declaring variables for the project, add three more.

1 In the Actions panel, below the code you just added, skip a line and use the following code to create three more variables:

```
var currSong:String;
var currVol:Number = .5;
var currPan:Number = 0;
```

The variable `currSong` will hold a string that contains the name of the currently selected song. The `currVol` and `currPan` variables will store numeric values for the current volume and pan settings. They are given initial values of 0.5 and 0 respectively. The range of values for volume and pan will be covered later in the lesson.

Next, you will add one more variable with a data type of Array to hold the playlist.

Creating the songList array

If you completed Lesson 7, "Using Arrays and Loops in ActionScript 3.0," you are familiar with the technique of storing a list of data in a single variable as an array. In this lesson, you will use an array to store the list of songs that the user can choose from. In a later lesson, you will change this array to an XML list that can be updated and modified easily, but for now, you will just add six songs directly to the array.

With Frame 1 of the `actions` layer still selected, add the following line below the existing code in the Actions panel:

```
var songList:Array = new Array("TapTouch.mp3", "Sparkles On Her
¬Dress.mp3", "Looking Up.mp3", "Shelter.mp3", "Healing
¬Invitation.mp3", "Faster.mp3");
```

You'll find these songs in the Lessons > Lesson09 > MP3s folder. After completing the lesson, you may want to change this list to use some of your own MP3 files, but unless you are already familiar with ID3 tags and know that your files have tags in the ID3 version 2.4 format, for now you should work with the files provided. ID3 tags will be discussed later in more detail.

Setting the song titles using a for loop

The six movie clips onstage that look like classic jukebox selections have instance names of `song1` through `song6`. You will use these as buttons with which the user can choose the various songs in the `songList` array. When the project runs, these song clips will display the titles of the songs. As you have seen, each song clip has a text field, named `title`, inside it. To control these text fields using ActionScript in the main Timeline, you can refer to them by the path (using `song1` as an example):

```
this.song1.title
```

The keyword `this` in ActionScript refers to the location from which the ActionScript is referenced, which in this case is the main Timeline.

Because the song clips have instance names that vary only by the number at the end, and the `songList` array has the same number of song clips as items, it will be easy to set up a `for` loop that assigns the names of the songs in the `songList` array to the `title` text fields in the clips.

1   Below the existing code in Frame 1 of the `actions` layer, add the following `for` loop:

```
for(var i = 0; i < songList.length; i++) {
 this["song" + (i + 1)].title.text = songList[i] as String;
 }
```

A number of useful techniques are being implemented here. In the first line of the `for` loop, notice that the number of times the code repeats is based on the length of the `songList` array (for a review of `for` loops and arrays, see Lesson 7):

```
for(var i = 0; i < songList.length; i++) {
```

The second line of code introduces the technique of evaluating the path of a movie clip using square brackets. Each time the `for` loop repeats, the text between the brackets is combined to produce one of the clip names. The `i` variable in the `for` loop begins at 0 and increments up to 5, with 1 added to the current value of `i` in each iteration, so the loop evaluates from 1 to 6, numbers which correspond with the song `MovieClip` instance names. The first time the `for` loop runs the code

```
this["song" + (i + 1)]
```

it will evaluate to `this.song1`, the second time to `this.song2`, and so on. This can be a very useful way to loop through a group of objects with similar names.

The remaining part of the line,

```
songList[i] as String
```

evaluates to a different element of the array each time the loop repeats. The result will set all six song clip titles to the six songs stored in the array.

2   Test the movie. The filenames of the songs appear in the text fields of the song clips.

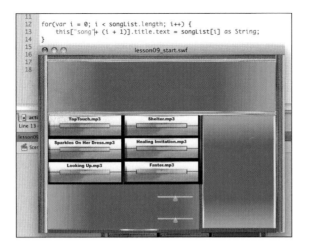

```
11
12  for(var i = 0; i < songList.length; i++) {
13      this["song"]+ (i + 1)].title.text = songList[i] as String;
14  }
15
16
17
18
```

lesson09_start.swf

TapTouch.mp3   Shelter.mp3

Sparkles On Her Dress.mp3   Healing Invitation.mp3

Looking Up.mp3   Faster.mp3

Modifying text fields with the replace() method

When you tested the movie, you probably noticed that the text fields display the full names of the song files, including the file extension suffix ".mp3." Since it's not really desirable to display the suffix in the interface, you can use a method of the TextField class to remove it. The replace() method takes two parameters between the parentheses. The first parameter is the text to be removed; the second is what you wish to add in place of the removed text. If you have used the find-and-replace feature in any software application, you are familiar with the concept of replace().

In this example, you will replace the suffix .mp3 with no text, which will be described by empty quotation marks ("").

To write the names of the songs without the suffixes, you will modify the for loop you just created. You'll add a new variable named str to store the original filenames of the songs, and then you'll modify that variable with the replace() method. This new string will then be what is placed in the title fields of the song clips.

1   Rewrite the code in the for loop that you added:

```
for(var i = 0; i < songList.length; i++) {
 this["song" + (i + 1)].title.text = songList[i] as String;
}
```

so that it instead reads:

```
for(var i = 0; i < songList.length; i++) {
 var str:String = songList[i] as String;
 str = str.replace(".mp3" , "");
 var clip = this["song" + (i + 1)].title;
 clip.text = str;
}
```

2 Test the movie. Notice that now the names of the songs appear without the file extension.

3 Close the lesson09_start.swf file to leave the testing environment.

Making the sliders invisible until needed

Since the two sliders that you added to the Stage won't be needed until the user selects a song to play, it makes sense to set their visible properties to `false` to hide them. Later in the lesson, you will add code to make them both visible and functional when a song is chosen.

1 With Frame 1 of the `actions` layer of the Timeline still selected, insert a new line in the Actions panel below your existing code and add the following two lines:

```
panSlide.visible = false;
volSlide.visible = false;
```

2 Test the movie once more. The sliders should no longer be visible.

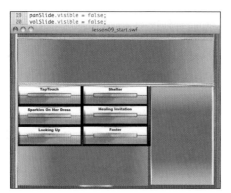

3 Close the lesson09_start.swf file to leave the testing environment.

Next, you will add the event listeners that will let users click to select a song.

Programming the buttons to select songs

The six song clips onstage will be used to call a function that will determine which song will be played. Start by creating six addEventListener() calls for these clips.

Adding event listeners to the song buttons

The six clips with the instance names song1 through song6 will all call the same function. This function will use a long conditional (switch) statement to determine which song to play.

First, add six addEventListener() methods to listen for mouse clicks on the clips.

1 On a new line below the existing code, add the following six listeners:

```
song1.addEventListener(MouseEvent.CLICK, chooseSong);
song2.addEventListener(MouseEvent.CLICK, chooseSong);
song3.addEventListener(MouseEvent.CLICK, chooseSong);
song4.addEventListener(MouseEvent.CLICK, chooseSong);
song5.addEventListener(MouseEvent.CLICK, chooseSong);
song6.addEventListener(MouseEvent.CLICK, chooseSong);
```

Creating the chooseSong() function

Next, you will create the shell for the chooseSong() function that all of these events will call.

1 On a new line below the existing code, add this function:

```
function chooseSong(e:MouseEvent):void {
}
```

This function will do much of the work for the entire project and will contain quite a bit of code. It will store the name of the sound that the user selects, create a new Sound instance, and create and set the properties for related SoundChannel and SoundTransform instances to control the sound. It will also make the sliders visible (since they will of course be needed once a song has been selected) and set the initial volume and pan settings for the sliders.

Creating a switch statement for the song selection

The first thing to be done in the chooseSong() function is to store the name of the song that the user selects. The selected song will be stored in the currSong variable that you created earlier. A long switch statement will be used to check which song was selected and set the currSong variable to contain a string that describes the path to that song. For example, when the first song in the songList array is selected (songList[0]), then the currSong variable will be set to:

```
"../MP3s/" + songList[0] as String;
```

The string "../MP3s/" refers to the folder in which songs are stored. The two dots and initial forward slash (../) tell that the MP3s folder is found in the parent folder of the current Flash file.

● **Note:** A switch statement is an alternative type of conditional statement that works very similarly to an if statement, but lots of developers prefer to use it when there are many conditions to be checked. A switch statement begins with the keyword switch followed by the condition to be checked. A series of case statements evaluates each value that you wish to check. If a case statement is ended with a break, then the entire switch statement is ended when one of the case statements is true; otherwise, the player proceeds through the entire statement. For more information about switch statements, see the "ActionScript 3.0 Reference for the Flash Platform."

1 Add the full switch statement to the chooseSong() function so that the entire function reads:

```
function chooseSong(e:MouseEvent):void {

  switch (e.currentTarget.name) {
   case "song1":
    currSong = "../MP3s/" + songList[0] as String;
    break;
   case "song2":
    currSong = "../MP3s/" + songList[1] as String;
    break;
   case "song3":
    currSong = "../MP3s/" + songList[2] as String;
    break;
   case "song4":
    currSong = "../MP3s/" + songList[3] as String;
    break;
   case "song5":
    currSong = "../MP3s/" + songList[4] as String;
    break;
   case "song6":
    currSong = "../MP3s/" + songList[5] as String;
    break;
  }
 }
```

Now the currSong variable will store any song the user selects.

You will now create and work with three instances. The variable you created called snd will be an instance of the Sound class, the variable called channel will be a SoundChannel instance that will contain the snd instance, and the trans instance will refer to the SoundTransform object you will create to manipulate the volume and pan of snd.

You will create all these instances and set their initial properties in the chooseSong() function.

Creating a Sound class instance and checking for existing instances

Since the `chooseSong()` function may be called at any time while a user is interacting with this project, you want to make sure that multiple songs don't overlap: that is, if a `snd` instance is already playing, it needs to stop before a new one begins. You will use an `if` statement to check whether the `snd` variable contains a value. If `snd` does have a value, then that sound should be stopped, and only after that will a new `snd` instance be created.

1   Below the closing curly brace of the `switch` statement and above the closing brace of the `chooseSong()` function, add the following code:

```
if (snd != null) {
 channel.stop();
}
snd = new Sound();
```

Keeping in mind that all audio in the `snd` instance will play through the `channel` instance (which you will be working with very soon), the code you just wrote states that if a sound already exists in the `snd` object (`snd != null`), then the sound playing in `channel` will be stopped (`channel.stop()`). After this, a new instance of the Sound class will be created in the `snd` object (`snd = new Sound()`).

The result of this code is that each time the user clicks one of the song clips, a new Sound object is created; if a song is playing, it will stop.

Loading a sound into a Sound instance

To load a sound into an instance of the Sound class, you use the `load()` method. This method takes a single parameter, `URLRequest`, which specifies the path to the file you want to load.

1   Keeping in mind that the song that the user wishes to play has already been stored in the variable `currSong`, add the following code below the code you just added and above the closing brace of the `chooseSong()` function:

```
snd.load(new URLRequest(currSong));
```

Creating the SoundChannel and SoundTransform instances

As mentioned, to control the stopping, panning, and volume of a Sound instance, the instance needs be associated with `SoundChannel` and `SoundTransform` instances. You will do this now.

1   Below the line that reads:

```
snd.load(new URLRequest(currSong));
```

Note: In projects where you are loading sounds from external locations, it is a good idea to track the loading progress of a sound and check for errors in the loading. For information on how to do this, look up `load()` in Flash Help. Because the files for this lesson are local, and to concentrate on the features in the Sound classes, this lesson does not track loading progress.

add a new SoundChannel instance in the variable called `channel`:

```
channel = new SoundChannel;
```

Next, you need an instance of the SoundTransform class in the variable called `trans`. The constructor for the SoundTransform class takes two required parameters: one for volume and one for pan.

2 On the next line, type the following code:

```
trans = new SoundTransform(currVol, currPan);
```

This SoundTransform instance takes its `volume` property from the `currVol` variable you created earlier; recall that this variable had an initial value of 0.5. The pan value comes from the value of the variable `currPan`, whose initial value is 0.

Values for volume and pan: listeners, beware!

The SoundTransform class has properties that take numeric values (or expressions that evaluate to numbers) to indicate the volume and pan settings.

Volume in ActionScript is measured between 0 (silent) and 1 (full volume of the original audio). A common mistake is to assume that volume is measured between 0 and 100. This can have dire consequences, because numbers over 1 overdrive the sound level. A volume setting of 2 will play the sound twice as loud as in the original file, a setting of 5 will be 500 percent of the original volume, and therefore a volume setting of 100 is—you got it—100 times louder than the original sound! This is obviously an unfortunate level for eardrums and sound cards, so it is important to remember the actual volume range.

Pan is measured between –1 and 1. A setting of –1 will play the sound exclusively in the left speaker. A pan setting of 1 will play the sound in the right speaker only. A pan setting of 0 will play the sound exactly in the center of the stereo field.

To play the sound that has been loaded into the `snd` instance inside of `channel`, use the `play()` method of the Sound class.

3 On the next line, type the following code:

```
channel = snd.play();
```

Next, you need to associate the sound playing in the `channel` object with the new SoundTransform instance.

4 Add the following code on the next line:

```
channel.soundTransform = trans;
```

This will apply the volume and pan settings in the `trans` instance to the `channel` object and therefore the play sound.

At this point, the entire `chooseSong()` function should read as shown here:

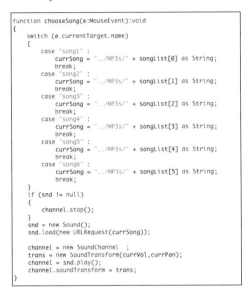

```
function chooseSong(e:MouseEvent):void
{
    switch (e.currentTarget.name)
    {
        case "song1" :
            currSong = "../MP3s/" + songList[0] as String;
            break;
        case "song2" :
            currSong = "../MP3s/" + songList[1] as String;
            break;
        case "song3" :
            currSong = "../MP3s/" + songList[2] as String;
            break;
        case "song4" :
            currSong = "../MP3s/" + songList[3] as String;
            break;
        case "song5" :
            currSong = "../MP3s/" + songList[4] as String;
            break;
        case "song6" :
            currSong = "../MP3s/" + songList[5] as String;
            break;
    }
    if (snd != null)
    {
        channel.stop();
    }
    snd = new Sound();
    snd.load(new URLRequest(currSong));

    channel = new SoundChannel   ;
    trans = new SoundTransform(currVol,currPan);
    channel = snd.play();
    channel.soundTransform = trans;
}
```

5 Test the movie. You should be able to click any of the song clips and hear the related song play back. Choose multiple songs, and notice that only one song at a time will play.

6 Close the lesson09_start.swf file to leave the testing environment.

There are still a few more things to add to the `chooseSong()` function, starting with the volume and pan sliders and their text fields.

Controlling the visibility of the volume and pan controls

Earlier, you set the volume and pan sliders to be invisible. Once the user selects a song to play, the sliders will of course be needed again to control the volume and pan. So in the body of the `chooseSong()` function, make the sliders visible.

1 Above the closing brace of the `chooseSong()` function and below the line that reads

```
channel.soundTransform = trans;
```

insert the following two lines to make the sliders visible:

```
panSlide.visible = true;
volSlide.visible = true;
```

Next, you will use the values of the `currVol` and `currPan` variables to display the volume and pan levels in the text fields next to the sliders.

2 Below the code you just added, insert these new lines:

```
volLabel.text = "Current Volume " + int(currVol * 100);
panLabel.text = "Current Pan " + int(currPan * 100);
```

Most users are intuitively more comfortable with volume and pan sliders that range up to 100 rather than up to 1, which is why the `trans.volume` and `trans.pan` values were multiplied by 100. These values will be used only for display in text fields.

Notice also that the values of `currVol` and `currPan` are both cast as integers. This is because, unlike instances of the data type `Number`, integers (`int`) cannot contain fractions. This specification will prevent numbers with decimal places from being displayed in the volume and pan text fields.

3 Test the movie once more. Notice that when a song is selected, the pan and volume sliders become visible and their initial settings are displayed in the text fields.

Notice that moving the sliders around has no effect at this point on the volume or panning of the music or the text in the text fields. You will add code soon to change this.

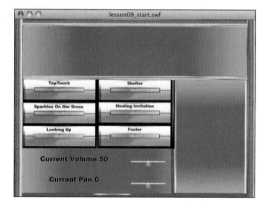

4 Close the lesson09_start.swf file to leave the testing environment.

Before you add the listeners to respond to movement of the volume and pan sliders, there is one more line of code to add to the `chooseSong()` function. This will be used to listen for data that is stored in MP3 files.

Adding a listener for the ID3 tags of an MP3 file

The MP3 file format allows the insertion of text-based data into the file. These *ID3* tags in an MP3 file are typically used to store information about the file, such as the names of the song, artist, and album and the date of release.

ActionScript is capable of reading and displaying this ID3 data from a loaded MP3 file. The Sound class even has a built-in event that responds to the successful loading of ID3 tags from an MP3 file. You will use this ID3 event to call a function to display information about the currently playing song in your interface.

1   Below the last line of code that you inserted and above the closing brace of the chooseSong() function, add the following line:

```
snd.addEventListener(Event.ID3, id3Handler);
```

When a load() method loads an MP3 file that has ID3 tags, the successful loading of those tags triggers the ID3 event. In this case, when the event occurs, a function named id3Handler() is called.

Next, you will create the id3Handler() function.

Creating the id3Handler() function

The ID3 format contains dozens of possible tags and also lets you create your own custom tags.

In this lesson, you will use three of the most common tags (you can look up other ID3 tags in Flash Help): the ones that contain the name of the song in the MP3 file, the artist, and the album that the song is from. The data you retrieve from these tags will be used to populate the songTitle and info text fields onstage.

First add the shell for the id3Handler() function.

1   With Frame 1 of the actions layer still selected, add a new line below all the existing code in that frame, and insert the following function structure:

```
function id3Handler(event:Event):void {
}
```

Remember that this function will be called every time new data from a loaded MP3 file is available. This data will be automatically stored in the id3 property of the Sound class instance that loaded the MP3 file—in this case, the snd instance.

The first thing you will add to the new function is a local variable to contain all the loaded ID3 data.

Using iTunes to check and set ID3 tags

Most MP3 files contain some ID3 tags, but not all of them are in the correct format to work with Flash and ActionScript. ActionScript 3.0 works best with ID3 tags in the version 2.4 format. You can view and create these tags, as well as save them in the correct version, with a number of audio applications. One of the most popular is Apple's iTunes (available free for Mac OS and Windows).

To view and set the ID3 tags of an MP3 file, open it in iTunes. If you see the song name, the artist name, and other information for the file in the iTunes library, ID3 tags are the sources of that data. To set the ID3 tags to the correct version, select the song in the iTunes library, right-click it (Control-click on a Macintosh with a single-button mouse) to open its context menu, and choose Convert ID3 Tags.

In the dialog box that opens, make sure that the ID3 Tag Version box is selected and choose v2.4. Then click OK.

Finally, to make sure that you are viewing the updated version of the file with the correct tags, right-click the song in the iTunes Library and choose Show in Finder (in Mac OS) or Show in Windows Explorer (in Windows).

You can now be confident that ActionScript can read and use the tags in this file.

2 In the id3Handler() function, add the following new line so that the function now reads:

```
function id3Handler(event:Event):void {
 var id3:ID3Info = snd.id3;
}
```

If an MP3 file has ID3 tags at all, most likely those tags include a songName property. However, it's a good idea to be certain of this before trying to use this information in a project, so you'll add a conditional statement to check whether a songName property exists. If it does, it will display the song name in the songTitle text field onstage.

3 Add code to the id3Handler() function so that it reads:

```
function id3Handler(event:Event):void {
 var id3:ID3Info = snd.id3;
 if (id3.songName != null) {
   songTitle.text = id3.songName;
 }
}
```

4 Test the movie. Select a song. The song should play, and in addition the title should now appear at the top of the screen. Try other songs; the title will update automatically.

5 Close the lesson09_start.swf file to leave the testing environment.

Adding the artist and album information

If songName information is available in the ID3 tags, then you can assume that artist and album information will also be available. In your own projects, you may want to use additional conditional statements to check for the existence of data in each tag separately.

1 Add code to the id3Handler() function to set the info text field to display information using the artist and album properties. The final function should read:

```
function id3Handler(event:Event):void {
 var id3:ID3Info = snd.id3;
 if (id3.songName != null) {
  songTitle.text = id3.songName + "\n";
  info.text = "Artist: \n" + id3.artist + "\n \n";
  info.appendText("Album: \n" + id3.album);
  info.appendText("\n\n" + "Available at: \n" +
  ¬"passionrecords \n.com");
 }
}
```

This new code has a few elements that you may not have encountered before. The first new line uses the tag \n to force new lines in a string of text in the text field.

The second and third new lines add text to the existing info text field, with the appendText() method.

2 Test the movie. Now when a song is selected, in addition to the title appearing at the top, artist and album information from the ID3 tags as well as the string for the label's website appear in the info field on the right side.

3 Close the lesson09_start.swf file to leave the testing environment.

Adding a text format object

In Lesson 8, you learned to format text with the TextFormat class. You will now create a TextFormat instance and apply it to the info field. Since most of this code is familiar from Lesson 8, add it all at once.

1 With Frame 1 of the actions layer still selected in the Timeline, insert a new line in the Actions panel below all the existing code.

2 Create a new TextFormat instance and set its properties with the following code:

```
var format:TextFormat = new TextFormat();
format.font = "Arial Black"; //If your computer does not have
//this font installed on it, use the installed font of
//your choice.
format.color = 0xFFFF00;
format.size = 14;
format.url = "http://www.passionrecords.com/";
```

If you completed Lesson 8, all of this code is familiar to you, with the exception of the url property of the TextFormat class. Setting the url property of a TextFormat instance is a very easy way to add a hyperlink to ActionScript formatted text. In this case, any text that has the format instance as its TextFormat property will go to www.passionrecords.com when clicked.

3 Apply the new format object to be the defaultTextFormat property of the info field by adding this line below all the existing code:

```
info.defaultTextFormat = format;
```

4 Test the movie. Choose a song and notice the formatting of the text on the right. Click that text. If you are connected to the Internet, your default browser should load and display www.passionrecords.com.

5 Close the lesson09_start.swf file to leave the testing environment.

Adding the slider controls

The last thing that you will add to this project is code to make the sliders control the volume and panning of the currently playing song.

Like the List component that you used in Lesson 5, "Using ActionScript and Components to Load Content," the Slider component has a built-in CHANGE event that occurs whenever the user drags a slider's handle.

Note: Many developers like to organize their files by placing all the addEventListener() calls in the same section of the file. If you would prefer to place the two lines that you just added with the rest of the addEventListener() methods for this file, feel free to cut and paste them below the addEventListener() methods for the six buttons that you created earlier. They will work exactly the same way in either location.

1   Below all the existing code for Frame 1, create an addEventListener() method that listens for the CHANGE event for each onstage Slider instance:

```
volSlide.addEventListener(SliderEvent.CHANGE, volumeChange);
panSlide.addEventListener(SliderEvent.CHANGE, panChange);
```

Adding the volumeChange() and panChange() functions

When the user changes the volume (using the volume slider), a function named volumeChange() is called. Add the shell for that function below all the existing code for Frame 1.

1   On a new line below all the existing code for Frame 1, add the following code:

```
function volumeChange(e:SliderEvent):void {
}
```

The syntax e.target.value will describe the value to which the slider gets moved. This value will update the volLabel text field as well as set the volume of the Sound object.

2   Add two new lines to the volumeChange() function to update the text property of volLabel to show the new volume setting. The function should now read:

```
function volumeChange(e:SliderEvent):void {
 currVol = e.target.value;
 volLabel.text = "Current Volume: " + int(currVol * 100);
}
```

To actually set the volume, you will use the slider's value as the volume property of the SoundTransform instance named trans. Each time you update the properties of a SoundTransform instance, the properties need to be reapplied to the SoundChannel instance for you to hear the change. The last line of this function will do that.

3 Add two more lines to the volumeChange() function to apply the slider's current value to be the volume of the playing song. The completed function should read:

```
function volumeChange(e:SliderEvent):void {
 currVol = e.target.value;
 volLabel.text = "Current Volume: " + int(currVol * 100);
 trans.volume = currVol;
 channel.soundTransform = trans;
}
```

Before you test the completed lesson file, add one final function, panChange(). This is very similar to the volumeChange() function, but uses the pan property of the SoundTransform class.

4 Insert the panChange() function below all the existing code:

```
function panChange(e:SliderEvent):void {
 currPan = e.target.value;
 panLabel.text = "Current Pan " + int(currPan * 100);
 trans.pan = e.target.value;
 channel.soundTransform = trans;
}
```

5 Test the completed movie. Select a song and try sliding the volume and pan controls. The volume slider should vary from silent to full volume, and, if you have stereo speakers, you should hear the panning control send the sound from the left speaker to the right.

Congratulations—you now can create projects with full interactive control over sound! This is a solid foundation on which you can build endless and powerful variations.

Some suggestions to try on your own

ActionScript provides a number of other ways to control sounds. You will see some of them in the coming lessons, but it would also be a good idea to consult the ActionScript 3.0 language reference found in Flash Help, especially reading through all the methods, properties, and events of the three sound-related classes used in this lesson. Play with some of the example code in the reference. In addition, here are a few suggestions for deeper exploration of how to control sound with ActionScript:

- Use the techniques covered in this lesson and add ID3 tags to your own MP3 files. Try replacing the sound files in the `songList` array of the lesson09_start.fla file with your MP3 files.

- Add information about some of the other ID3 tags in your MP3 files to the text fields onstage. Add more text fields. For information about other default tag names, see Flash Help.

- Create a new `TextFormat` object and set its properties to your taste. Set the object to format the `songTitle` field at the top of the Stage.

- Research the `Microphone` and `SoundMixer` classes in Flash Help. These two ActionScript 3.0 classes offer many other audio capabilities. New to Flash Player 10.1 is the capability to record audio from a user's microphone without the need for external server software.

- Research the `computeSpectrum()` method of the `SoundMixer` class in Flash Help. This method can be used to create graphics from audio data.

- Research the Sound class's `sampleData` event, which can be used to create new sounds entirely with ActionScript.

Review questions

1 What are three ActionScript classes you can use to load, play, and control an external audio file?

2 What are two properties of a sound file that can be controlled with the SoundTransform class?

3 What method of the TextField class can be used to replace text in a text field? What method can be used to add to an existing text field?

4 What event of the Sound class can respond to the loading of text data from an MP3 file?

Review answers

1 The Sound class, the SoundChannel class, and the SoundTransform class all work together in ActionScript to load, play, and control sound files with ActionScript.

2 The SoundTransform class can control the volume and panning of sound with ActionScript.

3 The replace() method of the TextField class can find and replace text in a field. The appendText() method can concatenate text to a text field.

4 The ID3 event of the Sound class occurs when the ID3 text data of an MP3 file has successfully loaded.

10 WORKING WITH AN XML PLAYLIST

Lesson overview

In this lesson, you will learn to do the following:

- Understand the basic structure of an XML file.

- Understand how you can use XML in a Flash project.

- Create an XML object in Flash with ActionScript.

- Use the URLLoader class to load an external XML file.

- Respond to COMPLETE and ERROR events of the URLLoader class.

- Access data in an XML file from Flash using the XML features of ActionScript 3.0.

- Use XML data to control a music player application.

This lesson will take approximately 2 hours.

This lesson will show how to use the data in external XML files in your Flash projects by taking advantage of the enhanced XML capabilities in ActionScript 3.0.

A music player powered by ActionScript and XML.

XML is a very easy-to-use markup language that has become a standard for organizing data. It is a tag-based language that is very similar to HTML; however, unlike HTML, XML does not have predefined tags and is therefore completely flexible—you can define your own tags to describe the data that you store in an XML file.

In this lesson, you will work with an XML file that includes a playlist and song information that will drive the music player application that was created in Lesson 9, "Controlling Sound with ActionScript."

Understanding the basic structure of an XML file

XML files are really just text files with the suffix ".xml," so they can be created and edited with any application that supports text files.

ActionScript 3.0 has very strong support for XML. ActionScript 3.0 is based on the ECMAScript programming standard defined by the ECMA International standards committee. Part of this standard includes native support for XML. (To learn more about XML and ECMAScript, visit www.ecma-international.org/publications/standards/Ecma-357.htm.)

ActionScript 3.0 is capable of reading and writing XML. Common uses of XML in Flash projects include:

- Working with RSS feeds

- Creating podcasts

- Creating blogging applications

- Communicating with server software

- Creating captioned applications and subtitles

- Working with video and audio playlists

To understand the basics of how an XML document is set up, open the XML file that you will use for this lesson: songlist.xml, in the Lessons > Lesson10 > Start folder. The images in this lesson show this file opened in Dreamweaver, but you can use any application that supports plain text files. If you do not own Dreamweaver but wish to use it to work with XML files, a free 30-day download is available at https://www.adobe.com/cfusion/tdrc/index.cfm?product=dreamweaver&loc=en.

It is helpful to remember that the code in an XML file is not intended to *do* anything—XML files are used only to store and organize data. If you have worked with data in spreadsheets before, then much of XML's structure should be familiar to you.

The songlist.xml file has a simple structure but contains the basic format common to all XML files. The following image shows songlist.xml open in Dreamweaver.

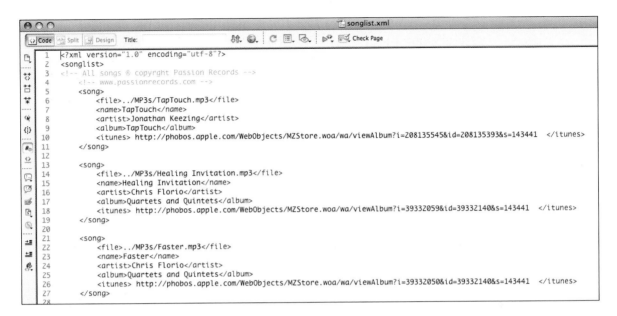

```
1   <?xml version="1.0" encoding="utf-8"?>
2   <songlist>
3   <!-- All songs © copyrght Passion Records -->
4       <!-- www.passionrecords.com -->
5       <song>
6           <file>../MP3s/TapTouch.mp3</file>
7           <name>TapTouch</name>
8           <artist>Jonathan Keezing</artist>
9           <album>TapTouch</album>
10          <itunes> http://phobos.apple.com/WebObjects/MZStore.woa/wa/viewAlbum?i=208135545&id=208135393&s=143441   </itunes>
11      </song>
12
13      <song>
14          <file>../MP3s/Healing Invitation.mp3</file>
15          <name>Healing Invitation</name>
16          <artist>Chris Florio</artist>
17          <album>Quartets and Quintets</album>
18          <itunes> http://phobos.apple.com/WebObjects/MZStore.woa/wa/viewAlbum?i=39332059&id=39332140&s=143441   </itunes>
19      </song>
20
21      <song>
22          <file>../MP3s/Faster.mp3</file>
23          <name>Faster</name>
24          <artist>Chris Florio</artist>
25          <album>Quartets and Quintets</album>
26          <itunes> http://phobos.apple.com/WebObjects/MZStore.woa/wa/viewAlbum?i=39332050&id=39332140&s=143441   </itunes>
27      </song>
28
```

The first line of an XML file contains a declaration tag that tells parsers which version of XML and what type of encoding the file uses.

```
<?xml version="1.0" encoding="utf-8"?>
```

Since by default ActionScript ignores this line, you don't have to be too concerned with it for now.

The two lines below the first `<songList>` tag in the songlist.xml file are comments. These serve the same purpose as ActionScript comments (discussed in Lesson 9), which is to leave notes for yourself and others. Comments in an XML file are contained between the characters `<!--` and `-->`, as in:

```
<!-- This is an XML comment -->
<!-- similar to an HTML comment -->
```

ActionScript ignores XML comments by default, so you can too.

After those initial lines comes the body of the songlist.xml document, which is made up of tagged data. Every XML document used with ActionScript must have a single root pair of tags. In this case, that tag pair is named `songlist`. An opening tag in XML is contained within angle brackets (for example, `<songlist>`), and a closing tag adds a forward slash after the opening angle bracket (`</songlist>`). All opening tags in XML must have a corresponding closing tag. Another word for a tag in XML is *element*.

All the additional elements of the XML document are contained between the opening and closing root tags. In your own XML documents you can make up any names you want for the tags, which is the main reason the language is so versatile and useful.

XML is set up in a hierarchy of parent and child tags.

Note: If you need to access XML comments using ActionScript, you can use the `ignoreComments()` method of the XML class. For more information, see the ActionScript 3.0 Language Reference.

In the songlist.xml file, the `<songlist>` tag is the parent of all 12 sets of `<song>` tags (elements).

Each song element has five child elements. These elements are named file, name, artist, album, and itunes.

```
<song>
    <file>../MP3s/TapTouch.mp3</file>
    <name>TapTouch</name>
    <artist>Jonathan Keezing</artist>
    <album>TapTouch</album>
    <itunes> http://phobos.apple.com/WebObjects/MZStore.woa/wa/viewAlbum?i=208135545&id=208135393&s=143441  </itunes>
</song>
```

Seeing the various tags or elements in a table format may help you understand the format of the songlist.xml file. Each song element could be considered the equivalent of a record or entry—or a row—in a spreadsheet or table. The child elements provide various values or information for each song element.

`<song>`	`<file>`	`<name>`	`<artist>`	`<album>`	`<itunes>`
`<song>`	../MP3s/TapTouch.mp3	TapTouch	Jonathan Keezing	TapTouch	http://phobos.apple.com…
`<song>`	../MP3s/Healing Invitation.mp3	Healing Invitation	Chris Florio	Quartets and Quintets	http://phobos.apple.com…
`<song>`	>../MP3s/Faster.mp3	Faster	Chris Florio	Quartets and Quintets	http://phobos.apple.com…
`<song>`	>../MP3s/Shelter.mp3	Shelter	David Horton	Looking out from inside	http://phobos.apple.com…
`<song>`	>../MP3s/Sparkles On Her Dress.mp3	Sparkles on her Dress	Chris Florio	Butterfly/Gymsock	http://phobos.apple.com…
`<song>`	etc.				

An XML file can have as many levels of nested child elements as needed. This simple example just contains a series of song elements, each with its child elements. You can add as many song elements as you like by repeating the structure.

For now, close the songlist.xml file. Later, you'll load the data in this file to a Flash project using ActionScript.

Examining the starting file

This lesson will begin with a slightly modified version of the completed file from Lesson 9. You'll delete the array that was used to determine the songs available in the music player and instead use the data from the songlist.xml file. By getting this data from the XML file, you make it easy for anyone to add to or modify the song list without having to re-create or even open the existing Flash file.

1 Open the lesson10_start.fla file in the Lessons > Lesson10 > Start folder.

2 Open the Actions panel if it is not visible, and examine the code on Frame 1 of the actions layer. If you completed Lesson 9, you will recognize the code from that lesson. With the exception of a few comments added for clarity, this file contains the same ActionScript as in the completed version of Lesson 9.

3 Examine the Stage. Notice that two new buttons have been added to the project. With the Properties panel visible, select the button in the lower left that has the text "more songs." Notice that this button has the instance name more_btn. In the interface, only six song choices are visible at a time, so you will add ActionScript to the file to allow the user to click this button to view additional songs.

4 Select the button in the upper right of the Stage that has the Apple iTunes logo. Notice in the Properties panel that this button has an instance name of link_btn. You will add ActionScript to the file so that when this button is clicked, it will launch iTunes and navigate to the iTunes location of the song that is currently selected in the Flash project. The iTunes locations of these songs are stored as URLs in the songlist.xml document.

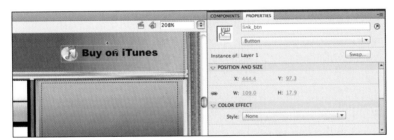

Now you can begin adding this new functionality to the file.

Replacing the songList array with an XML instance

As mentioned earlier, this project replaces the songList array from Lesson 9 with the contents of the songlist.xml file. You'll begin by deleting the array from the existing code.

1 With Frame 1 of the actions layer selected, locate the songList array in the Actions panel.

2 Select the entire array (as well as related comments) and press Delete.

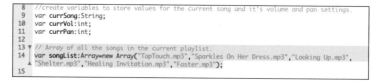

Next, you will insert two new variables into the file. These will be used later in the lesson to keep track of current songs.

3 In the Actions panel, on Frame 1, locate the code that declares these variables:

```
var currSong:String;
var currVol:int;
var currPan:int;
```

4 Below this code, insert the following lines:

```
var songCount:int = 0;
var songNum:int;
```

Now you will create a new XML object that will be used to contain the data from the songlist.xml file and a URLLoader object to load the XML into Flash.

Creating new XML and URLLoader instances

The XML class is used to store XML data that has been created in a Flash project or loaded from an external XML file. The XML class also has methods and properties for working with XML data.

The class that is used for loading data into Flash is called the URLLoader class. If you completed Lesson 5, "Using ActionScript and Components to Load Content," you used the URLLoader class to load text into Flash from external files. In this lesson, you will use an instance of this class to load the songlist.xml file.

Add code to this project to create a new instance of the XML class and a new instance of the URLLoader class.

1 Locate the following variables declarations:

```
var currSong:String;
var currVol:int;
var currPan:int;
var songCount:int = 0;
var songNum:int;
```

2 Place the cursor below these lines and press Enter/Return to add a new line.

3 Add the following two lines of code:

```
var songList_XML:XML;
var xmlLoader:URLLoader = new URLLoader();
```

The `songList_XML` variable will contain the data from the songlist.xml file. That data has not loaded yet, so this variable has no initial value.

You have also created the `xmlLoader` variable and given it a new instance of the `URLLoader` class.

Loading an external playlist using the URLLoader class

The `URLLoader` class uses the `load()` method to bring data from an external source into a Flash project. When `URLLoader` data is requested, events of the `URLLoader` class provide feedback that lets you respond after data has loaded or after an error occurs.

This `load()` method requires one parameter: the URL of the data you wish to load. Often that parameter takes the form of a new `URLRequest` object. You will use the `load()` method to load the data from the songlist.xml file.

1 On a new line, below the line that reads:

```
var xmlLoader:URLLoader = new URLLoader();
```

insert the following code:

```
xmlLoader.load(new URLRequest("songlist.xml"));
```

Note: The line that you just added assumes you have a file named songlist.xml in the same folder as your Flash file (which you do). If the file that you want to load is on a remote server, you would type the entire URL to that file as the `URLRequest` parameter.

Responding to COMPLETE and IO_ERROR events

The `URLLoader` class has built-in events that give feedback on the loading of data. In this project, you will use two of them. The `COMPLETE` event fires once when the data that you have instructed it to load has successfully completed loading. You should get in the habit of using the `COMPLETE` event to check that data is available before writing code that requires the use of that data. If for some reason the data fails to load, then the `IO_Error` event occurs. It is also a good idea to listen for this event, to help you take into account situations in which your users are unable to load data that might be an important part of your projects.

An additional URLLoader event—not used in this lesson but worth knowing about—is the PROGRESS event, which can be used to monitor the progress of larger files that may take a while to load. As you may recall from Lesson 6, "Creating Preloaders in ActionScript 3.0," the PROGRESS event is central to the creation of preloaders.

You will add event listeners to this project for the COMPLETE and IO_ERROR events.

1 In the Actions panel, below the previous line of code that you entered, add the following two addEventListener() methods:

```
xmlLoader.addEventListener(Event.COMPLETE, xmlLoaded);
xmlLoader.addEventListener(IOErrorEvent.IO_ERROR,
¬errorHandler);
```

If the songlist.xml file fails to load, then the listener you just added calls a function named errorHandler(). Next, you need to insert that function.

2 On a line below the code you just added in the previous step, insert the following code:

```
function errorHandler(event:IOErrorEvent):void {
 songTitle.text = "XML loading error: " + event;
}
```

Now if an error occurs, an error message is placed in the songTitle text field in the upper part of the Stage. In your own projects, you may want to use error events to take the user to alternative content that does not require the material that failed to load.

If the file loads successfully, the xmlLoaded() function will be called instead of errorHandler(). The xmlLoaded() function performs much of the setup for the music player.

Start by adding the shell for this function.

3 Below the errorHandler() function, add the following code:

```
function xmlLoaded(event:Event):void {
}
```

Now that you know the songlist.xml data has loaded successfully, you can place that data in the XML instance you created previously.

4 Between the curly braces of the xmlLoaded() function, add the following line:

```
songList_XML = new XML(xmlLoader.data);
```

Now all the elements from the songlist.xml file can be accessed from within the songList_XML instance, and you can be confident that the XML data is loaded and stored. Next, you will copy some of the existing ActionScript from the previous lesson into the xmlLoaded() function, secure in the knowledge that code requiring the XML elements will not execute until the XML data is available.

Moving the event listeners into the xmlLoaded() function

Right now, this file has six `addEventListener()` methods: one for each of the song clips onstage. They are currently set to start listening as soon as the file launches. A safer approach is to put them in the `xmlLoaded()` function so that the clip listeners won't be active until the song list data is available.

1 Below the code that you just added, locate the following lines:

```
song1.addEventListener(MouseEvent.CLICK, chooseSong);
song2.addEventListener(MouseEvent.CLICK, chooseSong);
song3.addEventListener(MouseEvent.CLICK, chooseSong);
song4.addEventListener(MouseEvent.CLICK, chooseSong);
song5.addEventListener(MouseEvent.CLICK, chooseSong);
song6.addEventListener(MouseEvent.CLICK, chooseSong);
```

2 Select all this code and cut it (Edit > Cut) to the clipboard.

3 Place the cursor above the closing curly brace of the `xmlLoaded()` function and paste the code. The `xmlLoaded()` function should now read:

```
function xmlLoaded(event:Event):void {
songList_XML = new XML(xmlLoader.data);

song1.addEventListener(MouseEvent.CLICK, chooseSong);
song2.addEventListener(MouseEvent.CLICK, chooseSong);
song3.addEventListener(MouseEvent.CLICK, chooseSong);
song4.addEventListener(MouseEvent.CLICK, chooseSong);
song5.addEventListener(MouseEvent.CLICK, chooseSong);
song6.addEventListener(MouseEvent.CLICK, chooseSong);
}
```

Creating the setSongs() function

The other thing that should not occur until the XML data has loaded is the labeling of the onstage song clips. This is now taking place inside a `for` loop below the code you just added. The loop currently reads:

```
for(var i = 0; i < songList.length; i++) {
 var str:String = songList[i] as String;
 str = str.replace(".mp3", "");
 var clip = this["song" + (i + 1)].title;
 clip.text = str;
}
```

You will modify this code so that it gets its information from the XML data, and you will move it into a new function called `setSongs()`. You will then call this function when the XML data is loaded.

About XML lists and accessing data from XML elements

The code that you just inserted:

```
var titleText:String = songList_XML.song[i].name;
```

takes advantage of a number of very useful features in ActionScript 3.0 for working with XML data.

Recall that the original songlist.xml file contained a series of song elements, each including a set of elements.

In ActionScript, you can access elements in XML data using the same dot notation that you would use for other ActionScript paths.

The XML instance in which the XML data was stored takes the place of the root element of the XML file. The child elements of the XML file can be accessed with dots. For example, to access the song elements of the XML data you are working with, you would write:

```
songList_XML.song
```

Requesting songList_XML.song would access all 12 separate song elements in this file. When there are repeating elements in XML data, ActionScript 3.0 automatically stores them in what is called an XML list. An XML list works similarly to an array. (For a review of arrays in ActionScript, see Lessons 7 and 9.)

For example, if you wish to access the first song element in the songList_XML data, you could write:

```
songList_XML.song[0]
```

If you want to get the value stored in the name tag of the third song element, you could write:

```
songList_XML.song[2].name
```

This feature makes working with XML data similar to working with other data, as you have done before. If you reexamine the for loop as it stands now:

```
for(var i = 0; i < 6; i++) {
var titleText:String = songList_XML.song.[i].name;
}
```

it is apparent that the loop will, one at a time, store the names of the first six song elements in the XML data.

1 Below the closing curly brace of the xmlLoaded() function, add the shell for the setSongs() function:

```
function setSongs():void {
}
```

2 Locate the for loop below the setSongs() function. It currently reads:

```
for(var i = 0; i < songList.length; i++) {
 var str:String = songList[i] as String;
 str = str.replace(".mp3", "");
 var clip = this["song" + (i + 1)].title;
 clip.text = str;
}
```

3 Select the entire for loop and cut it (Edit > Cut) to the clipboard.

4 Paste the code between the curly braces of the setSongs() function. The setSongs() function should now read:

```
function setSongs():void {
for(var i = 0; i < songList.length; i++) {
 var str:String = songList[i] as String;
 str = str.replace(".mp3", "");
 var clip = this["song" + (i + 1)].title;
 clip.text = str;
}
}
```

Be sure you have the correct number of curly braces in this function, remembering that both the for loop and the function itself require closing curly braces.

Now, taking one line at a time, modify this for loop to work with the XML array.

The first line of the for loop now reads:

```
for(var i = 0; i < songList.length; i++) {
```

This was appropriate when you were working with an array whose length property represented the only six songs that were available for play in the Lesson 9 project. However, now this project uses an external XML file that can be modified to store an indefinite number of songs. The length of the song list is no longer restricted to just the six song choices that appear on the screen.

The purpose of this for loop is to set the song clips' text fields to the currently available songs. Since you are using six clips, you will set the for loop to repeat six times.

5 Change the first line of the for loop to read:

```
for(var i = 0; i < 6; i++) {
```

Accessing the song title and artist from the XML data

The second line of the `for` loop you are working with currently reads:

```
var str:String = songList[i] as String;
```

The `str` variable stored the names of the songs from the `songList` array that you removed. The XML file contains significantly more information than the array, and you will be working with some of it soon. The first modification of this line is a simple name change that makes this variable's purpose clearer.

1   Change the variable name `str` to `titleText`. The line should now read:

```
var titleText:String = songList[i] as String;
```

2   Further modify this line by changing the value of the `titleText` variable to take the song title information from the XML `name` property.

```
var titleText:String = songList_XML.song[i].name;
```

Since artist information is available from the XML data in the same manner, it makes sense to create an additional variable to store that information.

3   Select and copy (Edit > Copy) the line that currently reads:

```
var titleText:String = songList_XML.song[i].name;
```

4   On the line directly below the line you just copied, paste a new copy of the line.

5   Change the new copy of the line to read:

```
var artistText:String = songList_XML.song[i].artist;
```

The entire `for` loop should now read:

```
for(var i = 0; i < 6; i++) {
 var titleText:String = songList_XML.song[i].name;
 var artistText:String = songList_XML.song[i].artist;
 str = str.replace(".mp3", "");
 var clip = this["song" + (i + 1)].title;
 clip.text = str;
}
```

Setting the song clips' title and artist fields

The last three lines of code in the `for` loop were used to set the text fields in the Lesson 9 project. These need to be modified for the XML version of the project.

The first of these three lines now reads:

```
str = str.replace(".mp3", "");
```

This code was used in the previous lesson to remove the file suffix (.mp3) from the array elements. This is no longer needed, since the filename and song title are separate elements in the XML data.

1 Select and delete the line that reads:

```
str = str.replace(".mp3", "");
```

The next line reads:

```
var clip = this["song" + (i + 1)].title;
```

This is used to store the path to the text field named `title` in the individual song clips. Recall from Lesson 9 that each time the `for` loop repeats, it evaluates this line to return `song1.title`, `song2.title`, `song3.title`, and so on. There is still a need to set the titles, but since you will also set the names of the artists in this example, the only modification you will make to this line is to change the name of the variable.

2 In the line that reads:

```
var clip = this["song" + (i + 1)].title;
```

change the name of the variable from `clip` to `clipTitle` so the line now reads:

```
var clipTitle = this["song" + (i + 1)].title;
```

The onstage clips named `song1` through `song6` have text fields in them with an instance name of `title`. You will use the `clipTitle` variable to set their text properties. These clips also have a second text field named `artist`, so create a second variable to store the path to those text fields. Since this path is nearly identical to the one you just created, you can copy and paste the previous line.

3 Select and copy the line you just modified, which currently reads:

```
var clipTitle = this["song" + (i + 1)].title;
```

4 On a new line below the line you copied, paste a new version of this line.

5 Modify the new line so that it reads:

```
var clipArtist = this["song" + (i + 1)].artist;
```

The `for` loop should now read:

```
for(var i = 0; i < 6; i++) {
 var titleText:String = songList_XML.song[i].name;
 var artistText:String = songList_XML.song[i].artist;
 var clipTitle = this["song" + (i + 1)].title;
 var clipArtist = this["song" + (i + 1)].artist;
 clip.text = str;
}
```

The final line within the brackets of the `for` loop sets the song clips' title text fields to the names of the songs gathered from the XML data. Since the variable that stores references to the song clips was changed from `clip` to `clipTitle` and the variable that stores the song names was changed from `str` to `titleText`, update the code to reflect these changes.

6 Change the code that currently reads:

```
clip.text = str;
```

so that it reads:

`clipTitle.text = titleText;`

This code sets the titles of the individual song clips when the for loop runs. One final line in the for loop will do the same for the artist names in the song clips.

7 Below the line that reads:

```
clipTitle.text = titleText;
```

insert the following code:

```
clipArtist.text = artistText;
```

You will make a slight modification to this code later, but for now this completes the for loop as well as the setSongs() function. The entire function should look like the code shown here:

```
function setSongs():void
{
    for (var i = 0; i < 6; i++)
    {
        var titleText:String = songList_XML.song[i].name;
        var artistText:String = songList_XML.song[i].artist;
        var clipTitle = this["song" + (i + 1)].title;
        var clipArtist = this["song" + (i + 1)].artist;
        clipTitle.text = titleText;
        clipArtist.text = artistText;
    }
}
```

Adding a call to the setSongs() function

The setSongs() function you just created needs to be implemented when the file is first launched, but not until after the XML data (which is used to set the songs) is available. You already have a function named xmlLoaded() that is called upon completion of the loading of the XML data; that would be a good place in which to call the setSongs() function.

1 In the Actions panel for Frame 1, scroll up to locate the xmlLoaded() function.

2 Above the closing curly brace of this function, insert this line to call the setSongs() function:

```
setSongs();
```

The xmlLoaded() function should now read:

```
function xmlLoaded(event:Event):void {
  songList_XML = new XML(xmlLoader.data);
  song1.addEventListener(MouseEvent.CLICK, chooseSong);
  song2.addEventListener(MouseEvent.CLICK, chooseSong);
  song3.addEventListener(MouseEvent.CLICK, chooseSong);
```

```
song4.addEventListener(MouseEvent.CLICK, chooseSong);
song5.addEventListener(MouseEvent.CLICK, chooseSong);
song6.addEventListener(MouseEvent.CLICK, chooseSong);

setSongs();
}
```

There are quite a few more features to add to this project, but you need to do just one more thing before you're ready to test the project: Update the `switch` statement that determines which song will be played when a song clip is clicked.

Updating the chooseSong() function

Recall from Lesson 9 that when any one of the song clips (`song1` through `song6`) is clicked, the `chooseSong()` function is called. For this lesson's version of the project, most of this functionality will remain the same. The one element that you will need to modify, to take into account the XML source of the song data, is the `switch` statement that determines the currently playing song.

1   Locate the `switch` statement in the `chooseSong()` function. The first few lines of this statement should read:

```
switch (e.currentTarget.name) {
 case "song1" :
 currSong = "../MP3s/" + songList[0] as String;
 break;
```

To keep track of the songs in the list, you'll give a different value (depending on which song clip is clicked) to the `songNum` variable that you created earlier.

2   Below the line that reads:

```
case "song1":
```

add the following new line:

```
songNum = 0;
```

Very soon it will be clearer how this value will be used.

Notice that the `currSong` variable is still taking its value from the `songList` array that you deleted earlier. Update this value so that it now gets the current song from the XML data.

3   Change the line that reads:

```
currSong = "../MP3s/" + songList[0] as String;
```

so that it now reads:

```
currSong = songList_XML.song[songNum + songCount].file;
```

This approach is similar to the way that you retrieved the title and artist information for the song clips, only now you are retrieving the file element from the XML data. Since the value of songCount is initially 0, the variable will have no effect when added to songNum at this point. However, you will make use of this variable soon.

The first condition in the switch statement should now read:

```
case "song1":
songNum = 0;
currSong = songList_XML.song[songNum + songCount].file;
break;
```

4 Update the rest of the switch statement in a similar manner. The full switch statement should read:

```
switch (e.currentTarget.name) {
 case "song1":
  songNum = 0;
  currSong = songList_XML.song[songNum + songCount].file;
  break;
 case "song2":
  songNum = 1;
  currSong = songList_XML.song[songNum + songCount].file;
  break;
 case "song3":
  songNum = 2;
  currSong = songList_XML.song[songNum + songCount].file;
  break;
 case "song4":
  songNum = 3;
  currSong = songList_XML.song[songNum + songCount].file;
  break;
 case "song5":
  songNum = 4;
  currSong = songList_XML.song[songNum + songCount].file;
  break;
 case "song6":
  songNum = 5;
  currSong =songList_XML.song[songNum + songCount].file;
  break;
}
```

You should now be able to test the file without getting error messages.

5 Test the movie to see the results so far.

The file should now work approximately the way that it did at the end of Lesson 9. The buttons should load and play the associated songs when clicked, and the volume and pan sliders should still work, with the ID3 tags displaying the same information as before. As a matter of fact, the only difference in this file for the user so far is that the artist's name appears on the song clips and there are two onscreen buttons that don't do anything yet ("more songs" and "Buy on iTunes").

That was a lot of effort to get a file that works about the same way as when you started. But you should congratulate yourself—you can now integrate XML data into a Flash project! You will soon add some new functionality to this project that uses some of the other data in the XML file.

Next, you will create the code to make the two additional buttons onstage functional.

Creating hyperlinks using XML data

The XML data that you loaded into the Lesson 10 file contains a link element with a URL for the location of each song on iTunes. The link_btn element in the upper-right corner of the Flash Stage will use ActionScript's navigateToURL() method with the link element's URL data to create a hyperlink for each song. In Lesson 1, "Using Code Snippets and Navigating the Flash Timeline," you used a code snippet to create a link using the navigateToURL() method. Now you will write the code yourself.

1 In the Actions panel for Frame 1 of the lesson10_start.fla file, locate the addEventListener() methods in the xmlLoaded() function.

Note: If you had any errors in your code, before proceeding you may want to compare it to the working code so far by viewing the lesson10_part1.fla file located in the Lessons > Lesson10 > Complete folder.

2 On a line below the existing addEventListener() methods for the six song clips, insert a new addEventListener() for link_btn with the following code:

```
link_btn.addEventListener(MouseEvent.CLICK, iTunesLink);
```

When the link_btn element is clicked, it will call a function called iTunesLink(), which you will now create.

3 Scroll to the end of the code for Frame 1 and, below all the existing code, add the shell for the iTunesLink() function:

```
function iTunesLink(e:MouseEvent):void {
}
```

You access the iTunes element of the XML data similarly to the way you accessed the name, artist, and file elements.

4 Within the curly braces of the iTunesLink() function, add this line:

```
var link:String = songList_XML.song[songNum + songCount].
¬itunes;
```

Which itunes element from the XML data will be used is determined by adding the number stored in the songNum variable to the number in the songCount variable. Recall that the switch statement sets the songNum variable based on the song clip that the user selected. Up until this point songCount equals 0, so the link element will match the song clip that was selected (you will work more with songCount soon).

Once the appropriate link from the XML data has been stored in the link variable, you can use that variable in a navigateToURL() method to create the actual hyperlink.

5 On a line above the closing curly brace of the iTunesLink() function, add the following code:

```
navigateToURL(new URLRequest(link), "_blank");
```

This code will open the URL stored in the link variable, and the link itself will launch iTunes and go to the appropriate location. The full function should read:

```
function iTunesLink(e:MouseEvent):void {
 var link:String = songList_XML.song[songNum + songCount].
 ¬itunes;
 navigateToURL(new URLRequest(link), "_blank");
}
```

6 Test the movie. Select a song and then click the iTunes link. If iTunes is installed on your machine, it should open and automatically navigate to the page for the song you selected, otherwise you will be taken to this song on Apple's iTunes website.

In the final step of this lesson, you'll add code for the button that contains the text "more songs," at the lower left of the Stage. This code will enable the Flash project to display and play as many songs as you want to include in the XML file.

Navigating through the song list

The more_btn element will be used to display additional songs from the songlist.xml file in the onstage song clips. When the songList data contains no more song titles to display, then the list will repeat so that the user can click this button repeatedly to cycle through the song list.

First add a new listener for this button.

1   In the Actions panel for Frame 1 of the lesson10_start.fla file, locate the addEventListener() methods in the xmlLoaded() function.

Below the existing addEventListener() methods, add the following line:

```
more_btn.addEventListener(MouseEvent.CLICK, moreSongs);
```

This code calls a function named moreSongs() when the button is clicked. This is the final function for this lesson, and you'll add it now.

2   Below all the existing code for this project, add the shell for the moreSongs() function:

```
function moreSongs(e:MouseEvent):void {
}
```

To understand what moreSongs() needs to do requires a little review of the functionality already in this file. When the user clicks one of the six buttons onstage, a switch statement is called. The switch statement determines which song will be played, using the number associated with the selected song clip. That number is stored in a variable called songNum. If you recall, it also adds the value of the songCount variable to that number. By default, songCount is 0, so the variable has no effect on which song is selected.

The reason for the "more songs" button is to allow the user to select from more than six songs. It does this by incrementing the songCount value. Each time the user clicks "more songs" (more_btn), the songCount value increases by one. When this button is clicked (one time), then the songCount goes from 0 to 1, and the six buttons—instead of selecting songs 0 through 5—will select songs 1 through 6. If the songCount variable equals 5, then songs 5 through 10 will be selected. You'll add a conditional statement to the moreSongs() function to make sure that songCount never exceeds the total number of songs in the XML data minus six (the number of buttons onstage for selecting songs).

3   Add code to the moreSongs() function so that it reads:

```
function moreSongs(e:MouseEvent):void {
 if(songCount < songList_XML.song.name.length() - 6) {
  songCount++;
 } else {
  songCount = 0;
 }
}
```

4   Test the movie. Click one of the song buttons. Now click the "more songs" button. Again, click the same song button you originally clicked. This time, a different song should play. Press the "more songs" button once more, and then press the same song button again; a totally different song plays. However, the labels on the buttons are not yet changing! This is a problem with an easy solution.

Updating the song buttons

The setSongs() method assigns the song labels, so that is where you will go to fix the label problem.

1   In the code for Frame 1 of the actions layer, locate the setSongs() function and find these lines:

```
var titleText:String = songList_XML.song[i].name;
var artistText:String = songList_XML.song[i].artist;
```

Because these two lines are within a for loop set to repeat six times, these lines are always going to set the labels of the song clips from the first six songs in the XML data, because the value of the variable i will always loop from 0 to 5.

However, if you add the value of the songCount variable to i, then when the "more songs" button is clicked, the song and artist labels will increment to match the songs in the XML data.

2   Alter the two lines in step 1 so that they read:

```
var titleText:String = songList_XML.song[i + songCount].name;
var artistText:String = songList_XML.song[i + songCount].
¬artist;
```

To update the song clip labels each time more_btn is clicked, you call the setSongs() function within the moreSongs() function.

3   Scroll all the way back down to the moreSongs() function and, above the closing curly brace, add the following line to call the setSongs() function:

```
setSongs();
```

The full moreSongs() function should now read:

```
function moreSongs(e:MouseEvent):void {
 if(songCount < songList_XML.song.name.length() - 6) {
  songCount++;
 } else {
  songCount = 0;
 }
 setSongs();
}
```

4   Test the movie once more. Now when you click the "more songs" button, all the labels will update. If you click enough times and go through all the songs in the XML data, you return to the original songs: a continuous loop through the song list.

No matter how many songs are added to the songlist.xml file, the ActionScript will continue to work and navigate through all the songs. This means that by using XML, all you need to do to add and remove content from the project after it is built is change the XML file.

The same principle that was applied here for a music player can be used for any type of content or data—as you will see in the next lesson using video content.

Some suggestions to try on your own

Here are a few things you can do on your own to get more comfortable with some of the techniques introduced in this lesson:

•   Try adding song elements to the songlist.xml file, making sure each element has the same child elements as the existing songs do.

- Add child elements to all the song elements in the songlist.xml file. For example, you could add elements for genre, time, rating, and so on.

- Try placing your own version of this file on a server and loading the files from that server. Use your favorite FTP software to modify the songlist.xml file on the server.

- Create multiple XML files with different playlists, and create buttons that let the user choose which XML files determine the playlist that is used. For example, create playlists for different artists or musical styles.

- Add an event listener for the PROGRESS event of the URLLoader instance in this lesson. Try tracing a message to the output window as the loading progresses.

- Use the navigateToURL() and URLRequest() methods to create links to other online content associated with artists in your XML playlists.

- Create your own XML files based on the structure of the songlist.xml file. Try loading and using that data in a Flash project.

Review questions

1 What is another term for an XML tag?

2 What is the main class used to work with XML in ActionScript 3.0?

3 What class can be used to load data in ActionScript 3.0?

4 Name and describe three events of the URLLoader class.

5 In XML data that has multiple versions of the same element, how can ActionScript access a specific element?

Review answers

1 Another term for an XML tag is element.

2 The main class in ActionScript 3.0 for working with XML is the XML class (not exactly a trick question).

3 The load() method of the URLLoader class can be used to load data into a Flash project.

4 The COMPLETE event of the URLLoader class is triggered by the successful loading of requested data. The IO_ERROR event is triggered if the requested data fails to load. The PROGRESS event is triggered repeatedly while data is loading.

5 ActionScript uses dot notation and array notation (square brackets) to locate the individual elements of an XML list. For example, to locate the title child element of the third song element in XML data, you could refer to it in ActionScript as song[2].title.

11 USING ACTIONSCRIPT AND COMPONENTS TO CONTROL VIDEO

Lesson overview

In this lesson, you will learn to do the following:

- Use the FLVPlayback component to work with Flash video files.

- Set the properties of the FLVPlayback component in the Property inspector.

- Set the properties of the FLVPlayback component with ActionScript.

- Use the ColorPicker component to set the background color of a video skin.

- Use the Slider component to adjust the transparency of a video skin.

- Use ActionScript cue points to trigger events from markers in a video file.

- Use the FLVPlaybackCaptioning component.

- Work with a Timed Text XML file for video captions.

- Create ActionScript that responds when a video file is finished playing.

- Create ActionScript that works with an XML video playlist.

- Use the Allow Full Screen template to view full-screen video in a browser.

This lesson will take approximately 3 hours.

In the past few years, Flash video has exploded in popularity and is now the dominant video format for the web. It is extremely easy to get started working with Flash video.

A video player with customizable controls connected
to an XML playlist.

Adobe Flash CS5 Professional ships with all the tools needed to create Flash video files and integrate them into Flash projects. You can place video in a Flash file and give the user video-player controls without using any ActionScript. However, integrating ActionScript with Flash video will offer vast creative possibilities. This lesson introduces many ActionScript techniques for working with the video components that ship with Flash CS5—but keep in mind that entire books have been written about ActionScript and Flash video. We hope the techniques in this lesson will inspire you to pursue the subject more deeply.

Examining the Lesson11 folder contents

This lesson will be created largely from external media and data files and from Flash CS5 components. You will use ActionScript to connect all these pieces and create a simple video player application.

If you open the Lessons > Lesson11 folder, you will see that in addition to the Start and Complete folders, there is a folder called Video. This folder contains seven F4V files. F4V is Adobe's version of the industry-standard H.264 video format.

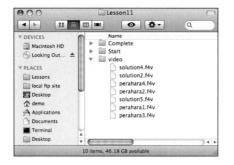

The Lessons > Lesson11 > Start folder contains two XML files and a FLA file. The captions.xml file will be used with a component in Flash to create synchronized subtitles for a video clip. The vidlist.xml file will work similarly to the way the songlist.xml file did in Lesson 10, "Working with an XML Playlist," and will supply filenames and information about a list of video clips to be played in your project.

The actual Flash file for this lesson contains no pre-created material. Open the Lessons > Lesson11 > Start > lesson11_start.fla file. You will create most of the Flash content for this project using Flash components. All the components and text that you will add to this file will be placed on the empty layer named content, and all the code will go on the actions layer.

F4V and FLV video files

F4V is one of two native Flash video file formats, the other being FLV. While F4V files tend to give better image quality than FLV files of the same size, F4V files require that your users have a more recent version of Flash Player (9.0.115 or later) and a faster processor. Also, F4V files do not support alpha channels. If you have video experience and are used to working with H.264 files with other suffixes (.mp4 and .mov), you can use some but not all of them with Flash. For more information about the F4V format, visit www.adobe.com/devnet/flv.

The FLV format does support full alpha-channel transparency (with On2VP6 compression), and FLV video files will work with versions as far back as Flash Player 7. FLV files also tend to perform better than F4V files on older machines. Flash CS5 Professional and the Adobe Media Encoder that ships with Flash can create both FLV and F4V files, making it easy for you to use whichever format is more appropriate for your projects.

Adding the FLVPlayback component

One of the most powerful components to ship with Flash CS5 is the FLVPlayback component. While it is possible to play and manipulate external video files in Flash without this component, the FLVPlayback component contains all the functionality most users need to work with Flash video, and in fact this component often provides the best way to work with video. You can use an FLVPlayback instance to play and manipulate any external FLV or F4V file. The FLVPlayback class in ActionScript is associated with the FLVPlayback component and has an extensive set of methods, properties, and events for working with video. FLVPlayback is worth serious study if you are interested in interactive video.

We will look at some of the ActionScript tools for working with the FLVPlayback component soon, but first let's look at how much can be done without any code.

1   With the Stage visible and the first frame of the content layer selected, open the Components panel (Window > Components).

Flash CS5 ships with two versions of the FLVPlayback component. One is just called FLVPlayback and is the same as the version that shipped in previous versions of Flash. The other is called FLVPlayback 2.5 and includes new features available in Flash CS5. This is the version that you will use in this lesson.

2 In the Video folder of the Components panel, locate the FLVPlayback 2.5 component.

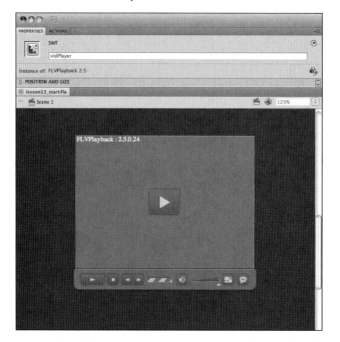

3 Drag an instance of the FLVPlayback 2.5 component to the lower right of the Stage.

4 In the Properties panel, give the onstage FLVPlayback 2.5 component the instance name **vidPlayer**.

Setting FLVPlayback properties in Flash

As mentioned earlier, much of the video functionality required by the average project can be accomplished easily without code, using Flash's intuitive component parameters to set common properties. In the case of the FLVPlayback component, you can use the Component Parameters section of the Property inspector to choose the initial video file that will play in the component as well as set the type and appearance of the controls with which the user can manipulate the video. This is what you will do now.

1 With the `vidPlayer` component selected onstage, open the Property inspector if it is not already visible (Window > Properties) and make sure that the Component Parameters are visible.

As you can see in the figure, there are many properties that can be set for the video and its playback. You will leave most of these settings at their defaults, but a few you will set now. Keep in mind that all these settings can also be controlled with ActionScript.

The most important setting for the FLVPlayback component is the one that determines which video file will play in the component. This is the `source` property. Soon you will set this property using ActionScript, but for now you will try choosing the initial `source` video here in the Property inspector.

2 In the Component Parameters area of the Property inspector, click the pencil icon to the right of the Source property.

3 In the dialog box that appears, browse to the Lessons > Lesson11 > Video folder and choose the Solution5.f4v file. Then click OK. The path to the video file that you selected will appear to the right of the `source` property.

Note: The path for the `source` property in the Component Parameters are written as an absolute path to the selected file on your local hard drive, so use care when using this technique.

4 Test the movie. The video that you selected will play inside the FLVPlayback component.

The set of controls that the user is given for an instance of the FLVPlayback component is known as the component's *skin*. Unless you consciously set the `skin` property of this component, the controls that appear for the video will be whatever skin was last selected and may not be what you want for your project. So you will next set the skin.

Setting the FLVPlayback controls

Flash CS5 ships with a large number of prebuilt sets of video controls that can be associated with instances of the FLVPlayback component. These skins are set with the `skin` property of the FLVPlayback component, either in the Component Parameters panel or with ActionScript. For now, you will set the initial skin in the Component Parameters.

1 With the `vidPlayer` instance still selected and the Component Parameters still visible, locate the `skin` property and click the pencil icon to open the Select Skin dialog box.

2 In the drop-down list that appears in the Select Skin dialog box, navigate to and select the SkinUnderAll.swf skin; then click OK.

Setting skin color and transparency

Next you will set the color and transparency of the skin for your video—first in the Component Parameters panel, and then using ActionScript to allow users to change these properties while the project is running.

1 With the `vidPlayer` component still selected, locate the `skinBackgroundColor` property in the Component Parameters panel and click the color chip to the right of the property name.

2 Select the color that you want your video controls to be.

About FLVPlayback skin files

The skins that appear in the Select Skin dialog box are actually SWF files created to work with the FLVPlayback component. All these SWF files, as well as the original FLA files from which they were created, are installed on your hard drive when you install Flash CS5 Professional. There are many variations of the possible controls; the filenames describe the controls each contains. For example, the skin named SkinOverPlayMuteCaptionFull.swf contains controls that appear directly *over* the video file. This skin will give the user control over playing the video and muting the audio as well as toggling captions on and off and viewing in full-screen mode. The skin you selected in this exercise, SkinUnderAll.swf, appears *under* the video and contains *all* the possible controls for the FLVPlayback component.

You will soon see that you can easily modify the color and transparency of these prebuilt skins. If the overall design of these skins doesn't match the intended look of your project, you can also very easily create custom-designed skins that offer the same functionality as the built-in skins. For more information, see Flash Help or visit the video section of the Flash developer site at www.adobe.com/devnet/video/.

3 Select the skinBackgroundAlpha property and enter a value between 0 and 1 to set the transparency of the color that you selected. A good initial setting would be between 0.7 and 1. Remember that a setting of 0 would mean that the background color you selected would not be visible.

4 Test the movie again. The video will play, but this time with the skin that you selected and with your color and transparency choices.

   Try some of the video controls. You should be able to play and pause the video, scrub the slider, and adjust the volume of the audio. Notice that at this point the two controls on the far right, which are for toggling captions on and off and switching to full-screen mode, don't do anything. You will add that functionality later in the lesson.

5 Close the lesson11_start.swf file to leave the testing environment.

Adding ActionScript control of FLVPlayback properties

Using ActionScript to set any of the properties of an FLVPlayback instance is as simple as setting the properties of a `MovieClip` or any other ActionScript class. For example, to set the `rotation` property of a movie clip instance named `clip1` to 90 degrees, you would write:

`clip1.rotation = 90;`

Similarly, if you wanted to set the `source` property of an FLVPlayback instance named `vid1` to play a movie named vid1.f4v, you could write:

`vid1.source = "vd1.f4v";`

Keeping this in mind, if you know the available properties for the `FLVPlayback` class (many of which you have already seen in the Component Parameters), then you can easily look up their possible values in Flash Help and control them with ActionScript.

Remember, when you want to set a property only once and leave it that way, you can do this in the Component Parameters, but when you want to make a property dynamic and interactive, then use ActionScript. As an example, you will use two UI components—the Slider and the ColorPicker—to let the user change the settings for the color and transparency of the FLVPlayback skin.

Adding a slider to control transparency

If you completed Lessons 9, "Controlling Sound with ActionScript," and 10, "Working with an XML Playlist," then you are already familiar with the Slider component and its use. It will be easy at this point to use the same technique for the `skinBackgroundAlpha` property of your video player.

1 Open the Components panel if it is not already visible.

2 From the User Interface components folder, select the Slider component.

3 With the `contents` layer of the Timeline selected, drag an instance of the Slider component to the upper-left area of the Stage.

4 In the Properties panel (Window > Properties), give the new Slider component the instance name of **alphaSlide**.

5 With the `alphaSlide` instance selected, make the Component Parameters in the Property inspector visible.

6 Set the `minimum` property of `alphaSlide` to 0 and the `maximum` property to 1. This range is the same as the range of the `skinBackgroundAlpha` property.

7 Set the other values for the `alphaSlide` instance as shown in the following image.

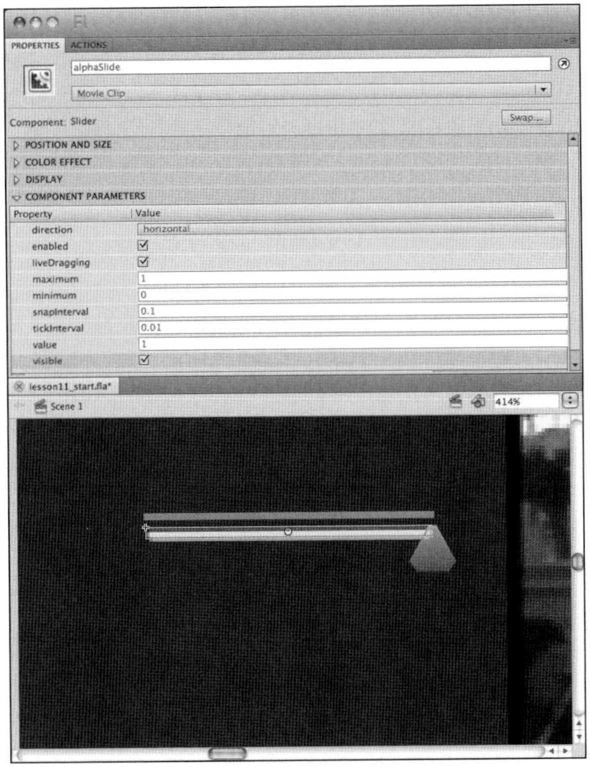

Now you'll create a text element to give the user a clue about the intended purpose of this slider.

8 Select the Text tool from the Tools panel and drag out a text field above the slider.

9 Type **Video Player Transparency** or a similar phrase in the text field. This text will be for display only.

10 Set the font style and color of the text any way that you wish.

Next, you'll add the ActionScript to make the slider work.

Adding the initial slider ActionScript

You learned in Lesson 9 that before you can work with the Slider component in ActionScript, you need to import the `SliderEvent` class.

1 With Frame 1 of the `actions` layer selected and the Actions panel open, insert the following code on the first line of the Actions panel:

```
import fl.events.SliderEvent;
```

Since you will soon be using a number of other classes that also must be imported, this is a good time to add those other `import` statements.

2 Below the line you just typed, add the following code:

```
import fl.controls.ColorPicker;
import fl.events.ColorPickerEvent;
import fl.video.*;
```

Now you will be ready to work with the ActionScript video classes and the ColorPicker component, but first finish the code for the alphaSlide instance.

You learned in Lesson 9 that the CHANGE event is what responds when the user moves a Slider instance. Add this event to your code.

3 On the line below the existing code, add the following line:

```
alphaSlide.addEventListener(SliderEvent.CHANGE, alphaChange);
```

The code for the alphaChange() function should be familiar to you from similar code you have used in previous lessons.

4 Add the alphaChange() function below the line you just added by typing:

```
function alphaChange(e:SliderEvent):void {
 vidPlayer.skinBackgroundAlpha = e.target.value;
}
```

As with the Slider components you worked with in previous lessons, the value to which the user drags the slider (e.target.value) is what is used to set a specific property: in this case, the skinBackgroundAlpha property of the FLVPlayback component.

5 Test your movie. While the video is playing, scrub the slider. The color of the skin background should fade in and out accordingly.

6 Close the lesson11_start.swf file to leave the testing environment.

Next you will use an additional component to let the user choose a color for the video controls.

Working with color

You may use color pickers regularly in many applications without really thinking about it. In fact, if you do any design work in Flash, you probably use a color picker to choose fills, strokes, and text colors. With the ColorPicker component in Flash, you can easily add this functionality to your own projects. For this lesson, you will add a standard color picker with the basic settings, but in other projects you can use ActionScript to modify the ColorPicker component in many ways, including offering your users custom palettes with as many colors as you wish.

Adding the ColorPicker component

Like the Slider and other components, ColorPicker fires off a CHANGE event when the user makes a change to a component instance—in this case, when the user selects a new color.

1   With the `contents` layer of the Timeline selected and the Component Parameters of the Property inspector visible, locate the ColorPicker component in the User Interface folder.

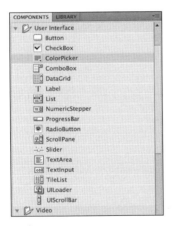

2   Drag an instance of the ColorPicker component to the Stage above the `alphaSlide` instance.

3   In the Properties panel, give the new ColorPicker component the instance name of **colorChoose**.

4 Give the `colorChoose` instance descriptive text by copying and pasting the text that you placed near the slider and changing the wording to **Video Player Color** or the equivalent. Position the text near the `colorChoose` instance.

5 Test the movie. The color picker responds when you click it because this is the component's built-in behavior, but the color you choose will not be applied to anything. You will set that next, with ActionScript.

6 Close the lesson11_start.swf file to leave the testing environment.

Setting the skin background color

As mentioned earlier, the CHANGE event is what ActionScript listens for to determine when the user has selected a color. You've already set up the `ColorPicker` component; now you'll insert the listener.

1 In the Actions panel, add the following code below the existing code for Frame 1 of the `actions` layer:

```
colorChoose.addEventListener(ColorPickerEvent.CHANGE,
¬changeHandler);
```

2 Add the `changeHandler()` function below that with this code:

```
function changeHandler(e:ColorPickerEvent):void {
 var cp:ColorPicker = e.currentTarget as ColorPicker;
 vidPlayer.skinBackgroundColor = Number("0x" + cp.hexValue);
}
```

Much of this should be starting to look familiar.

Note that in both lines within the function's braces, the data type of the value that is set is specifically indicated.

Your code so far should read:

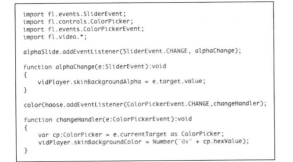

```
import fl.events.SliderEvent;
import fl.controls.ColorPicker;
import fl.events.ColorPickerEvent;
import fl.video.*;

alphaSlide.addEventListener(SliderEvent.CHANGE, alphaChange);

function alphaChange(e:SliderEvent):void
{
    vidPlayer.skinBackgroundAlpha = e.target.value;
}

colorChoose.addEventListener(ColorPickerEvent.CHANGE,changeHandler);

function changeHandler(e:ColorPickerEvent):void
{
    var cp:ColorPicker = e.currentTarget as ColorPicker;
    vidPlayer.skinBackgroundColor = Number("0x" + cp.hexValue);
}
```

About casting to a data type

There are many situations in which ActionScript will not recognize data as being in the format in which you want to use it. For example, ActionScript might be treating data as a string of literal characters when you want the data to be treated as a number. Or maybe you want to get a list of movie clips from an array, but ActionScript doesn't recognize the objects listed in the array as movie clips. Telling ActionScript that specific data should be recognized as belonging to a certain data type is called *casting*. You have already written code that casts data in earlier lessons, but it's worth taking a closer look here at the two main ways of casting in ActionScript. The function you just wrote uses both techniques.

In the line of the changeHandler() function that says

var cp:ColorPicker = e.currentTarget as ColorPicker;

e.currentTarget is the item that triggers the function, and it is explicitly identified or cast as the data type ColorPicker. In this line, the ActionScript keyword as is used to indicate that the preceding term should be cast as a specific type of data—in this case, *as* a color picker.

Similarly, in the second line

vidPlayer.skinBackgroundColor = Number("0x" + cp.hexValue);

the skinBackGroundColor value is selected by combining in parentheses the literal characters "0x" (remember 0x identifies a hexadecimal color in ActionScript) with the hexadecimal value that the user chooses from the color picker. This combined phrase is cast as a number. This is an example of the other way that data can be cast to a data type.

Most of the time these two casting techniques can be used interchangeably, but there are a few situations, such as when casting arrays, that the first technique (using the as keyword) should be used. If you are not certain which to use, then use the as type of casting.

3   Test your movie. Now when you select a new color with the color picker, that color will be assigned to the background of the video controls. While the movie is running, you should be able to freely modify the background color with the color picker and the transparency with the slider.

4   Close the lesson11_start.swf file to leave the testing environment.

Next you will set the source property of the vidPlayer component using ActionScript.

Setting the source property of the FLVPlayback component

You already set the source property of the vidPlayer component using the Component Parameters panel in Flash CS5. However, it is good to be able to do this in ActionScript because ActionScript can provide dynamic control over which videos play in a given component. Also, as mentioned earlier, if you set the source property in the Property inspector, you run the risk that the path to your local hard drive will be retained even when your project is uploaded to a web server. If you set a relative path using ActionScript, this will not occur.

1   In the Actions panel, add the following code below the existing code for Frame 1 of the actions layer:

```
vidPlayer.source = "../video/solution5.f4v";
```

2   If you want, test the movie again. You will see that the functionality has not changed at all. The only difference is that the source of the FLVPlayback component is obtained from your ActionScript code and not from the Component Parameters settings. When a property of a component is set in both ActionScript and the Flash interface, the ActionScript always overrides the settings in the interface.

Using cue points with Flash video

One of the most useful features for working with video in Flash is the capability to add and use cue points. A cue point is a marker that is associated with a specific location in time in a Flash video file. Using ActionScript, you can add cue points to a Flash video file when it is encoded or at runtime. You can use cue points to navigate to specific locations in a video file or to trigger ActionScript events at specific locations in the video.

You can use cue points in nearly infinite ways to make video clips into tightly integrated parts of your interactive projects in Flash. In this lesson, you will use an ActionScript-generated cue point to trigger a function that changes the text in a field and adds a listener when that text field is clicked.

Before you create an ActionScript cue point, examine the Property inspector to see how to identify the cue points in a Flash video clip.

1   On the Flash Stage, select the vidPlayer instance of the FLVPlayback component.

2   In the Property inspector, scroll down below the Component Parameters panel and open the Cue Points panel for vidPlayer.

Notice that this component has five cue points listed. These are cue points that were embedded in the source video file when the file was encoded. This particular file was encoded with Adobe Media Encoder, which ships with Flash CS5, but there are many software packages that can create Flash video files and embed cue points in them.

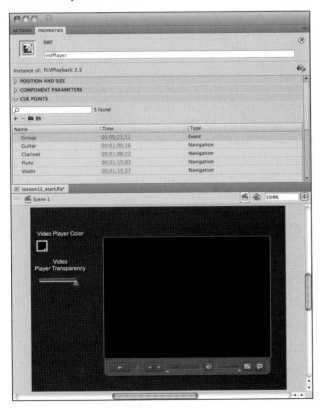

There are two types of embedded cue points: Event cue points and Navigation cue points. Event cue points can be used to trigger ActionScript events that can call a function, and Navigation cue points can be used to navigate to specific locations in a video file using ActionScript. Notice in the Property inspector that each cue point has a name, a time location (specified in hours, minutes, seconds, and frames), and a type. Embedded cue points are extremely useful and worth further study. However, rather than use the existing Event and Navigation cue points in this file, you will create your own cue points using a third type of cue point called an ActionScript cue point. These can be both created and edited in Flash.

ActionScript cue points can be created either in the Property inspector or using ActionScript. You will use code to create an ActionScript cue point in this file, but first you will add a new text field that will be controlled using cue points.

Adding a title text field

You will create a new text field that will be used to display text that is triggered by cue points.

1 With Frame 1 of the contents layer selected, choose the Text tool from the Tools panel and drag out a new text field above the FLVPlayback instance onstage.

2 Give the new text field the instance name of **title_txt**.

3 Choose any font or formatting that you wish for this field. You can do this in the Properties panel, or you can be ambitious and create a TextFormat object in ActionScript.

4 Type some text in the field. This will be the text that appears onscreen while the first video is playing. You will replace this text with ActionScript when cue points occur in video files.

Working with ActionScript cue points

Cue points are created in ActionScript using a simple method called createASCuePoint(). You will use this method now.

1 With Frame 1 of the Actions layer selected and the Actions panel visible, locate the line that reads:

```
vidPlayer.source = "../video/solution5.f4v";
```

2 On a new line below this code, add an ActionScript cue point by inserting this code:

```
vidPlayer.addASCuePoint(10, "BuyCD");
```

This creates a new ActionScript cue point for the vidPlayer instance. The first parameter within the parentheses indicates the location in the video clip that is associated with this cue point. In this case, the cue point will be located 10 seconds into the video clip. The second parameter is a string that refers to the name of the cue point, in this case BuyCD. When a Flash video with ActionScript cue points is played, an event is automatically triggered each time a cue point location is reached. You will use this CUE_POINT event to call a function that writes text in the title_txt field and adds a listener that links to a URL where users can purchase CDs of the music in the video file.

3   Below the last line that you typed, add this line to listen to vidPlayer for CUE_POINT events:

```
vidPlayer.addEventListener(MetadataEvent.CUE_POINT,
cuePointNav);
```

Now you will create the cuePointNav() function that will be triggered when a cue point is reached.

4   Below the line you just added, insert the shell for the cuePointNav() function:

```
function cuePointNav(e:MetadataEvent):void
{
}
```

This function will be called each time any cue point is reached, but you want to change the text in the title_txt field only when the specific cue point named BuyCD is reached. You will add a conditional statement that uses the information that arrives with the cue point metadata to determine when the desired cue point is reached.

5   Within the curly braces of the cuePointNav() function, add the following conditional statement:

```
if (e.info.name == "BuyCD")
  {
    title_txt.text = "Click to Purchase Music by Nan Jing";
  }
```

6   Test the movie. The video should begin playing immediately, and 10 seconds into the video when the ActionScript cue point you added is reached, the text field should display the string "Click to Purchase Music by Nan Jing."

7 Close the lesson11_start.swf file to return to the authoring environment.

You will now add an event listener so that the user can click this text to link to a URL.

8 In the Actions panel, locate the cuePointNav() function you just created.

9 In the conditional statement in this function, add code to listen for the CLICK event on the title_txt field. Below the line that reads:

```
title_txt.text = "Click to Purchase Music by Nan Jing";
```

add this line:

```
title_txt.addEventListener(MouseEvent.CLICK, buyCD);
```

The full function should now read:

```
vidPlayer.addEventListener(MetadataEvent.CUE_POINT,
¬cuePointNav);
function cuePointNav(e:MetadataEvent):void
{
 if (e.info.name == "BuyCD")
 {
  title_txt.text = "Click to Purchase Music by Nan Jing";
  title_txt.addEventListener(MouseEvent.CLICK, buyCD);
 }
}
```

Now you will add the buyCD function that will occur when the title_txt field is clicked. Since the code in this function should be familiar to you by this time, you can do this all in one step.

10 Below all of the existing code in the Actions panel, add the following function:

```
function buyCD(e:MouseEvent):void{
navigateToURL(new URLRequest("http://www.cdfreedom.com/
¬artists/passionrecords/catalog/nanjing/"));
}
```

11 Test the movie again. The text should still appear when the video has reached 10 seconds, but now when the text is clicked, your default browser should navigate to the URL in your code.

This exercise shows just one example of the many ways that you can use cue points to create interactive video in Flash.

Another common use of cue points is to create captions and subtitles that are synchronized with video clips. When you need to create many captions in a video clip, you can make the process easier by using another built-in component in Flash called the FLVPlaybackCaptioning component. This component uses external XML files that contain caption information to generate cue points. In the next steps, you will add an instance of the FLVPlaybackCaptioning component to add captions to this project.

Adding the FLVPlaybackCaptioning component

In Lesson 10, you learned how to use an XML file as a playlist. You wrote ActionScript to load and use the playlist information in a Flash project. Later in this lesson, you will get some additional practice with this technique using an XML file as a video playlist.

Another use of an XML file is to store captions or subtitles for a video file. You can create an XML file that contains the specific times in a video clip at which captions should appear as well as the text that should be displayed at that point in the video. You can even store information about how that text can be formatted. Of course, you could then write ActionScript to load and use the information from that XML file, as you already have seen in Lesson 10. However, there is an even easier way to do this.

If you create the XML file with your captions using a specific protocol called the Timed Text format, then the FLVPlaybackCaptioning component in Flash will take care of all the ActionScript for you! The component will load the XML file and connect all the information in the XML file with the video that is played in an FLVPlayback instance. ActionScript cue points will automatically be generated at the time locations indicated in the XML file, and those cue points will generate events that change the text in an indicated area.

For this lesson, an XML file in the Timed Text format has been provided. You will add captions to your video using this file with an instance of the FLVPlaybackCaptioning component. First, let's look at the Timed Text code in the captions.xml file.

Examining the captions.xml file

In the Lessons > Lesson11 > Start folder, locate the captions.xml file and open it in Dreamweaver or the text editor of your choice.

If you completed Lesson 10 or are familiar with XML, then the basic format of the file should be familiar.

```xml
<?xml version="1.0" encoding="UTF-8"?>
  <tt xml:lang="en" xmlns="http://www.w3.org/2006/04/ttaf1"  xmlns:tts="http://www.w3.org/2006/04/ttaf1#styling">

      <body>
          <div xml:lang="en">
              <p begin="00:00:00.50" dur="7000ms" tts:textAlign="center" tts:color="#cccc99" tts:backgroundColor="#333300">Seven Possible Solutions</p>
              <p begin="00:00:11.50" tts:textAlign="center" tts:color="#cccc99">Live at the Goethe Institute, Boston, Mass<br/>June 10, 2008</p>
              <p begin="00:00:22.40" dur="10s">Hiro Honshuku - <span tts:fontWeight="bold" tts:color="#ccc333" tts:fontStyle="italic">Flute and Electronics</span> </p>
              <p begin="00:00:33.50" dur="10s" tts:textAlign="left">Mimi Rabson <span tts:fontWeight="bold" tts:color="#ccc333" tts:fontStyle="italic">Violin</span> </p>
              <p begin="00:00:44.50" tts:textAlign="center">Peter Cokkinias <span tts:fontWeight = "bold" tts:color="#ccc333" tts:fontStyle="italic">Saxophone and Bass
Clarinet</span></p>
              <p begin="00:00:54.50" tts:textAlign="center">  Thomas Sanger Elnaes <span tts:fontWeight = "bold" tts:color="#ccc333" tts:fontStyle="italic">Piano</span>
</p>
              <p begin="62s" tts:textAlign="right">Chris Florio   <span tts:fontWeight="bold" tts:color="#ccc333" tts:fontStyle="italic">Guitar Composition</span></p>
              <p begin="74s" dur="10s" tts:textAlign="right">Mike Rivard  <span tts:fontWeight="bold" tts:color="#ccc333" tts:fontStyle="italic"> Contrabass</span></p>
          </div>
      </body>
  </tt>
```

The top-level `<tt>` tag in this file indicates that this file is in the Timed Text format.

The body of code contains a series of tags to indicate where the captions should appear while a video file plays. The <begin> tags indicate the place at which a caption begins. These times are indicated in hours:minutes:seconds:milliseconds format (for example, 00:03:40:50). The <dur> tags indicate how long the text will appear onstage; this can be measured in seconds (s) or milliseconds (ms). The file also contains a variety of <tts> formatting tags to format the caption text. Most of these tags are fairly intuitive (textAlign, color, fontStyle, and so on), especially if you have worked with HTML code.

You can use this file as a template for your own Timed Text files. For more information about the Timed Text format, see http://help.adobe.com/en_US/AS3LCR/ Flash_10.0/TimedTextTags.html.

When you have finished examining the captions.xml file, close that file and return to the lesson11_start.fla file in Flash, where you will integrate the captions.xml file into your project.

Adding the FLVPlaybackCaptioning component

The FLVPlaybackCaptioning component adds no graphical content to your project. Instead, it contains the functionality to connect the captions in a Timed Text file to an instance of the FLVPlayback component. When you drag an instance of the FLVPlaybackCaptioning component to the Stage, a rectangular placeholder appears, but this is not visible to your users.

1 Back in the lesson11_start.fla file, with the contents layer selected and the Components panel open, locate the FLVPlaybackCaptioning component in the Video folder.

2 Drag an instance of this component to anywhere on the Stage.

3 With the new FLVPlaybackCaptioning instance selected onstage, go to the Component Parameters section of the Property inspector.

4 In the Component Parameters, set the flvPlaybackName property to vidPlayer. This connects your captions with the FLVPlayback instance onstage.

5 Set the source property to captions.xml. This is the XML Timed Text file that you previously examined. The component will automatically load this file and associate the tags in the file with the video that plays in the vidPlayer instance.

6 Notice that captionTargetName is set to auto. When this is the case, the FLVPlaybackCaptioning component will create a new text field automatically and display the captions of the video. If you wish to create a text field specifically for your captions, you could indicate its instance name here, in the captionTargetName property. For now, leave the property set to auto.

7 Test the movie. The captions with their formatting should appear at the times indicated in the captions.xml file.

8 While a caption is visible, try toggling the button on the far right of the FLVPlayback skin.

Now that you have working captions, this button will let your users toggle them on and off. This feature is great for giving your users the option of subtitles. You could even use a technique similar to the one covered in Lesson 2, "Working with Events and Functions," to give your users the option of subtitles in multiple languages, by using a conditional statement that chooses between multiple caption files.

9 Close the lesson11_start.swf file to leave the testing environment.

The next feature that you will add to this project will change it from an application that plays a single video file to one that automatically plays a series of video files using an XML file as a playlist.

Playing multiple video files from an XML playlist

The process of adding a video playlist to this project will review a number of techniques from previous lessons. It will also introduce techniques for playing multiple video files in the same FLVPlayback component, and for listening and responding when a video file that was playing has reached its end.

You will load a list of video files from a simple XML playlist. Then you'll create an event listener that will play the next video file from the playlist when the current video is complete.

Examining the vidlist.xml file

The first step in this section will be to take a look at the code in the vidlist.xml file that will be used as a video playlist.

1   In Dreamweaver or the text editor of your choice, open the vidlist.xml file found in the Lessons > Lesson11 > Start folder.

```
<?xml version="1.0" encoding="utf-8"?>
<vidlist>
<!-- All vids © copyrght Passion Records -->
    <!-- www.passionrecords.com -->
    <vid>
        <file>../video/solution5.f4v</file>
        <name>Nan Jing in Performance</name>
    </vid>

    <vid>
        <file>../video/solution2.f4v</file>
        <name>7 Possible Solutions (mvmt.2)</name>
    </vid>

    <vid>
        <file>../video/solution4.f4v</file>
        <name>Hope (excerpt)</name>
    </vid>

    <vid>
        <file>../video/perahara1.f4v</file>
        <name>Kandy Perhara</name>
    </vid>

    <vid>
        <file>../video/perahara2.f4v</file>
        <name>Filmed in Kandy Sri Lanka</name>
    </vid>
```

If you completed Lesson 10, then the code in this file should be familiar to you. It is similar to the songlist.xml file that you used for that lesson but is even simpler. There is only one main element within the root vidlist tags, called vid. Each vid element contains two child elements. The file elements contain the names of video files. The name element contains text that you will use in a text field in Flash.

2   Close the vidlist.xml file and return to the lesson11_start.fla file in Flash.

You will now add the ActionScript to work with the vidlist.xml file. As mentioned, the technique you will use to load and use the vidlist.xml file is similar to the technique you used for the songlist.xml file in the previous lesson.

Loading the vidlist.xml file with ActionScript

Now for some ActionScript. First you will add a few variables.

1   With Frame 1 of the `actions` layer selected in the Timeline and the Actions panel open and visible, locate the code that contains all the initial `import` statements:

```
import fl.events.SliderEvent;
import fl.controls.ColorPicker;
import fl.events.ColorPickerEvent;
import fl.video.*;
```

2   On a new line below this code, create a new variable named **vidList_XML** that will be used to store an XML object:

```
var vidList_XML:XML;
```

3   Insert the following code below the line you just added:

```
var vidTitle:String;
```

This variable will be used to store the name associated with each `vid` element in the vidlist.xml file.

It will be necessary to keep track of which video from the playlist should be played next. To do that, you will need to create a variable called `count`.

4   Add the following on the line below the code you just entered:

```
var count:int = 0;
```

Notice that the initial value of `count` is 0. This variable will be used soon to determine the first video that will play from the vidlist.xml data.

To load the data from the XML file, you will use an instance of the `URLLoader` class.

5   Insert a variable on the next line to contain this instance:

```
var xmlLoader:URLLoader = new URLLoader();
```

Now you will use the `load()` method of the `URLLoader` class instance to load the vidlist.xml file.

6   On the line below the code you just added, insert the following line:

```
xmlLoader.load(new URLRequest("vidlist.xml"));
```

In the previous lesson, you learned that it is important to confirm that data has been loaded before using that data. You will listen for the COMPLETE event of the URLLoader class to make sure the data in the vidlist.xml file has completely loaded before working with it.

7   On the line below the load() method that you just added, create an addEventListener() function for the COMPLETE event:

```
xmlLoader.addEventListener(Event.COMPLETE, xmlLoaded);
```

Creating the xmlLoaded() function

The xmlLoaded() function, which will be called when the vidlist.xml data is available, will be used to work with the XML data.

1   Below the code listener you last added, insert the shell for the xmlLoaded() function:

```
function xmlLoaded(event:Event):void {
}
```

The first thing this function should do is store the XML data that was loaded in the XML object you created in the preceding task.

2   Between the curly braces of the xmlLoaded() function, insert this line:

```
vidList_XML = new XML(xmlLoader.data);
```

The next thing you will add within this function is an event listener that responds whenever video in the vidPlayer instance finishes playing. The event that will do this is the COMPLETE event of the FLVPlayback class.

Distinguishing between COMPLETE events

You have already worked with COMPLETE events a number of times in this and earlier lessons. You have worked with the COMPLETE event of the URLLoader class, the Loader class, and the UILoader class. In all of these cases, the COMPLETE event is listening for the successful completion of the loading of external content.

Even though the name is the same, when you are listening for the COMPLETE event of the FLVPlayback component, you are not listening for the moment when a video file is completely loaded. Instead, you are listening for the moment when a video file has reached the end of its playback and is complete. Because video files are streaming files, they can be downloading and playing at the same time and therefore don't need to be completely loaded before they can begin playing. It is therefore much more common to need to listen for the moment when video is finished *playing* than when it is finished *loading*. This is what you add ActionScript to listen for in this lesson.

3 On the next line of the xmlLoaded() function, add a listener for the vidPlayer COMPLETE event with this code:

```
vidPlayer.addEventListener(VideoEvent.COMPLETE, changeVid);
```

The complete function should now read:

```
function xmlLoaded(event:Event):void {
 vidList_XML = new XML(xmlLoader.data);
 vidPlayer.addEventListener(VideoEvent.COMPLETE, changeVid);
}
```

Next you will add the changeVid() function that will be triggered each time a video file completes playing.

Creating the changeVid() function

Remember that the changeVid() function occurs every time the vidPlayer instance fires the COMPLETE event. The purpose of changeVid() is to identify the next video from the loaded playlist and set it to be the source file of vidPlayer. The final step of the changeVid() function will be to increment the count variable so that it can be used to play a different video each time the changeVid() function is called.

1 On a line below the closing brace of the xmlLoaded() function, insert the shell of the changeVid() function:

```
function changeVid(e:VideoEvent):void {
}
```

The first thing this function will do is store the string for the next video in the list. This string will be stored in a new variable using the value of count to determine the element of the vidlist.xml data from which to get the file information.

2 Between the curly braces of the changeVid() function, add the following line:

```
var nextVid:String = vidList_XML.vid[count].
¬file;
```

Next you will use the value of this new variable as the source of the vidPlayer instance.

3 Add this line below the code you just typed:

```
vidPlayer.source = nextVid;
```

Now you will use the name element from the current vid element (vid[count]) as the text in the onscreen title_txt field.

4 Below the last line you entered, add the following lines of code:

```
vidTitle=vidList_XML.vid[count].name;
title_txt.text = vidTitle;
```

Just because you can, next set the background color of vidPlayer to change every time a new video plays.

5 On the next line of code, add the following:

```
vidPlayer.skinBackgroundColor = Math.random() * 0xFFFFFF;
```

Finally, to make sure that a new video is played the next time this function is called, increment the value of the count variable by 1.

6 Add this line above the closing curly brace of the changeVid() function:

```
count++;
```

The completed changeVid() function should read:

```
function changeVid(e:VideoEvent):void {
 var nextVid:String = vidList_XML.vid[count].
 ¬file;
 vidPlayer.source = nextVid;
 vidTitle = vidList_XML.vid[count].name;
 title_txt.text = vidTitle;
 vidPlayer.skinBackgroundColor = Math.random() * 0xFFFFFF;
 count++;
}
```

The code for the entire file should now read:

```
import fl.events.SliderEvent;
import fl.controls.ColorPicker;
import fl.events.ColorPickerEvent;
import fl.video.*;

var vidList_XML:XML;
var vidTitle:String;
var count:int = 0;
var xmlLoader:URLLoader = new URLLoader();
xmlLoader.load(new URLRequest("vidlist.xml"));
xmlLoader.addEventListener(Event.COMPLETE, xmlLoaded);

function xmlLoaded(event:Event):void
{
 vidList_XML = new XML(xmlLoader.data);
 vidPlayer.addEventListener(VideoEvent.COMPLETE, changeVid);
}
```

```
function changeVid(e:VideoEvent):void
{
 var nextVid:String = vidList_XML.vid[count].file;
 ¬vidPlayer.source = nextVid;
 vidTitle = vidList_XML.vid[count].name;
 title_txt.text = vidTitle;
 vidPlayer.skinBackgroundColor = Math.random() * 0xFFFFFF;
 count++;
}
alphaSlide.addEventListener(SliderEvent.CHANGE, alphaChange);

function alphaChange(e:SliderEvent):void
{
 vidPlayer.skinBackgroundAlpha = e.target.value;
}


colorChoose.addEventListener(ColorPickerEvent.CHANGE,
¬changeHandler);

function changeHandler(e:ColorPickerEvent):void
{
 var cp:ColorPicker = e.currentTarget as ColorPicker;
 vidPlayer.skinBackgroundColor = Number("0x" + cp.hexValue);
}


vidPlayer.source = "../video/solution5.f4v";
vidPlayer.addASCuePoint(10, "BuyCD");

vidPlayer.addEventListener(MetadataEvent.CUE_POINT,
¬cuePointNav);
function cuePointNav(e:MetadataEvent):void
{
 if (e.info.name == "BuyCD")
 {
  title_txt.text = "Click to Purchase Music by Nan Jing";
  title_txt.addEventListener(MouseEvent.CLICK, buyCD);
 }
}
function buyCD(e:MouseEvent):void
{
 navigateToURL(new URLRequest("http://www.cdfreedom.com/
 ¬artists/passionrecords/catalog/nanjing/"));
}
```

Note: As always, if you had any trouble with your code, try troubleshooting by using the error messages that you receive as guides. If you still have problems, compare the code to the lesson11_complete. fla file in the Lessons > Lesson11 > Complete folder.

7 Test the movie. When the first video is finished playing (you can scrub toward the end if you get impatient), the next video in the `vidlist` data should automatically start. Notice that the `title_txt` field changes each time a new video file loads. If you let the movie continue, it will play through all of the video files contained in the vidlist.xml file. Also notice that each time a new video file is loaded, the background color of the skin changes.

8 There is one last detail to attend to in the test file. If you click the second button from the right, which is designed to switch the video to full-screen mode, you'll see that nothing happens. Fortunately, this small problem is simple to fix. Unfortunately, full-screen mode does not work in the testing environment, so close the lesson11_start.swf file.

After adjusting the publish settings, you'll preview the full-screen feature in the browser.

Using the full-screen publish settings

The easiest way to make full-screen video work in Flash is to use the FLVPlayback skins that enable full-screen viewing and to let Flash write code in your HTML file to allow the page to make use of full-screen mode. Since you have already used an FLVPlayback component with a full-screen mode button, the final step of the lesson is to set the publish settings to use the Allow Full Screen template.

1　With the lesson11_start.fla file still open in Flash, choose File > Publish Settings. On the Formats tab of the Publish Settings dialog box, make sure that the Flash and HTML options are selected.

2　Click the HTML tab.

3　From the Templates drop-down list, choose Flash Only – Allow Full Screen and then click OK.

4 Test this project in your default browser by choosing File > Publish Preview > Default – (HTML).

5 Your project should play in the browser the same way it did when you viewed it in the Flash testing environment. Now, however, when you click the full-screen button, the video file that is playing should take over the full screen. Press the Escape key to return to the normal view of the project.

Some suggestions to try on your own

Having made it all the way through the lesson, you now have a great collection of tools for integrating Flash video into your projects. By experimenting with the other features in the classes and components that you used in this lesson, you will discover many other easy-to-use options for working with video in Flash.

Digging a little deeper and exploring other video-related ActionScript classes, including `NetConnection`, `Video`, `Camera`, and particularly `NetStream`, will open up even more options.

Finally, to go even further with Flash video, investigate the Adobe Flash Media Server technology and its possibilities. You will find that there are many good reasons why Flash video has become such a popular format.

You may also want to make a few modifications to the project file for this lesson to solidify your understanding of the topics covered here:

- Research the Adobe Media Encoder and learn to create your own Flash video files with embedded cue points. If you own Adobe After Effects or Premiere Professional, you can also use them to make Flash video files with cue points.

- Add ActionScript cue points to this project that call other functions. Try to think of creative and practical uses for cue points.

- Try experimenting with the captions.xml file. Change the timing, text, or formatting of the captions. (It is a good idea to save a backup copy of the original file before you do this.)

- Try adding to or replacing the video files supplied in the Video folder with your own FLV or F4V files. You can create video files in these formats from many standard video formats, including QuickTime movies and AVI files. For help doing this, see Flash Help.

- Create additional `vid` elements in the vidlist.xml file to add your videos to the playlist.

- Add child tags to the `vid` elements in the vidlist.xml playlist. Use your new elements in the Flash project to display additional information in text fields or in other creative ways.

- Explore the other properties of the `FLVPlayback` class. Try changing some of these settings in the Component Parameters panel or with ActionScript.

Review questions

1 Name a Flash component that is used to play and control Flash video files.

2 What are the two Flash video file formats?

3 What are the three types of cue points that work with Flash video?

4 What is the format for creating files that work with the FLVPlaybackCaptioning component?

5 What event is used by the FLVPlayback class to respond when a video has reached the end of the file?

Review answers

1 The FLVPlayback component is used to play and control Flash video files.

2 Flash supports the FLV and F4V video formats.

3 The three types of cue points that work with Flash video are Event cue points, Navigation cue points, and ActionScript cue points. Event and Navigation cue points are both embedded cue points that are stored as part of an FLV or F4V video file. ActionScript cue points are stored in a SWF file and can be created and edited in Flash.

4 The FLVPlaybackCaptioning component reads XML files in the Timed Text format.

5 The COMPLETE event of the FLVPlayback class fires any time a video playing in an FLVPlayback instance reaches its end.

12 DELVING DEEPER INTO GRAPHICS AND ANIMATION WITH ACTIONSCRIPT

Lesson overview

In this lesson, you will learn to do the following:

- Use the inverse kinematics (IK) tools in Flash CS5.

- Use the IK classes in Flash CS5 to create advanced animation with ActionScript.

- Check whether users have a video camera or webcam available to their computers.

- Add sound effects to your animation.

- Access and display video from a webcam or connected camera using ActionScript.

- Create bitmap graphics with ActionScript.

- Take screen captures of Flash objects and save them as bitmap data.

- Examine the Adobe Pixel Bender Toolkit.

- Work with filters in ActionScript.

- Use an external class file to load filters created in the Pixel Bender Toolkit.

- Apply Pixel Bender filters to a snapshot from a live camera.

- Use a slider to perform live modifications to the properties of a filter.

This lesson will take approximately 3.5 hours.

In this lesson, you will take advantage of some terrific and fun tools available in ActionScript 3.0 for creating and manipulating graphics and animations.

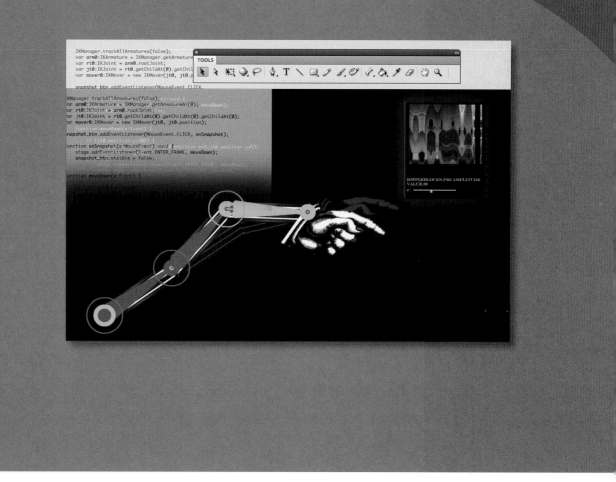

Inverse kinematics and Pixel Bender filters are some
of the Flash CS5 features controlled with ActionScript
in this lesson.

Inverse kinematics in Flash CS5

One of the most exciting features in Flash CS5 is a full set of tools to work with *inverse kinematics* (IK), which is the process of calculating the movement of a series of objects that are connected with bones at joints. For example, in an animation of a human walk cycle, rather than separately animating a character's feet, lower legs, upper legs, and hips, you can use the IK tools in Flash to link the individual parts together with bones so that when one part is animated, the entire chain moves. By setting the range of motion for each joint, you can then easily create realistic movements. Flash CS5 offers tools for setting up an IK animation in the Timeline, including new features for realistic springing. It also offers full ActionScript control over IK using a number of new classes.

You should be aware that you can't create IK systems with ActionScript. These systems are created only in the Flash interface itself. However, once they are created, they can be manipulated either in the interface or with ActionScript. As always, the interface is often best for linear animation, and ActionScript makes more sense for interactive animation, such as in a game.

This lesson will work with IK using ActionScript, but before you begin the project here, open a file that contains an IK example that can be controlled in the Timeline so that you can see how IK is created in Flash.

Viewing the IKSample file

An *IK system* is a group of graphics that are connected to move together in a system of joints. IK systems can be created in Flash from shapes or from symbols. However, if you intend to work with IK using ActionScript, it's best if the individual pieces of the system are `MovieClip` instances.

Open the Lessons > Lesson12 > IKSample.fla file. If you have not worked with IK in Flash before, a number of features may be new to you. On the Timeline, you'll see that there is only one layer with a single frame. The layer is called Armature and has a new icon on it. An armature layer is automatically generated by Flash for each IK system that is created.

You create an IK system in Flash by connecting graphics using the Bone tool in the Tools panel. This system, referred to as an armature in Flash, can be thought of as a chain of graphics connected at joints. These joints control the movement of all the objects in the system when any one of the objects is moved.

To create a connection between two graphics, you simply select the Bone tool from the Tools panel and drag from the desired joint location in one object to the desired location of a joint in another object. In this sample file, this has been done for you, but you may want to experiment with creating your own files and with creating IK animations.

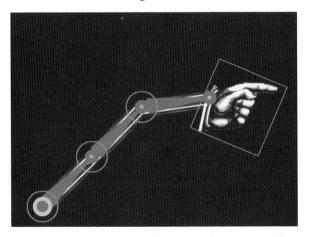

About IK bones

Bones allow symbol instances and shapes to move in relation to each other. You can add bones to multiple symbol instances or to the interior of a single shape. You can use the Properties panel or ActionScript to constrain the movement of the separate parts of an IK system, and new to Flash CS5 you can add springing values to IK bones to get a range of new motion possibilities. Bones cannot be created with ActionScript; they must be created in the Flash interface. They can then be controlled in the Timeline or with ActionScript. For more information about how to create bones in Flash, see "Using Inverse Kinematics" in Flash CS5 Help.

The armature in the sample file is composed of four movie clips that make up a robotic arm: three rectangular clips and a fourth clip with a hand pointer. If you select any one of these graphics, you will see the bones (represented in purple) that have been created to connect them. When a specific bone is selected, it turns green. Click anywhere on the armature and move the mouse; the entire system moves, and the individual pieces bend at the joints. Try selecting different parts of the armature and moving them.

Notice that even when it's not selected, the joint farthest from the hand remains green. This indicates that it is the root joint. In any armature, there is only one root: the origin point for the armature. When you work with IK and ActionScript, the root joint will be a useful point of reference.

Creating animation in the Timeline with IK in Flash is similar to working with other Flash animation techniques. If you are already used to working with "regular" Flash animation, you should have no trouble getting up and running using the IK features in the Timeline. (For details, see "Using Inverse Kinematics" in Flash CS5 Help.) However, in this lesson, you will focus on using ActionScript to create IK animation.

Switching between authortime and runtime IK

IK animation created in the Timeline is considered *authortime* IK. IK animation created with ActionScript is considered *runtime* IK. Once an armature layer is created, you can indicate whether it will be used for authortime or runtime animation by setting the properties for that layer. Remember that either way, the IK system must be created in the Timeline.

1 In the IKSample.fla file, select Frame 1 of the `Armature` layer.

2 With the Properties panel visible, select the Type drop-down list from the Options section. You will see that the two options are Authortime and Runtime.

Remember that if you intend to create an IK system that will be controlled with ActionScript, the system must be set to Runtime. This has been done for you in the Lesson 12 project file, which you will begin next. Feel free to experiment with IK in the Timeline as much as you like before moving on.

Examining the starting files

This lesson includes quite a few new techniques, starting with ActionScript control of IK. Before beginning, take a look at the contents of the Lessons > Lesson12 > Start folder.

Notice that in addition to the lesson12_start.fla file, there are two MP3 audio files. You will use ActionScript to control these sound effects files in your project. In addition, there is an external ActionScript class file for this lesson. You will work with this file later in the lesson.

Now open the Lessons > Lesson12 > Start > lesson12_start.fla file in Flash CS5 and look at the assets that are provided with the file.

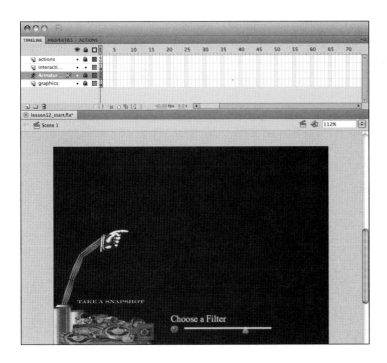

There are four layers in the Timeline of this file. The `actions` layer is currently empty. All the code that you will add to this project will go here.

The `interactive content` layer contains two buttons: a text field and a Slider component. Select them one at a time. If you select the area at the lower left that includes the text that reads Take A Snapshot, you will see that it is a button instance. Make the Properties panel visible while this button is selected, and you will see that the button has an instance name of `snapshot_btn`.

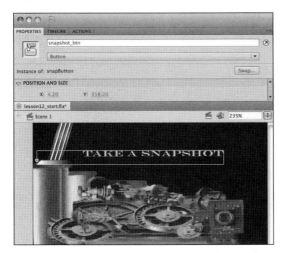

The text that says Choose A Filter is a text field that has been given the instance name valueText. The slider below that text is an instance of the Slider component that has the instance name fSlider, and the red button to the left of the slider has the instance name filter_btn. You will write ActionScript in this lesson to interact with all four of these elements.

The Armature_1 layer contains a copy of the same armature that you viewed in the IKsample.fla file. With the Properties panel visible, select Frame 1 of this layer in the Timeline. Notice that the Type option for the armature is set to Runtime. That is because you will create animation for this armature with ActionScript. This layer has been locked to maintain the initial position of the graphics. You won't have to unlock the layer for this lesson, but if you wish to unlock it to experiment with this graphic, you should make a backup copy first, since the initial position of the graphics is essential to the functionality you're adding in this lesson.

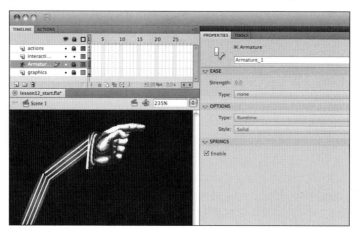

The bottom layer (graphics) in the Timeline contains static design elements that will not be made interactive.

The first ActionScript you will work with in this lesson will introduce the IK classes in Flash CS5.

Working with IK animation in ActionScript

Flash CS5 has a number of classes you can use to work with inverse kinematics. The first code you will add to this project imports all these classes so they will be available to the project.

1 With Frame 1 of the actions layer selected and the Actions panel visible, add this line of code:

```
import fl.ik.*;
```

Using the wildcard (*) to import all classes in a package

In ActionScript, the asterisk is a wildcard that tells the `import` statement to import all the class files found in the package indicated. Collections of related ActionScript class files are usually stored in the same package. You use the wildcard (*) symbol when you intend to work with all or many of the classes found in a specific package. For example, you could write separate lines to import specific multiple event classes like this:

```
import fl.events.ColorPickerEvent;
import fl.events.ListEvent;
import fl.events.ScrollEvent;
import fl.events.SliderEvent;
```

Or if you needed to use more than a few classes from the events package, you could save some coding by typing:

```
import fl.events.*;
```

This code would import all the classes in the events package and make them available to your file.

Since you will be using many of the IK classes in this project, you're importing the entire IK package with the `import fl.ik.*;` shortcut).

Using the IKArmature and IKManager classes

The IKManager class is used to keep track of all the IK armatures in a single Flash document. The IKArmature class is used to describe a single IKArmature instance in the document. Unlike with most other ActionScript classes that you've worked with so far, you don't have to create new instances of the IKManager or IKArmature classes. As already mentioned, IK systems can be created only in the Flash interface, and when you create IK on the Flash Timeline, an IKManager instance is generated in the background automatically. An IKArmature instance is automatically created for each armature in the Timeline as well.

▶ **Tip:** If you have a project containing multiple armatures, you can reference them by their number using getArmatureAt() or give them names and refer to them with the getArmatureByName() method.

If you wanted to let the user drag IK armatures the same way you did in the IKSample file, you'd set the `trackAllArmatures` property of IKManager to `true`. But for this project, ActionScript, rather than the user, should move the armature, so set this property to `false`.

1   Below the `import` statement in the Actions panel, add this line of code:

```
IKManager.trackAllArmatures(false);
```

The IKManager instance for a file automatically keeps a list of all the IKArmature instances in the file. You can make a reference to any armature in a Flash file using the `IKManager.getArmatureAt()` method. You will use this method to make an ActionScript reference to the onstage armature so that you can manipulate it in code.

2   Below the previous line of code you added, type the following code:

```
var arm0:IKArmature = IKManager.getArmatureAt(0);
```

The new variable `arm0` stores a reference to the armature onstage. Since there is only one armature on the Stage, it's an accurate assumption that it is in position 0 in the `IKManager` list.

You can keep track of the individual joints in an IK armature using the `IKJoint` class. Once you have stored a reference to an `IKJoint`, you can animate it using the `IKMover` class. When a single joint in an IK system is moved using ActionScript, the whole system will automatically respond accordingly, just as you saw on the Timeline of the IKsample file. In this project, the goal is to move the joint that is farthest from the root to animate the whole system.

As mentioned, each IK armature in Flash has only one root joint. You can reference this root using the `rootjoint` property of `IKArmature`.

3   On the line below the existing code, create a reference to the root joint of the onstage armature:

```
var rt0:IKJoint = arm0.rootJoint;
```

Once a reference to the root of the armature has been stored, all the other joints can be referenced as children of the root. For example, the first joint attached to the root could be referenced as:

```
rt0.getChildAt(0);
```

4   To reference the third joint away from the root, which is the one you will animate, add the following code below the line you added in step 3:

```
var jt0:IKJoint = rt0.getChildAt(0).getChildAt(0).
¬getChildAt(0);
```

Now you will apply animation to the joint stored in `jt0`. Remember that animation applied to one joint of an IK armature will move the entire armature chain similarly to the way you saw the armature move in the IKSample file. You will use the `IKMover` class to create the animation.

Using the IKMover class

The `IKMover` class is used to animate joints in an IK armature. Once a new instance of the `IKMover` class is created, you can use the `moveTo()` method of this class to move any joint to any location. You'll create an instance of this class now.

Add this code below all the code you have added so far:

```
var mover0:IKMover = new IKMover(jt0, jt0.position);
```

The first required parameter of a new `IKMover` instance is the name of the joint that will be moved—in this case, `jt0`. The second parameter is the starting point of the movement. In this case, that point will be derived from the current position of `jt0`. Once that's established, the `moveTo()` method can be used to move the `jt0` joint to a new location.

This movement will be initiated when the `snapshot_btn` instance is clicked.

Adding an event listener to snapshot_btn

A function that occurs when the user clicks the Take A Snapshot button onstage will trigger an ENTER_FRAME function that will start the armature animating. You've already had quite a bit of experience with the basics of this technique, so much of it will be familiar to you.

1 Below the existing code, insert an `addEventListener()` method for `snapshot_btn`:

```
snapshot_btn.addEventListener(MouseEvent.CLICK, onSnapshot);
```

2 Add the shell for the `onSnapshot()` function below the previous line:

```
function onSnapshot(e:MouseEvent):void {
}
```

As mentioned, this function will initiate an ENTER_FRAME function.

3 Within the curly braces of the `onSnapshot()` function, add this code:

```
stage.addEventListener(Event.ENTER_FRAME, moveDown);
```

The `moveDown()` function will animate the armature. While that is occurring, it would not be desirable for the user to take another snapshot, so while this function occurs the snapshot button should be hidden.

4 Below the last line you typed and above the closing curly brace of the `onSnapshot()` function, add this line:

```
snapshot_btn.visible = false;
```

The full `onSnapshot()` function should now read:

```
function onSnapshot(e:MouseEvent):void {
    stage.addEventListener(Event.ENTER_FRAME, moveDown);
    snapshot_btn.visible = false;
}
```

Adding the moveDown() function

When the user clicks the Take A Snapshot button, the armature should animate down to the camera graphic on the Stage, take a picture, and animate back up. You will add the code to "take the picture" later in the lesson. Now you will add the up and down animation. Because a number of things will be occurring in your code when the animation has finished moving down, you will separate the down movement and the up movement into separate ENTER_FRAME functions. A moveDown() function is triggered when the user clicks the snapshot_btn instance, and a moveUp() function is triggered when the downward movement is complete.

Start by adding the shell for the moveDown() function.

1 Below the existing code, add the following:

```
function moveDown(e:Event) {
}
```

The moveDown() function, which will occur on every frame, should move the armature a little closer to its target on each frame. The armature will have reached its target when it gets to a y position of 305, so you will use a conditional statement to check whether the target has been achieved. When it has been, you will turn off the moveDown() listener and initiate the moveUp() function.

2 Add a conditional statement to the moveDown() function so that it now reads:

```
function moveDown(e:Event) {
 if(jt0.position.y < 305) {

 } else {


 }
}
```

Now you will add to this function the actual movement of the armature, using the moveTo() method of the IKMover class. The moveTo() method takes a single parameter. This is the point that the joint, stored in the IKMover instance, should be moved to. In this case, the amount that will be moved in each frame will be relative to the current position of jt0, so you will first create a variable that stores a point that is five pixels to the right and five pixels below the jt0 joint's current location. That point will be used as the parameter for the moveTo() method.

3 Below the line that reads:

```
if(jt0.position.y < 305) {
```

add the following two lines:

```
var pt0:Point = new Point(jt0.position.x + 5,jt0.position.y + 5);
mover0.moveTo(pt0);
```

As mentioned, when the target position has been reached, this function should be disabled and a new ENTER_FRAME function initiated that will move the armature back to its original location.

4 Below the line that reads:

```
} else {
```

add the following lines:

```
stage.removeEventListener(Event.ENTER_FRAME, moveDown);
stage.addEventListener(Event.ENTER_FRAME, moveUp);
```

The entire moveDown() function so far should read:

```
function moveDown(e:Event) {

    if(jt0.position.y < 305) {
        var pt0:Point = new Point(jt0.position.x + 5, jt0.position.y + 5);
        mover0.moveTo(pt0);
    } else {
        stage.removeEventListener(Event.ENTER_FRAME, moveDown);
        stage.addEventListener(Event.ENTER_FRAME, moveUp);
    }
}
```

If you tested the movie at this point, you would get an error, because the moveUp() function has been referred to but does not yet exist. So before you test what you have so far, add the shell for the moveUp() function.

5 Below all the existing code, add the following:

```
function moveUp(e:Event):void {

}
```

Your code now should read:

```
import fl.ik.*;

IKManager.trackAllArmatures(false);
var arm0:IKArmature = IKManager.getArmatureAt(0);
var rt0:IKJoint = arm0.rootJoint;
var jt0:IKJoint = rt0.getChildAt(0).getChildAt(0).getChildAt(0);
var mover0:IKMover = new IKMover(jt0, jt0.position);

snapshot_btn.addEventListener(MouseEvent.CLICK, onSnapshot);

function onSnapshot(e:MouseEvent):void {
    stage.addEventListener(Event.ENTER_FRAME, moveDown);
    snapshot_btn.visible = false;
}

function moveDown(e:Event) {

    if(jt0.position.y < 305) {
        var pt0:Point = new Point(jt0.position.x + 5, jt0.position.y + 5);
        mover0.moveTo(pt0);
    } else {
        stage.removeEventListener(Event.ENTER_FRAME, moveDown);
        stage.addEventListener(Event.ENTER_FRAME, moveUp);
    }
}

function moveUp(e:Event):void {

}
```

6 Test the movie. In the testing environment, click the Take A Snapshot button.

The arm graphic should animate down and land on the camera graphic. Notice that even though you added code to control the movement of only one joint, the entire armature moved down and bent at all of its joints.

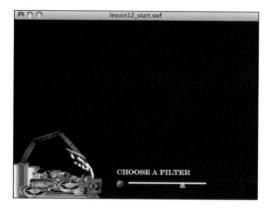

7 Close the lesson12_start.swf file to leave the testing environment.

Next you will add code to the moveUp() function to return the armature to its original position.

Coding the moveUp() function

After the moveDown() function sends the armature to its target location near the camera graphic, the moveUp() function will return it to its original position.

The code for the moveUp() function is similar to that for the moveDown() function, but reversed.

1 Between the curly braces of the moveUp() function, add code so that the function reads:

```
function moveUp(e:Event):void {
 if(jt0.position.y > 165) {
  var pt0:Point=new Point(jt0.position.x - 5,
  ¬jt0.position.y - 5);
  mover0.moveTo(pt0);
 } else {
  stage.removeEventListener(Event.ENTER_FRAME, moveUp);
  snapshot_btn.visible = true;
 }
}
```

Notice that this function sends the jt0 joint back five pixels on each frame (jt0.position.x - 5, jt0.position.y - 5) until its y location has returned to 165.

When the armature is back in its original position, there is no further reason for this function to continue, so it is removed. At this point, the `snapshot_btn` instance is made visible so that it can be used again.

2 Test the movie. The arm graphic should now move up and down. Notice the Take A Snapshot button disappear for the duration of the animation.

You will add code to both the `moveUp()` and `moveDown()` functions, but first let's use ActionScript to load some sound effects into this project. These will be used to enhance the armature movement.

Creating Sound and SoundChannel instances

The two sound files that accompany this lesson, robotArm.mp3 and click.mp3, will be triggered to play while the armature is animating. The robotArm.mp3 sound will play when the arm is moving up and down. The click will play each time the arm reaches its target location over the camera graphic to create the impression that a snapshot has been taken.

You will create two separate `Sound` instances so that the two sounds can be controlled independently and overlap a little. A `SoundChannel` instance will be used for each sound so that it can be stopped and played. If you completed Lesson 9, "Controlling Sound with ActionScript," this code will be familiar to you.

Add code to create the `Sound` and `SoundChannel` instances and to load the two MP3 files.

1 In the Actions panel for Frame 1 of the `actions` layer, scroll to locate the line that reads:

```
var mover0:IKMover = new IKMover(jt0, jt0.position);
```

2 Starting on a new line below this line, insert the following code:

```
var fx1:Sound = new Sound();
fx1.load(new URLRequest("robotArm.mp3"));
var channel1:SoundChannel = new SoundChannel();
var fx2:Sound = new Sound();
fx2.load(new URLRequest("click.mp3"));
var channel2:SoundChannel = new SoundChannel();
```

Now that the sounds are loaded and available, you will set them to play and stop as the armature animation plays. In this lesson, you will assume that the MP3 files will load successfully because the files are local and in the same folder. You should already know how to confirm loading from earlier lessons, and in fact, you should confirm loading in all your online projects.

Playing and stopping the sound effects

The first sound in this animation will begin playing as soon as the user presses the Take A Snapshot button, so the code for this will go in the onSnapshot() function.

1   In the onSnapshot() function and below the line that reads:

```
snapshot_btn.visible = false;
```

insert the following line:

```
channel1 = fx1.play();
```

The onSnapshot() function should now read:

```
function onSnapshot(e:MouseEvent):void {
 stage.addEventListener(Event.ENTER_FRAME, moveDown);
 snapshot_btn.visible = false;
 channel1 = fx1.play();
}
```

The robotArm.mp3 sound should play, continuing until the arm has completed its descent. At this point, this first sound should stop and the "click" sound, which is very short, should play once. The robot arm sound should then restart for the ascent of the arm back to its original location.

All of the code for this should be inserted at the point at which the arm reaches the target over the camera graphic. In your code, this point occurs at the else statement in the moveDown() function. This is where you will add the next bit of code for the sounds.

2   Locate the moveDown() function, and below the line in the moveDown() function that reads:

```
} else {
```

insert the following three lines:

```
 channel1.stop();
 channel2 = fx2.play();
 channel1 = fx1.play();
```

The full moveDown() function should now read:

```
function moveDown(e:Event) {
 if(jt0.position.y < 305) {
  var pt0:Point = new Point(jt0.position.x + 5,
  ¬jt0.position.y + 5);
  mover0.moveTo(pt0);
 } else {
  channel1.stop();
  channel2 = fx2.play();
  channel1 = fx1.play();
  stage.removeEventListener(Event.ENTER_FRAME, moveDown);
```

```
    stage.addEventListener(Event.ENTER_FRAME, moveUp);
  }
}
```

The last Sound control that you will add will stop the sound when the arm has returned to its original position. In your code, this occurs in the `else` statement within the `moveUp()` function.

3 Locate the `moveUp()` function in your code, and below the line that reads:

```
snapshot_btn.visible = true;
```

insert the following line:

```
channel1.stop();
```

The full `moveUp()` function should now read:

```
function moveUp(e:Event):void {
 if(jt0.position.y > 165) {
  var pt0:Point = new Point(jt0.position.x - 5,
  ¬jt0.position.y-5);
  mover0.moveTo(pt0);
 } else {
  stage.removeEventListener(Event.ENTER_FRAME, moveUp);
  snapshot_btn.visible = true;
  channel1.stop();
 }
}
```

4 Test the movie. Click the Take A Snapshot button. Now when the arm animates, the sound effects should play in sync with the movement.

5 Close the lesson12_start.swf file to leave the testing environment.

The next sections will add the capability to take an actual snapshot and display it onstage each time the Take A Snapshot button is clicked. These snapshots will be taken from a feed from the user's live webcam using ActionScript's Camera class.

Accessing the user's webcam or video camera using ActionScript

If your users have webcams or external video cameras connected to their computers, Flash Player will recognize them, and you can use ActionScript to access a live feed from those cameras to work in Flash. You accomplish this using the Camera class in ActionScript. To test the code you are about to add, you (and your users) must have a video camera connected to your computer. Assuming that a camera is available, the code you will now write will take the feed from the camera and display it within the interface of this project. Later in the lesson, you will write code that can take snapshots from this camera feed.

Note: Even though ActionScript will let you or your user choose among multiple cameras if more than one video source is connected, Flash can display the feed from only one camera at a time.

Using the getCamera() method

To connect the feed from the user's video camera to your Flash project, you use the `getCamera()` method of the `Camera` class. This method accesses the data from a camera but doesn't display it; you create an instance of the `Video` class to display the feed.

Add the code to create an instance of the `Camera` class and access the user's camera.

1   Locate the line of code for Frame 1 of the `actions` layer that reads:

```
var channel2:SoundChannel = new SoundChannel();
```

2   On a new line below it, insert the following line:

```
var camera:Camera = Camera.getCamera();
```

Remember that the line you just added will access, but not display, the user's camera.

You'll create a new instance named `video` to display the camera if one is available.

Note: Instead of a specific data type, the variable `video` has a wildcard (*) for the data type. The wildcard will allow any type of data to be contained in the variable. You will see the reason for this when you check for the presence of a video camera.

3   Below the line you just typed, add the following code:

```
var video:*;
```

If the user has an installed video camera, then this variable will contain an instance of the `Video` class to display the camera feed. Soon you'll use a `Video` object to display the camera, but first you will write the code to check whether there actually *is* a recognized video camera. You will do this in a conditional statement.

Checking for the presence of a video camera

The instance of the `Camera` class you just created is called `camera`. If there is a video camera or cameras connected to the user's machine, then `camera` will have a value representing that specific camera. Otherwise, it will return `null`. So if the `camera` value is not `null`, you know the user has a camera that Flash can access.

1   On a line below the last code you typed, insert the shell for a conditional statement that checks for a camera's presence:

```
if(camera != null) {

} else {

}
```

If a camera is available, then you want to create a new `Video` object with which to display the camera's input. If there is no camera, you will just trace a message to the Output panel with that information.

2 Add code to the conditional statement so that it now reads:

```
if(camera != null) {
 video=new Video(160, 120);
 video.attachCamera(camera);
 addChild(video);
} else {
 trace("There is no recognized camera connected to your
 ¬ computer.");
}
```

In the line that reads `video=new Video(160, 120);`, a new `camera` instance is created and given two properties that represent the size of the video window. In this case, these parameters are set to display the video at 160 by 120 pixels.

The next line, `video.attachCamera(camera);`, uses the `attachCamera()` method of the `Video` class to connect the live camera feed to the `Video` object.

A `video` instance is a display object. Like movie clips, text fields, and other display objects you've worked with, instances created with ActionScript use the `addChild()` method to place them in the display list and onstage. The next line, `addChild(video);`, places the `Video` object with the camera feed onstage.

To take into account that some users may not have connected video cameras, the library of the lesson12_start.fla file has an alternative video file embedded in a movie clip named AltVid. Because you did not specify a data type for the `video` variable, the variable can contain either a `Video` instance (if the user has a connected camera) or a `MovieClip` instance (if there is no camera available) without displaying an error message. You'll add code to the `else` statement so that if there is no connected camera, the clip from the library will play instead, making it possible for users without a camera to use the rest of this lesson's functionality.

3 Add code to the `else` statement so that the full conditional statement now reads:

```
if(camera! = null) {
 video=new Video(160, 120);
 video.attachCamera(camera);
 addChild(video);
} else {
 trace("There is no recognized camera connected to your
 ¬ computer.");
 video = new AltVid();
 addChild(video);
}
```

Your full code so far should read:

```
import fl.ik.*;
var arm0:IKArmature = IKManager.getArmatureAt(0);
var rt0:IKJoint = arm0.rootJoint;
var jt0:IKJoint = rt0.getChildAt(0).getChildAt(0).
¬getChildAt(0);
var mover0:IKMover = new IKMover(jt0, jt0.position);
var fx1:Sound = new Sound();
fx1.load(new URLRequest("robotArm.mp3"));
var channel1:SoundChannel = new SoundChannel();
var fx2:Sound = new Sound();
fx2.load(new URLRequest("click.mp3"));
var channel2:SoundChannel = new SoundChannel();
var camera:Camera=Camera.getCamera();
var video:*;
if(camera! = null) {
 video = new Video(160, 120);
 video.attachCamera(camera);
 addChild(video);
} else {
 trace("There is no recognized camera connected to your
 ¬computer.");
 video = new AltVid();
 addChild(video);
}
snapshot_btn.addEventListener(MouseEvent.CLICK, onSnapshot);
function onSnapshot(e:MouseEvent):void {
 stage.addEventListener(Event.ENTER_FRAME, moveDown);
 snapshot_btn.visible = false;
 channel1 = fx1.play();
}
function moveDown(e:Event) {
 if(jt0.position.y < 305) {
  var pt0:Point = new Point(jt0.position.x + 5,
  ¬jt0.position.y + 5);
  mover0.moveTo(pt0);
 } else {
  channel1.stop();
  channel2 = fx2.play();
  channel1 = fx1.play();
  stage.removeEventListener(Event.ENTER_FRAME, moveDown);
  stage.addEventListener(Event.ENTER_FRAME, moveUp);
 }
}
function moveUp(e:Event):void {
 if(jt0.position.y > 165) {
```

```
  var pt0:Point = new Point(jt0.position.x - 5,
  ¬jt0.position.y - 5);
  mover0.moveTo(pt0);
} else {
  stage.removeEventListener(Event.ENTER_FRAME, moveUp);
  snapshot_btn.visible = true;
  channel1.stop();
 }
}
```

4   Test your movie to see the results of this camera code.

In the testing environment, you should see either a message telling you that no video camera is connected to your machine (or that Flash is not recognizing your camera) or a Flash Player Settings dialog box requesting access to the camera that has been recognized.

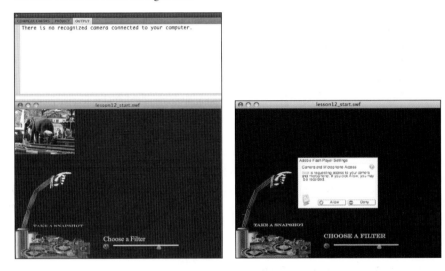

About the camera and microphone settings

If a SWF file contains ActionScript, like the getCamera() method you used in this lesson, that requests access to a user's camera or microphone, then the security that is built into Flash Player will display a screen giving the user the option of permitting or denying this access. As a developer, there is nothing you can do to override this security, but you can write code that will inform your application as to whether or not the user granted permission, so that you can then write alternative content in case the user denies camera access.

5 Assuming you see the dialog box requesting access to your camera, click Allow to grant Flash Player access to your camera. You should see the live video feed in the upper-left corner of the Stage.

The live video camera reveals that the diligent author is sleep deprived and needs a shave.

6 Close the lesson12_start.swf file to leave the testing environment.

You will doubtless think of many creative and fruitful uses for the Camera class in your own projects. In this project, you will use the Take A Snapshot button to create still images from the video feed. To do this, you'll use some very robust ActionScript classes for creating and manipulating bitmap images. After that, you'll use some new tools that ship with Flash CS5 to manipulate the snapshots.

Using the Bitmap and BitmapData classes

If you wish to create and manipulate bitmap graphics with ActionScript, you'll want to get to know the Bitmap and BitmapData classes well. In this lesson, you will learn to use a few features of these classes.

The BitmapData and Bitmap classes work together in a manner not unlike the way the Camera and Video classes did in the previous section. Typically, a BitmapData instance is used to store the pixel information for a bitmap image, and that data is passed to an instance of the Bitmap class to be displayed onstage.

A method of the BitmapData class called draw() lets you draw a bitmap copy of any display object in Flash and display it in a Bitmap instance. You will use this draw() method to take snapshots from the video feed.

First, however, you will create a new variable to store a bitmap image.

1 Near the top of the Actions panel for Frame 1, locate the line that reads:

```
var mover0:IKMover = new IKMover(jt0, jt0.position);
```

2 On a new line below this code, create a new variable with the data type `Bitmap`:

```
var bmp:Bitmap;
```

When the Take A Snapshot button has been clicked and the armature reaches its bottom target, you have already set a "click" sound to play. It is at this point that a snapshot should be taken and displayed. This functionality all belongs in the `else` portion of the `moveDown()` function. You will add this snapshot functionality now.

3 Locate the `else` statement of the `moveDown()` function in the Actions panel.

4 Below the line of code that reads:

```
channel1 = fx1.play();
```

insert the following code:

```
var bData:BitmapData = new BitmapData(camera.width, camera.
¬height);
```

This line creates a new instance of the `BitmapData` class. The two parameters are for the `width` and `height` of the new bitmap data; here, they are set to match the size of the onstage camera feed.

Next, you will use the `draw()` method of the `BitmapData` class to capture a still from the camera feed.

5 On the line below the code that you added, insert the following:

```
bData.draw(video);
```

The parameter of the `draw()` method indicates which display object will be drawn in the `BitmapData` instance. In this case, the `video` instance is being drawn. As mentioned earlier, the `BitmapData` instance doesn't display the bitmap data; to do this, you create a `Bitmap` instance in the variable you set up for this purpose.

6 On the line below the code you just added, type the following:

```
bmp = new Bitmap(bData);
addChild(bmp);
```

The new `Bitmap` instance takes the `BitmapData` instance as its parameter. The subsequent line (`addChild(bmp);`) adds the new `bitmap` instance to the display list and puts it onstage.

When elements are added to the Stage using `addChild()`, they are given the default position of the Stage's upper-left corner (0,0). Since this is already the location of the camera feed, you need to move the `Bitmap` object.

7 Below the last line you added, type the following lines:

```
bmp.x = 220;
bmp.y = 20;
```

As you might surmise, this code shifts the object 220 pixels to the right and 20 pixels down.

Before you test the movie, scale the bitmap up a little by setting its scaleX and scaleY properties.

8 Add this line below the last code you entered:

```
bmp.scaleX = bmp.scaleY = 2;
```

The full moveDown() function should now read:

```
function moveDown(e:Event) {
 if(jt0.position.y < 305) {
  var pt0:Point = new Point(jt0.position.x + 5,
  ¬ jt0.position.y + 5 );
  mover0.moveTo(pt0);
 } else {
  channel1.stop();
  channel2 = fx2.play();
  channel1 = fx1.play();
  var bData:BitmapData=new BitmapData(camera.width, camera.
  ¬ height);
  bData.draw(video);
  bmp = new Bitmap(bData);
  addChild(bmp);
  bmp.x = 220;
  bmp.y = 20;
  bmp.scaleX = bmp.scaleY=2;

  stage.removeEventListener(Event.ENTER_FRAME, moveDown);
  stage.addEventListener(Event.ENTER_FRAME, moveUp);
 }
}
```

9 Test the movie.

● **Note:** Beyond the basic methods you've learned here, the Bitmap and BitmapData classes contain many additional methods and properties that offer a wide range of possibilities for code-driven graphics.

After you click the Allow button to grant permission to access the camera, the video feed should appear (if there is not a connected camera, then the AltVid clip will play instead). When you click the Take A Snapshot button, the arm lowers, and a still image of the current video image should appear on the right.

Examining the Pixel Bender Toolkit

There are already a lot of cool things going on in this project, but we'll discuss one final set of features that will take advantage of some tremendous creative possibilities in Flash CS5. The Shader classes in ActionScript 3.0 work with the Adobe Pixel Bender technology to let you write your own image-manipulating filters and apply them dynamically in your Flash projects. The Pixel Bender Toolkit lets you write, test, and compile these filters. It is beyond the scope of this book to cover these processes in detail, but it is worth taking a brief look at these tools to get a feel for how they work.

When you install Flash CS5 on your machine with the default installer, the Pixel Bender Toolkit is also installed. (If it is not, you can install it from the original installation disc or download it from www.adobe.com.) On the Macintosh, this application is located under Applications/Utilities/Adobe Utilities/Pixel Bender Toolkit. On Windows, it is typically found under /Program Files/Adobe/Adobe Utilities – CS5/Pixel Bender Toolkit 2. You can launch it in Windows by choosing Start/Programs/Adobe/Adobe Utilities – CS5/Adobe Pixel Bender Toolkit 2. If you do not find Pixel Bender in this location, try using the search tool in your operating system or reinstall Pixel Bender Toolkit 2 from the disc that you originally used to install Flash CS5.

1 Locate or install the Pixel Bender Toolkit application on your machine, and then launch it.

The Pixel Bender Toolkit lets you create filters using a relatively easy-to-learn language and save them to be used in Flash. It also lets you import, modify, and test existing filters. These operations provide a good way for you to get a sense of how the Pixel Bender Toolkit works.

To work with the Pixel Bender Toolkit, you need to create or open an existing filter and load an image to test the filter. Start by loading an image.

2 In the Pixel Bender Toolkit, choose File > Load Image 1.

Note: In Flash, Pixel Bender filters can be applied to movie clips, buttons, video, text fields, or bitmap data using ActionScript. However, in the Pixel Bender Toolkit, they can be tested only on JPEG and PNG files.

The Open Image File dialog box displays a default folder of sample images. Select one of these, or navigate to select any JPEG or PNG image on your computer. Click OK.

The next step is to load a filter.

3 Choose File > Open Filter.

Note: The twirl.pbk filter is one of the many filters that come with the Pixel Bender Toolkit; many more are available online at www.adobe.com and other locations.

Navigate to the Lessons > Lesson12 > filters4PixelBenderToolkit folder, select twirl.pbk, and click Open.

4 Choose Build > Run to see this filter applied to your selected image.

When the filter runs, it is compiled and applied to the selected image. The parameters for the loaded filter can be controlled using the sliders on the right.

You can export these filters for use in Flash by choosing File > Export Kernel Filter For Flash Player.

You will not need to do this right now, since you will be working with pre-created filters in this lesson, but digging deeper into the possibilities available with this application via Flash Help and resources at Adobe.com would be time well spent.

For now, quit the Pixel Bender Toolkit and return to Flash, where you will use a provided ActionScript file to add Pixel Bender capabilities to your lesson file.

Examining the PBFilter.as file

To help keep the Timeline code in the lesson file from getting too long, an external ActionScript file has been provided that you will integrate into the lesson project to let users select and use the Pixel Bender filter of their choice. It is beyond the scope of this lesson to go through every line in the PBFilters class, but it is worth taking a look at the code in this file and noting a couple of significant points.

1 In Flash CS5, choose File > Open and navigate to the Lessons > Lesson12 > Start folder.

2 Open the PBFilter.as file.

3 Notice lines 12 through 16. These variable declarations indicate much of what this class will do.

This file contains an instance of the FileReference class. This class is used to let users upload files to a server and browse locations on their hard drives. In this project, it will allow users to choose the location of a Pixel Bender filter on their computers.

```
12        private var fr:FileReference;
13        private var shader:Shader;
14        private var shaderFilter:ShaderFilter;
15        public var filterValue:Number;
16        public var filterName:String;
```

Line 13 creates a variable to store an instance of the Shader class, which is used to represent a Pixel Bender filter in ActionScript.

Line 14 references the ShaderFilter class, which is used to apply a Pixel Bender filter using ActionScript.

Notice that lines 15 and 16 create public variables called filterValue and filterName. These variables are both set to public, so they can be referenced in external files. You will work with both these variables soon in this lesson's project.

4 Examine line 18.

Since this function (PBFilter) has the same name as the file (PBFilter.as), it is clearly the constructor function (see Lesson 4, "Creating ActionScript in External Files," for a review of constructor functions). Notice that this function takes two parameters. The first has a data type of Bitmap, and the second a data type of Number. This means that when an instance of the class is created, it can pass a bitmap reference and a number. You will use these parameters in your Flash file to tell this class which bitmap image will receive the filter selected by the code in this file. The numeric value will set an initial property of that filter.

```
18          public function PBFilter(image:Bitmap=null, val:Number = 0):void
19          {
20              filterValue = val;
21              image2Filter = image;
22              fr = new FileReference();
23              fr.addEventListener(Event.SELECT, onSelect);
24              fr.addEventListener(Event.COMPLETE, onComplete);
25              fr.browse();
26          }
27
```

5 Scroll down to line 35 and examine the `onComplete()` function.

Notice that this function is set to be `public`. This function will be called once each time the user selects a filter to apply to an image, but it will also be called from the `Slider` instance in the lesson file to manipulate the filter's parameters. Since each Pixel Bender filter can have many parameters with various names, this function looks to see if the selected filter has one of the most common parameter names; if it does, it will let the user adjust that parameter. You will work with the Slider component in the lesson file to give the user the capability to adjust whichever of these parameters is available.

```
35          public function onComplete(e:Event=null):void
36          {
37              shader = new Shader(fr.data);
38              filterName = fr.name;
39              if(shader.data.radius!= undefined){
40                  filterName += ": radius";
41                  shader.data.radius.value = [filterValue];
42              }else if(shader.data.amount != undefined){
43                  filterName += ": amount";
44                  shader.data.amount.value = [filterValue];
45              }else if(shader.data.amplitude != undefined){
46                  filterName += ": amplitude";
47                  shader.data.amplitude.value = [filterValue];
48              }else if(shader.data.Radius!= undefined){
49                  filterName += ": Radius";
50                  shader.data.Radius.value = [filterValue];
51              }
52              shaderFilter = new ShaderFilter();
53              shaderFilter.shader = shader;
54              image2Filter.filters = [shaderFilter];
55          }
56      }
```

You may want to come back to this file and use it as a starting point for your own experiments, but for now, close the PBFilter.as file. You will import it into your project file for this lesson.

Working with the PBFilter class

There are three interface elements on the Stage of the lesson12_start.fla file that you have not yet used. These will work with the `PBFilter` class you just examined to add live filtering to the snapshots taken using this project.

1 If it's not still open, reopen the Lessons > Lesson12 > Start > lesson12_start.fla file.

2 Select Frame 1 of the `actions` layer in the Timeline and make the Actions panel visible.

You will soon be working with the `Slider` instance that is onstage. If you recall from previous lessons, the `SliderEvent` class needs to be imported so you can work with its events in ActionScript.

3 Below the first line of the Actions panel that reads:

```
import fl.ik.*;
```

insert an `import` statement for the `SliderEvent` class:

```
import fl.events.SliderEvent;
```

Now create a new variable that will be used to store an instance of the `PBFilter` class you just examined.

4 Below the line that reads:

```
var bmp:Bitmap;
```

add the following code:

```
var filter:PBFilter;
```

Using the onstage interface elements to add filters

Three interface elements onstage give the user control over the application of filters to snapshots. The `filter_btn` instance will be used to let the user select a filter. The `valueText` field will be used to give the user textual feedback on the filters. The `fSlider` instance will be used after the user has applied a filter to alter a parameter of the filter.

Your users will not need to be able to place a filter on a snapshot until they have actually taken a snapshot, so when the file first launches you will hide all three of the interface elements; you will subsequently make them visible as needed.

1 On the line below the code you added in the previous step, insert these lines:

```
valueText.visible = false;
fSlider.visible = false;
filter_btn.visible = false;
```

The code you just added will make the text field, the slider, and the button invisible when the project starts. Remember that snapshots are taken within the `else` statement of the `moveDown()` function, so that is also the place where the user will need to use the button and see the text field.

Insert code into this function to make the button and text field visible. You will also insert text into the text field to instruct the user to select a filter.

2 Locate the `else` statement of the `moveDown()` function, and below the line that reads:

```
bmp.scaleX = bmp.scaleY = 2;
```

insert the following lines:

```
valueText.visible = true;
valueText.text = "\n" + "Choose a Filter";
filter_btn.visible = true;
fSlider.visible = false;
```

With this code in place, when a snapshot has been taken, the user will see the button and the text that instructs the user to select a filter.

The full (and final) moveDown() function should now read:

```
function moveDown(e:Event) {
 if(jt0.position.y<305) {
  var pt0:Point = new Point(jt0.position.x + 5,
  ¬ jt0.position.y + 5);
  mover0.moveTo(pt0);
 } else {
  channel1.stop();
  channel2 = fx2.play();
  channel1 = fx1.play();

  var bData:BitmapData = new BitmapData(camera.width, camera.
  ¬ height);
  bData.draw(video);
  bmp = new Bitmap(bData);
  addChild(bmp);
  bmp.x = 220;
  bmp.y = 20;
  bmp.scaleX = bmp.scaleY = 2;

  valueText.visible = true;
  valueText.text = "\n" + "Choose a Filter";
  filter_btn.visible = true;
  fSlider.visible = false;

  stage.removeEventListener(Event.ENTER_FRAME, moveDown);
  stage.addEventListener(Event.ENTER_FRAME, moveUp);
 }
}
```

Adding a function to the filter_btn instance

The filter_btn instance will enable users to select a filter and apply it to the snapshots they have taken. Most of the work to accomplish this will be done by an instance of the PBFilter class that will be created when the user clicks this button.

1 Below all the existing code in this file, add an event listener for filter_btn with the following code:

```
filter_btn.addEventListener(MouseEvent.CLICK, onFilter);
```

2 Below the line you just typed, add the shell for the onFilter() function that filter_btn will call:

```
function onFilter(e:MouseEvent):void {
}
```

The first thing this function will do is create a new instance of the PBFilter class.

3 Within the curly braces of the onFilter() function, add this line:

```
filter = new PBFilter(bmp, fSlider.value);
```

Recall that the constructor function of the PBFilter class takes two parameters, the first being Bitmap. Here you send the function the onstage bitmap (bmp) that contains the current snapshot. The second parameter that is passed is the number currently stored as the value of fSlider.

When this filter_btn instance is clicked, the PBFilter instance opens a dialog box that lets the user select a filter to apply to the current snapshot.

Next, you'll add code to this function to enable the slider.

4 Below the line you just typed, add the following two lines:

```
fSlider.visible = true;
valueText.text = "\n" + "Choose a Value";
```

The first of these lines makes the slider visible. Now that a filter has been selected, fSlider should be available to change its parameters.

The second line changes the text in the text field to instruct the user to choose a value with the slider.

5 Test the movie. Notice that when the movie launches, the button, text field, and slider are not visible.

6 Click the Take A Snapshot button. When the snapshot appears, the Choose A Filter button and text field become visible.

7 Click the Choose A Filter button. A dialog box opens to let you select a filter.

8 Browse to the Lessons > Lesson12 > filters4Flash folder and select one of the filters.

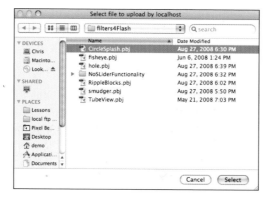

The filter you selected should be applied to your snapshot. Experiment with some of the other filters in the filters4Flash folder. If you create your own Pixel Bender filters or download filters from the web, they can also be used with this project.

9 Notice that even though the slider is now visible, moving it has no effect.

10 Close the lesson12_start.swf file to leave the testing environment.

The final step of this project is to program the `fSlider` instance to manipulate a filter parameter.

Manipulating a filter parameter with the Slider component

In previous lessons, you have used the Slider component a number of times. In those lessons, you have used the CHANGE event of the `SliderEvent` class to make something happen when the user drags the slider. The CHANGE event fires only when the user stops dragging, so it occurs only once for each drag. To get real-time updates for a filter while the user drags `fSlider`, you will use a different Slider event. This one is called the THUMB_DRAG event (the little thingy that the user slides around is known as the thumb), and it occurs repeatedly while the slider is being dragged.

1 Below all the existing code for this file, add an event listener for the THUMB_DRAG event:

```
fSlider.addEventListener(SliderEvent.THUMB_DRAG, valueChange);
```

The `valueChange()` function communicates with the `PBFilter` instance to change the values of the loaded filter.

2 Add the shell for this function:

```
function valueChange(e:SliderEvent):void {
}
```

Recall that the `PBFilter` class had a `public` property called `filterValue`. Because that property is public, it can be set using the value of the slider.

3 Insert the following line between the curly braces of the `valueChange()` function:

```
filter.filterValue = fSlider.value;
```

Now you'll add code that changes the text in the `valueText` field to display the name of the selected filter as well as the current value of `fSlider`.

4 On the next line, add the following code:

```
valueText.text = filter.filterName + " \n" + "Value: " +
¬filter.filterValue;
```

The final step is to call the public function named `onComplete()` in the `PBFilter` instance. Recall that this function scans a number of common filter parameters, and if it finds one that is contained in the currently applied filter, it will set that parameter value from the slider's value. Most of the supplied filters have a parameter that this function will recognize.

Note: Many developers frown upon the practice of allowing properties in a class file to be set from outside the file. They deem it desirable, in many situations, to keep the classes independent of any other files, so they can be more flexible in their use. To accomplish tasks like the one you're doing here, you could use `get` and `set` functions instead of setting the class files properties directly. This is probably something you don't need to worry about now, but you may want to keep this in mind for the future. For more information, see Colin Moock's *Essential ActionScript 3.0*.

5 On the line below the code you just entered, add this code:

```
filter.onComplete();
```

The final valueChange() function should read:

```
fSlider.addEventListener(SliderEvent.THUMB_DRAG, valueChange);
function valueChange(e:SliderEvent):void {
 filter.filterValue = fSlider.value;
 valueText.text = filter.filterName + " \n" + "Value: " +
 ¬filter.filterValue;
 filter.onComplete();
}
```

Here's the completed code for the entire file:

```
import fl.ik.*;
import fl.events.SliderEvent;
var arm0:IKArmature = IKManager.getArmatureAt(0);
var rt0:IKJoint = arm0.rootJoint;
var jt0:IKJoint = rt0.getChildAt(0).getChildAt(0).
¬getChildAt(0);
var mover0:IKMover = new IKMover(jt0, jt0.position);
var bmp:Bitmap;
var filter:PBFilter;
valueText.visible=false;
fSlider.visible = false;
filter_btn.visible = false;
var fx1:Sound = new Sound();
fx1.load(new URLRequest("robotArm.mp3"));
var channel1:SoundChannel = new SoundChannel();
var fx2:Sound = new Sound();
fx2.load(new URLRequest("click.mp3"));
var channel2:SoundChannel = new SoundChannel();
var camera:Camera = Camera.getCamera();
var video:*;
if(camera != null) {
 video=new Video(160, 120);
 video.attachCamera(camera);
 addChild(video);
} else {
 trace("There is no recognized camera connected to your
 ¬computer.");
 video = new AltVid();
 addChild(video);
}
snapshot_btn.addEventListener(MouseEvent.CLICK, onSnapshot);
function onSnapshot(e:MouseEvent):void {
 stage.addEventListener(Event.ENTER_FRAME, moveDown);
```

```
  snapshot_btn.visible = false;
 channel1 = fx1.play();
}
function moveDown(e:Event) {
 if(jt0.position.y < 305) {
  var pt0:Point = new Point(jt0.position.x + 5,
  ¬jt0.position.y + 5);
  mover0.moveTo(pt0);
 } else {
  channel1.stop();
  channel2 = fx2.play();
  channel1 = fx1.play();
  var bData:BitmapData = new BitmapData(camera.width, camera.
  ¬height);
  bData.draw(video);
  bmp = new Bitmap(bData);
  addChild(bmp);
  bmp.x = 220;
  bmp.y = 20;
  bmp.scaleX = bmp.scaleY = 2;

  valueText.visible = true;
  valueText.text = "\n" + "Choose a Filter";
  filter_btn.visible = true;
  fSlider.visible = false;

  stage.removeEventListener(Event.ENTER_FRAME, moveDown);
  stage.addEventListener(Event.ENTER_FRAME, moveUp);
 }
}
function moveUp(e:Event):void {
 if(jt0.position.y > 165) {
  var pt0:Point = new Point(jt0.position.x - 5,
  ¬jt0.position.y - 5);
  mover0.moveTo(pt0);
 } else {
  stage.removeEventListener(Event.ENTER_FRAME, moveUp);
  snapshot_btn.visible = true;
  channel1.stop();
 }
}
filter_btn.addEventListener(MouseEvent.CLICK, onFilter);
function onFilter(e:MouseEvent):void {
 filter = new PBFilter(bmp, fSlider.value);
 fSlider.visible = true;
```

(code continues on next page)

```
  valueText.text = "\n" + "Choose a Value";
}
fSlider.addEventListener(SliderEvent.THUMB_DRAG, valueChange);
function valueChange(e:SliderEvent):void {
 filter.filterValue = fSlider.value;
 valueText.text = filter.filterName + " \n" + "Value: " +
 ¬filter.filterValue;
 filter.onComplete();
}
```

6   Test the movie. Go through the process of taking a snapshot and selecting a filter. When a filter is selected, the slider should appear, and if that filter has one of the coded properties in the onChange() function, you should be able to perform live manipulations of that property of the filter.

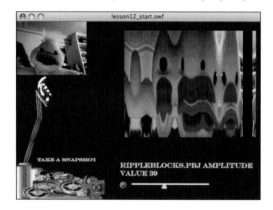

Whew! If you made it successfully through this lesson, you are probably starting to get comfortable with ActionScript 3.0. You've just covered a lot of very formidable new material. Again, it is important to remember that almost all the classes used in this lesson have many capabilities that were not even touched on. To make full use of them, it is worth taking time to look up each class in Flash Help and see what else it can do.

When you have time, experiment with the many topics introduced in this lesson, and when you feel ready, try to work some of these features into your real-world projects.

Suggestions to try on your own

You could enhance the project in this lesson in an infinite number of ways. Here are just a few:

- In a copy of the lesson project, try to alter the graphics in the library used in the Armature layer.

- Make your own IK armatures with authoring (Timeline) animation and integrate them into the project as design elements.

- Change the parameters of the moveTo() methods and experiment with runtime IK animation.

- Set the jt0 variable to refer to different joints in the armature and check out the resulting animations.

- Use the draw() method of the BitmapData instance to draw other display objects in the file and then modify the lesson to add filters to those objects.

- Experiment with the Pixel Bender Toolkit. Try creating your own filters or modifying existing ones. Load the filters into the lesson file.

Review questions

1 What step is necessary in the Flash interface to indicate that an IK armature will be controlled with ActionScript?

2 What two IK classes are created automatically when an armature is created in Flash?

3 Describe the process in ActionScript of displaying the feed from a user's video camera on the Flash Stage.

4 Describe the process of creating a bitmap graphic in ActionScript that draws a copy of another display object.

5 What application ships with Flash CS5 and allows you to program your own filters for Flash?

6 What event can be used with the Slider component to perform live tracking as the user moves a slider's thumb?

Review answers

1 An IK armature that will be controlled by ActionScript must have its option in the Properties panel set to Runtime.

2 When an IK Armature is created in the Flash authoring environment, an instance of the `IKManager` class and of the `IKArmature` class are created automatically.

3 To display a feed from a camcorder or webcam, an instance of the `Camera` class is created in ActionScript that uses the `getCamera()` method to connect to a video camera. An instance of the `Video` class is created to display the camera feed. The `Video` instance is connected to the `Camera` instance using the `attachCamera()` method of the `Video` class, and then the `Video` instance is placed onstage using an `addChild()` method. Here's an example:

```
var camera:Camera = Camera.getCamera();
var video = new Video(160, 120);
video.attachCamera(camera);
addChild(video);
```

4 To create a bitmap in ActionScript that is drawn from another display object, you create an instance of the BitmapData class and then use the draw() method of that class to draw an existing display object to the BitmapData instance. Next, an instance of the Bitmap class is passed the BitmapData, and finally the Bitmap instance is displayed onstage with the addChild() method. Here's an example:

```
var bd:BitmapData = new BitmapData(400, 300);
bd.draw(someDisplayObject);
bmp = new Bitmap(bd);
addChild(bmp);
```

5 Pixel Bender Toolkit 2 ships with Flash CS5 and allows users to create and compile filters that can be used in Flash as well as After Effects, Photoshop, and other programs.

6 The SliderEvent named THUMB_DRAG will fire continuously while a Slider instance is being dragged. This can be used to perform live tracking of the slider's value.

13 PRINTING AND SENDING EMAIL WITH ACTIONSCRIPT 3.0

Lesson overview

In this lesson, you will learn to do the following:

- Send email from a Flash project.

- Work with a PHP script that will receive email information from ActionScript.

- Send data from Flash to a PHP script using the URLVariables class.

- Create new variables in a URLVariables instance.

- Print content from a Flash file using the PrintJob class.

- Control printing using the methods and properties of the PrintJob class.

- Catch errors that may occur while attempting to print by using a try/catch statement.

This lesson will take approximately 2.5 hours.

One of the great features of ActionScript is the ease with which it can send and receive data from external sources. You have already taken advantage of this in a number of ways in earlier lessons. In this lesson, you will use ActionScript to control the printing and sending of email from a Flash application. You will learn two different techniques for sending email from Flash and explore the basics of the ActionScript PrintJob class, which is used to communicate with the printing capabilities of the user's operating system.

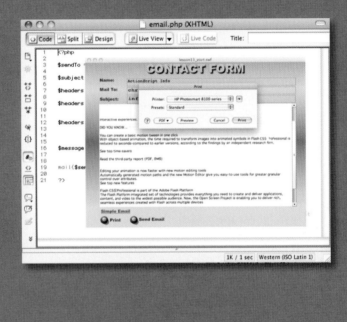

A Flash project can include powerful printing and emailing capabilities.

Examining the starting file

The starting file for this lesson is actually very simple. It consists of a few text fields and buttons that will be used to type text that can then be printed or sent as an email. By successfully accomplishing this task, you'll have learned how to add email capability and a wide range of printing options to your projects.

1   Open the lesson13_start.fla file from the Lessons > Lesson13 > Start folder.

The Timeline for this lesson has five layers. Two layers with background graphics and a `static text` layer have graphic elements that will be unaffected by ActionScript. The `actions` layer, of course, is where you will place the code for this lesson. The `interactive content` layer has a collection of text fields and a pair of buttons that you will use in this lesson.

2   With the Property inspector visible, one at a time select each of the five empty text fields that are on the Stage, and notice their instance names and types.

There are four editable text fields, with the instance names of `name_text`, `email_txt`, `subject_txt`, and `note_txt`. Because the `note_txt` field is intended to let users type as much text as they want, it has a UIScrollBar component to make that text field scrollable. There is also a read-only text field called `feedback_txt`.

The read-only text field at the lower left that reads Simple Email is also on this layer. You will use this text in the next task.

3   Select the buttons in the lower-left corner, and notice that they have the instance names `print_btn` and `send_btn`. Much of the code for this file will be written to take place when these buttons are clicked.

The first features you will add to this project will let the user send email from this file. You will add two types of email capability: one that is simple but limited, and one that is more robust but requires an external server script. By understanding both options, you can use whichever technique is appropriate in your own projects.

Adding a simple email link

You can add a simple link to any text field in Flash using the Properties panel—no ActionScript required. Typically, you would use this technique to create a simple hyperlink to a URL in a browser. You can also use this feature as a simple tool for prompting the user to send email. Try this now by adding an email link to a static text field.

1   Select the text field that reads Simple Email in the lower-left corner of the Stage.

2 In the Properties panel, open the Advanced Character section of the text field's properties and locate the Link field for the Simple Email text field.

3 Populate the Link field to create a mailto link similar to the following (with your own address, of course):

```
mailto:yourName@yourISP.com?subject=From Lesson 13 link&body=
¬This message was sent from Flash
```

Caution: You may have noticed that ActionScript is very forgiving about spaces between names and values. For example, in ActionScript, `clip.x=30;` and `clip.x = 30;` would be treated the same. The spaces are ignored, so you can choose whether to use spaces based on your personal preference. However, when you create code that will be sent as a URL, as you are doing here for this email link, it is important to not use any spaces at all between names and values.

If you have worked with `mailto:` syntax in HTML pages, then you are familiar with this type of link. After the email address, a question mark is used to indicate the addition of parameters such as `subject` and `body`. Each parameter is separated by an ampersand (&). You can change the value of the subject and body parameters to anything you wish.

4 Test the movie. When the text that contains the link is clicked, your default email application will open and come to the foreground with the address, subject, and body filled in from the link.

5 Close your email application.

6 Return to Flash and close the lesson13_start.swf file to leave the testing environment.

This technique is very simple. However, it relies on an external email application and requires the user to manually complete the process of sending and potentially altering the email. There are times when you may want to ensure that an email is sent automatically to the user with specific information included. That's when you'd want a more sophisticated alternative that uses a server script.

Sending email from Flash

Sending email directly from Flash without using the user's email application as an intermediary involves posting the email data directly from Flash to a server script. The server script can then send the email directly to the email addresses. There are many server-side languages you could use to process an email address; in this example, you will use a simple PHP script. This script will reside on a PHP-supported server. The PHP script will receive ActionScript variables and use them to create an email that it will then send to an address supplied in the Flash data.

For this lesson, a PHP file has been created for you. The one that you will actually use to test this lesson is installed on a server at www.actionscript.tv/email.php. A copy of this file is in the Lesson13 folder.

First, let's examine this file.

1 Open the email.php file from the Lessons > Lesson13 folder.

The PHP file contains a simple email function. For this lesson, you don't need to have had any experience with PHP; you just need to know that all the references in this file to variables that begin with the "s" prefix represent variable names that will be passed from your Flash project. You will write ActionScript to create and pass values for these variables based on the information your users enter. The PHP file will take care of the rest.

Sending values using the URLVariables class

When you want to send variables and their values from Flash to an external URL, you can use the ActionScript URLVariables class. You can create an instance of this class and assign variables as properties of the instance. You can then use the instance of the URLVariables class as the data parameter of a URLRequest instance. When you use the sendToURL() or navigateToURL() functions, all the variables that were appended to the URLRequest instance are sent to that URL.

If the description of this technique left you scratching your head, it will likely make more sense when you go through it yourself. The first ActionScript you will add to this project will create instances of the URLVariables and URLRequest classes.

1   With Frame 1 of the actions layer selected and the Actions panel visible, add the following code to the top of the Actions panel:

```
var variables:URLVariables = new URLVariables();
var mailAddress:URLRequest = new
¬ URLRequest("http://www.actionscript.tv/email.php");
```

The parameter for the mailAddress instance is the online location of the email.php script you just examined. The text fields onstage will be the source of the text to be emailed.

Next you will write the code that passes information to this PHP file when the Send Email button onstage is clicked.

Sending URLVariables to the PHP file

The text the user types in the onstage text fields will be stored as variables in the URLVariables instance you created named variables. Those variables will be set and sent any time the user clicks the send_btn instance (the Send Email button onstage).

Start by adding an event listener to this button.

1 Below the existing code in the Actions panel for Frame 1, add the following line:

```
send_btn.addEventListener(MouseEvent.CLICK, onSubmit);
```

2 On a new line below the code you just added, create the shell for the onSubmit() function:

```
function onSubmit(e:Event):void {
}
```

Recall from Lesson 7, "Using Arrays and Loops in ActionScript 3.0," that a dynamic class is one that can have properties and methods added to its instances from external files. The URLVariables class is a dynamic class. Properties added to instances of the URLVariables class are the variables that will be sent when that instance is used as the data for a URLRequest.

In the onSubmit() function, you will create a few properties for the variables instance that will store the text that the user types in the input text fields.

3 Within the curly braces of the onSubmit() function, add the following lines:

```
variables.sName = name_txt.text;
variables.sEmail = email_txt.text;
variables.sSubject = subject_txt.text;
  variables.sMessage =variables.sName + " has sent this note:"
  ¬+ "\n\n"+note_txt.text;
```

Note that the values of these properties (variables) are set similarly to the way that normal string variables are set. The first three lines simply take text from the onstage text fields. The sMessage property joins, or concatenates, the text from two text fields with some literal text and two carriage returns ("\n\n"). The sMessage property (variable) will be used as the email message.

Now you will set all these URLVariables properties as the data property for the URLRequest instance named mailAddress that you created earlier. The data property is used to contain data that is sent to the URL stored in a URLRequest instance.

4 Above the closing curly brace of the onSubmit() function, add this line:

```
mailAddress.data = variables;
```

The URLRequest class's method property determines the HTTP form-submission type. When sending data, this property is typically set to POST. You will send the variables using the POST method. Set that property now.

5 Add this code below the line you just added:

```
mailAddress.method = URLRequestMethod.POST;
```

Now that all the URLVariables properties are appended to the URL that you stored in mailAddress (remember that this URL was the location of the PHP file), you can send those variables to this address using the sendToURL() function.

6 Below the last line you typed, add the following code:

```
sendToURL(mailAddress);
```

The final line of this function gives the user some feedback by putting text in the feedback_txt field. In a more robust application, you might want to get confirmation from the PHP file that the email was successfully delivered. In this example, you are just confirming that the data was sent to the PHP file.

7 Add the following line above the closing curly brace of the onSubmit() function:

```
feedback_txt.text = "Your mail has been sent";
```

The final onSubmit() function should now read as follows:

```
send_btn.addEventListener(MouseEvent.CLICK, onSubmit);

function onSubmit(e:Event):void {

    variables.sName = name_txt.text;
    variables.sEmail = email_txt.text;
    variables.sMessage = variables.sName + " has sent this note:" + "\n\n"+note_txt.text;
    variables.sSubject = subject_txt.text;
    mailAddress.data = variables;
    mailAddress.method = URLRequestMethod.POST;
    sendToURL(mailAddress);

    feedback_txt.text = "Your mail has been sent";
}
```

8 Test your movie. Fill out the text fields using your own email address in the Mail To field.

9 Click the Send Email button. The `feedback_txt` field should inform you that the email was sent.

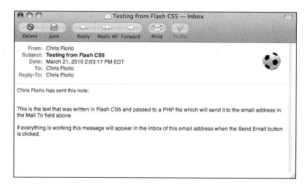

10 Open your default email application and check your email.

It may take a few moments, but an email should arrive with the information that you typed in Flash.

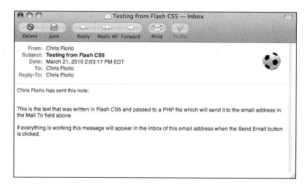

You can use and modify the email.php file and place it on your own server to add email functionality to your projects.

Now you will add printing capabilities, using the `PrintJob` class.

Adding printing capabilities with the PrintJob class

The `PrintJob` class allows Flash projects to communicate with the printing capabilities of the user's operating system. It can initiate printing, confirm the user's printing settings, and send multiple pages of specified content to the user's printer. However, a Flash SWF file cannot directly control the user's printer, and the success of a print job from Flash will depend not only on the user's having (of course) a properly connected printer, but also on the user's clicking to confirm the Print dialog box as presented by the operating system.

Once a `PrintJob` instance is created, the process of printing proceeds in three steps, using three methods of the `PrintJob` class. The `start()` method opens the operating system's Print dialog box. At this point, the ActionScript will pause until the user either confirms or cancels the printing. If the user confirms the printing, then the `start()` method will return `true`; if not, it will return `false`.

Assuming that the user has allowed the printing to proceed, the second step of the process is to use the `addPage()` method of the `PrintJob` class. This method can send any sprite or frame of a movie clip to the printer. You can add as many pages as you wish to a print job by calling the `addPage()` method multiple times. You have tremendous control over the properties of the print job: what to print and how to print it (we will touch on only a few of those properties, so consult Flash Help for more information).

Finally, when the pages have been added, the `send()` method of the `PrintJob` class initiates the printing of the added pages.

In this lesson, you give users the option of printing the information that they have entered in the text fields with some additional text added in your ActionScript. On your own projects, you have complete control over what is sent to the printer from Flash. As an example, in Lesson 14, "Creating Adobe AIR Applications with Flash and ActionScript," you will add a bitmap image to the document that is sent to the printer.

The printing process will be initiated when the user clicks the `print_btn` button, so start by adding an event listener to that button.

1   On the line below all your ActionScript for Frame 1, add this line:

    ```
    print_btn.addEventListener(MouseEvent.CLICK, onPrint);
    ```

    If you guessed that the next step is the shell for the `onPrint()` function, you guessed right.

2   Add the shell for the `onPrint()` function below the last line:

    ```
    function onPrint(e:MouseEvent):void {
    }
    ```

Capturing the current date and time with the Date class

It's become a standard convention in email client software that printed emails include some automated header or footer indicating the recipient and the date or time that the email was printed or sent. To add this functionality in this project, you will take advantage of the constructor function of the Date class. This class offers many versatile methods and properties for working with time- and date-related information. In this case, you will use the Date class in a very simple way: You'll create an instance of the Date class that will return the current date and time, which will then be placed at the top of a document that the user prints.

Create an instance of the Date class in the same manner as you have for other classes you've used.

1   Within the curly braces of the onPrint() function, add this line:

```
var now:Date = new Date();
```

You will use the Date instance you just created in documents that the user prints.

This is an example of a situation in which tracing the code you just typed might be useful. Remember, tracing is just a developer tool to help you get feedback on your ActionScript as you work. In this case, if you haven't worked with the Date() constructor before, it might be helpful to see what it returns.

2   Add this line below the previous one:

```
trace(now);
```

3   Test the movie. When you click the Print button, the Output panel will present the current date and time in its default format.

Get in the habit of tracing code as you work whenever you're not sure what the results of a specific action might be. You will probably encounter many situations in which trace() statements can be helpful.

4   Close the lesson13_start.swf file to leave the testing environment.

5   The trace() statement has served its purpose, so if you like, you can delete it or comment it out by placing two forward slashes at the beginning of the line:

```
//trace(now);
```

Creating the content to print

When the user clicks the Print button, the user's name, the date, and whatever text was typed in the note_txt field should print. Remember that the PrintJob class will be looking for a Sprite or MovieClip instance to print. You will first store all the text to be printed in a variable; then you'll place the data in that variable in a new Sprite instance and print that Sprite instance. All of this will go in the onPrint() function.

Start by creating the string of text that will be sent to the printer. This will go in a new variable named note.

1. Above the closing curly brace of the onPrint() function, add the following line:

```
var note:String = name_txt.text + " has sent this note on:" +
¬ "\n" + String(now) + "\n\n" + note_txt.text;
```

As already described, this line combines the name that the user typed in the Name field with the date and time from the Date instance and the message that the user typed in the note_txt field.

Soon you will place this text in a new TextField instance, but first you'll create the PrintJob instance.

2. On a line below the previous line you typed, add the following:

```
var printNote:PrintJob = new PrintJob();
```

As mentioned earlier, when a print job is started, it will return either true or false, depending on whether the user chose to print (true) or cancel (false). Therefore, it is a good idea to confirm that the start() method returns true before proceeding with processing the print job. You do this with a conditional statement.

3. Below the last line that you typed, create the shell for a new conditional statement that checks to see whether the start() method returns the value true:

```
if(printNote.start()) {
}
```

Remember that the code in Flash stops until the printNote.start() method returns either true or false. If it returns true, the conditional statement runs; if false, the conditional statement ends. Whatever code you type in the if statement will run only when the user clicks to confirm the printing.

This all seems fairly predictable and straightforward, and in most cases, printing should proceed uneventfully at this point. However, anyone who has ever used a printer knows that after the user confirms a print job, there are any number of potential problems that could cause an error in the printing. If any of these problems occurs, it could cause a runtime error in your Flash project that would stop the Flash project from running altogether. There is nothing you can do in ActionScript to fix a problem with the user's printer, but you can prevent printer problems from stopping your Flash movie. You will do this next, with a try/catch statement.

Using try/catch statements in ActionScript

You can use a try/catch statement in ActionScript any time there is potential for a runtime error that could halt your application. A try/catch statement is used for errors similarly to the way an if/else statement is used for conditions. In a try/catch statement, if no errors occur, then the code within the try block of the statement runs. If an error occurs, then the catch block of the code runs: that is, it handles the error. The act of "catching" the error prevents the file from being halted by the error.

1 Below the line that reads

```
if(printNote.start()) {
```

add the shell for a try/catch statement with this code:

```
try {

} catch(e:Error) {

}
```

Notice that the shell of the try/catch statement resembles the basic syntax of an if/else statement.

The try statement contains the code that will run if no printing errors occur. The first things you will create in the try statement are the TextField instance to contain the text to be printed and a new Sprite instance to contain the TextField instance.

2 Beneath the code that reads

```
try {
```

create two new instances with these lines:

```
var pageSprite:Sprite = new Sprite();
var noteText:TextField = new TextField();
```

When the user clicks OK in the Print dialog box, the current printer settings are sent to Flash. These settings can be accessed as properties of the PrintJob instance. The paperWidth and paperHeight properties tell you the printable area of the selected paper size on the user's printer. You can use these properties to set the size of the text field to match the printable area. Do this now.

3 Beneath the previous line that you added, enter this code:

```
noteText.width = printNote.paperWidth;
noteText.height = printNote.paperHeight;
```

Now place the text from the note variable in the new text field.

4 On the line below the code you just typed, add the following line:

```
noteText.text = note;
```

Now that the TextField and Sprite instances are ready to go, place the Sprite instance in the display list and the text field in the Sprite instance. (You will leave them in the display list only long enough to print, so the user will never see these objects onstage.)

5 Add this code below the last line you typed:

```
addChild(pageSprite);
pageSprite.addChild(noteText);
```

Now that the pageSprite is set to print, add it to the PrintJob instance using the addPage() method.

6 On the line below the code you just added, type this code:

```
printNote.addPage(pageSprite);
```

This completes the code that runs in the try statement. You will just add a simple trace statement in the catch block to report an error if one occurs.

7 Below the line that reads

```
} catch(e:Error) {
```

insert this line:

```
trace("There was an error");
```

This completes the try/catch statement. There should be a single closing curly brace below the line you just typed, and two more closing braces below that: one for the if statement and one for the entire onPrint() function.

Sending the job to the printer

The last two lines you'll add to this project will send the pageSprite instance to the printer and then remove it from the display list.

1 Below the first of the three closing curly braces (the one for the try/catch statement), add these two lines:

```
printNote.send();
removeChild(pageSprite);
```

The entire onPrint() function should now read as follows:

```
function onPrint(e:MouseEvent):void {
 var now:Date = new Date();

 var note:String = name_txt.text + " has sent this note on:" +
 ¬"\n"+String(now) + "\n\n" + note_txt.text;

 var printNote:PrintJob = new PrintJob();
 if(printNote.start()) {
  try {
   var pageSprite:Sprite = new Sprite;
   var noteText:TextField = new TextField();
   noteText.wordWrap = true;
   noteText.width = printNote.paperWidth;
   noteText.height = printNote.paperHeight;
   noteText.text = note;
   addChild(pageSprite);
   pageSprite.addChild(noteText);
   printNote.addPage(pageSprite);
  } catch(e:Error) {
   trace("There was an error");
  }
  printNote.send();
  removeChild(pageSprite);
 }
}
```

Don't forget to double-check that you have the right number of braces.

The code for the entire file should read:

```
var variables:URLVariables = new URLVariables();
var mailAddress:URLRequest = new URLRequest
¬("http://www.actionscript.tv/email.php");

name_txt.tabIndex = 1;
email_txt.tabIndex = 2;
subject_txt.tabIndex = 3;
note_txt.tabIndex = 4;
print_btn.tabIndex = 5;


send_btn.addEventListener(MouseEvent.CLICK, onSubmit);
```

```
function onSubmit(e:Event):void {

  variables.sName = name_txt.text;
  variables.sEmail = email_txt.text;
  variables.sMessage =variables.sName + " has sent this note:"
  ¬+ "\n\n"+note_txt.text;
  variables.sSubject = subject_txt.text;

  mailAddress.data = variables;
  mailAddress.method = URLRequestMethod.POST;
  sendToURL(mailAddress);

  feedback_txt.text = "Your mail has been sent";
}

print_btn.addEventListener(MouseEvent.CLICK, onPrint);

function onPrint(e:MouseEvent):void {
  var now:Date = new Date();
  var note:String = name_txt.text + " has sent this note on:" +
  ¬"\n" + String(now) + "\n\n" + note_txt.text;
  var printNote:PrintJob = new PrintJob();

  if (printNote.start()) {
    try{
      var pageSprite:Sprite = new Sprite  ;
      var noteText:TextField = new TextField();
      noteText.wordWrap = true;
      noteText.width = printNote.paperWidth;
      noteText.height = printNote.paperHeight;
      noteText.text = note;
      addChild(pageSprite);
      pageSprite.addChild(noteText);
      printNote.addPage(pageSprite);
    } catch(e:Error) {
      trace("There was an error");
    }
    printNote.send();
    removeChild(pageSprite);
  }

}
```

2 Test your movie. Fill in all the fields on the Stage.

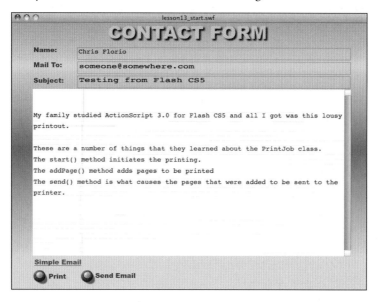

3 Click the Print button. The normal Print dialog box of your operating system will appear.

4 Click Print. If you have a printer connected to your computer, the text you typed in the name and note fields, along with the date, will print.

> Chris Florio has sent this note on:
> Sun Mar 21 14:33:27 GMT-0400 2010
>
> My family studied ActionScript 3.0 for Flash CS5 and all I got was this lousy printout.
>
> These are a number of things that they learned about the PrintJob class.
> The start() method initiates the printing.
> The addPage() method adds pages to be printed
> The send() method is what causes the pages that were added to be sent to the printer.

Being able to print and send email from Flash offers countless creative options for your projects—enabling you to print and send messages as diverse as game scores, product receipts, and test results. Bear in mind that you do not have to create a sprite specifically for printing, as you did in this lesson, but could instead print any existing sprite, any frame of any movie clip, or the root timeline of any Flash file. Remember that you determine what is printed with a parameter in the addPage() method.

In the next lesson, you'll see that by using the new Adobe AIR 2.0 technology you can have even more interaction with the user's operating and file systems.

Some suggestions to try on your own

This lesson introduced a number of features that you may want to pursue more deeply, particularly the methods and properties of the PrintJob and Date classes. You can also try some of these ideas:

- Try uploading the email.php file to your own server. Experiment with the code in this file to format the email in other ways.

- Add text fields to the screen. Create corresponding variables in the URLVariables instance to add this text from the new text fields to your emails.

- Study the methods and properties of the Date class in Flash Help and format the date and time in your emails any way you like.

- Study the parameters of the addPage() method of the PrintJob class and modify the way the document is printed.

- Add graphics to the sprite that will print. Use techniques covered in earlier chapters to include images in your printing.

- Create a TextFormat object to set the style or size of the text that is printed.

Review questions

1 What are the limitations of sending email using a text-field link?

2 Which class is used to send variables to a URL?

3 What three methods of the `PrintJob` class are used to control printing from ActionScript?

4 What is a process used in ActionScript to prevent a runtime error from halting playback?

Review answers

1 While an email link on a text field is very convenient, it has the limitations of relying on the user and the user's default email application to ensure that the email is sent. It also gives the user the opportunity to delete or alter data that was included in the email from Flash.

2 The `URLVariables` class is used to create variables for sending to a URL.

3 The `start()` method opens the operating system's Print dialog box to initiate printing. The second step (assuming the user has allowed the printing to proceed) adds pages to print using the `addPage()` method. Finally, the `send()` method sends the pages to the printer.

4 A `try/catch` statement is used in ActionScript to catch potential runtime errors that could halt the application. In a `try/catch` statement, the `try` block of code is executed with code that has the potential to cause an error. If no error occurs, the code in the `try` statement proceeds normally. If an error does occur, however, the code in the `catch` block of the statement occurs instead. The basic syntax of a `try/catch` statement is as follows:

```
try {
 something that could produce an error();
}
catch(errObject:Error) {
 someReponseToError()
}
```

14

CREATING ADOBE AIR APPLICATIONS WITH FLASH AND ACTIONSCRIPT

Lesson overview

In this lesson, you will learn how to do the following:

- Use Flash CS5 to create cross-platform desktop applications.

- Assign the Flash publish settings for Adobe AIR applications.

- Customize the AIR application and installer settings.

- Set custom icons for an AIR application.

- Create a digital signature for an AIR application.

- Use AIR-only `PrintJob` settings.

- Use AIR-only classes in ActionScript to create interaction with the user's operating system.

- Create drag-and-drop functionality in an AIR application using ActionScript.

- Use the `File` and `FileStream` classes to read data from external files.

- Publish and install an AIR application.

 This lesson will take approximately 2 hours.

Although Flash has always been used to create content for both online and offline work, it has traditionally been considered primarily a web tool. Flash developers typically create Flash content designed to be viewed as SWF files in the user's browser.

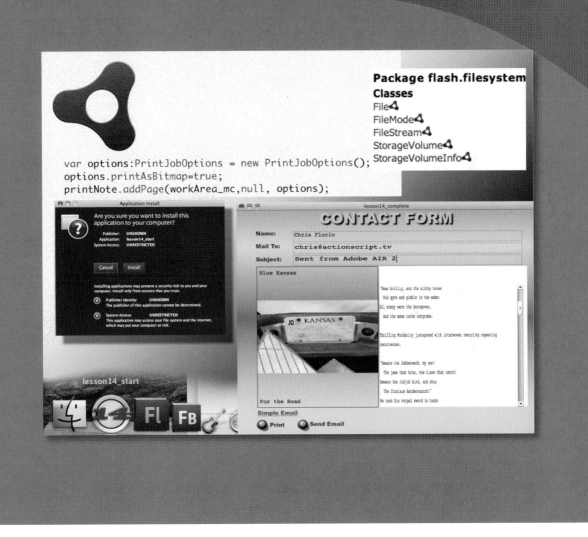

```
var options:PrintJobOptions = new PrintJobOptions();
options.printAsBitmap=true;
printNote.addPage(workArea_mc,null, options);
```

Standard Flash development tools can be used to
create desktop AIR applications.

With the Adobe Integrated Runtime, or AIR, technology, Adobe has created a platform that lets you leverage your existing Flash skills to create desktop applications. AIR 2 introduces a number of improvements and is fully supported in Flash CS5.

You create AIR applications in Flash with the same tool set you use to create traditional Flash web projects. Instead of publishing the finished project for Flash Player, however, you publish the project as a stand-alone AIR application. The resulting file plays as a true desktop application on Macintosh, Windows, and Linux computers and mobile devices that have the AIR runtime installed. Users who do not have the AIR runtime and try to view an AIR application are prompted to download and install the runtime for free.

AIR applications can be built with standard web tools like Flash CS5, Flash Builder 4, and Dreamweaver, using languages including ActionScript, JavaScript, and HTML. All the design and interactive features in Flash can be incorporated into an AIR application, and the entire ActionScript 3.0 language is supported in AIR applications. This means that you can make use of all your existing Flash skills and ActionScript knowledge as you create desktop applications.

In addition, applications created in Flash for distribution as AIR applications can offer capabilities not available to projects intended to play as SWF files in a browser. For security reasons, online Flash projects have very limited access to your user's operating system, but AIR applications have the same access as other desktop applications: They can read and write files to the user's machine, copy and paste to the clipboard, drag and drop into and out of other applications, and more. In addition, AIR applications can include browser capabilities, integrate PDF files, and create local databases on the user's machine using built-in SQLite features.

This lesson is not intended to be a full overview of Adobe AIR, but rather to give you a sense of how Flash can be used to create AIR applications and to show you some of the features available in ActionScript for AIR projects. If you are interested in pursuing development of Adobe AIR applications, there are a number of good books on the subject as well as plenty of information at the Adobe AIR Developer Center for Flash, found at www.adobe.com/devnet/air/flash/.

In this lesson, you will use a variation of the project in Lesson 13, "Printing and Sending Email with ActionScript 3.0," converting it to an AIR application and then adding some AIR-specific ActionScript to give the project drag-and-drop capabilities. The resulting file from this lesson will be a stand-alone, cross-platform AIR application.

Using AIR-specific ActionScript

As mentioned, AIR applications can take advantage of the entire ActionScript 3.0 language, but quite a bit of ActionScript is created specifically for AIR and cannot be used in regular Flash web projects.

The ActionScript 3.0 Reference for the Adobe Flash platform, which can be found within Flash Help as well as online at Adobe.com, has information about every class in the ActionScript language. If you look through the list of classes in this reference, you will notice that a number of them have the red AIR logo next to the class name. The classes that display this logo contain ActionScript that will work in an AIR application but should not be used in a regular Flash SWF file.

You will also see within some classes available for creating SWF files that certain properties, methods, and events are marked with the AIR-only logo. This means that those specific features of an ActionScript class can be used only when creating AIR applications.

![Screenshot of the Adobe Community Help window displaying the ActionScript 3.0 Reference for the Adobe Flash Platform, showing the NativeWindowInitOptions class documentation with a Packages list on the left and class details on the right.]

As you can see from even a brief look at this list, ActionScript offers many AIR-specific classes, which can add numerous capabilities to your applications. Many developers are creating applications in AIR or creating projects that are a combination of online Flash applications and offline AIR applications. For examples of work created in AIR, visit the Adobe AIR showcase at www.adobe.com/products/air/showcase/.

Before you start writing AIR-specific ActionScript, you need to set up Flash to turn your Flash project into an AIR application. That will be your first task here.

Specifying Flash publish settings for an AIR project

To turn a Flash project into an AIR application, you need to set the Flash publish settings to indicate that your file should be published for AIR. You will do this for the Lesson 14 project file.

1 From the Lessons > Lesson14 > Start folder, open the lesson14_start.fla file.

   This file is a variation on the completed file from Lesson 13. You will take a closer look at its content and code soon, but first you'll set its publish settings to turn it into an AIR project.

2 From the File menu, choose Publish Settings.

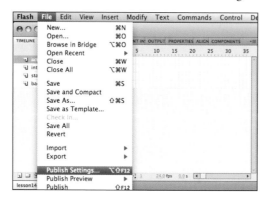

3 In the Publish Settings dialog box, click the Flash tab. The Player menu is currently set to Flash Player 10, indicating that publishing will create a SWF file for that version. From the Player menu, switch to Adobe AIR 2. (That's the latest version at the time of writing, but if you have a more recent version, choose that.)

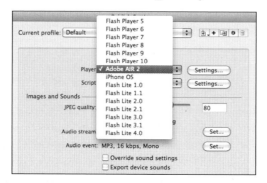

   You have selected to publish your project as an AIR application. Now you can adjust the settings for this AIR file.

4 Click the Settings button to the right of the Player menu.

When an AIR file is created, it uses an XML descriptor file to determine many of its settings, including how the AIR application's default window will be displayed and what icons the operating system will use to represent the application. This file is created, and the settings chosen, via the Application & Installer Settings dialog box in Flash. Alternatively, in this dialog box you can point to an existing descriptor file to determine these settings.

Detailed discussion of all these application and installer settings is beyond the scope of this book, and you'll leave most of the settings at their defaults for this project. You will, however, set some custom icons and create a digital signature for the project.

Setting custom icons

Because AIR applications are true desktop applications, they are represented in the operating system with icons the same way as any other application. You can choose your own graphics to be used as icons, creating or fine-tuning them in Photoshop or any other graphics application. Up to four files can be used for any one icon, they must be PNG format, and they must be in the specific sizes of 128 × 128, 48 × 48, 32 × 32, and 16 × 16 pixels. The user's operating system will use the different-sized icons under different circumstances. For example, the larger icons might appear in the Macintosh dock and in the Windows system tray.

The Lesson14 folder has some graphics provided in the correct format for icons. You'll assign those files as the icons for your AIR application.

1   At the top of the Application & Installer Settings dialog box, click the Icons tab (third from the left).

Here you will see a menu listing the four icon sizes. To replace the default icons, you'll select each of the four icon sizes and then click the Browse button below the list of icon sizes.

2   Select the icon 16×16 setting and then click the folder icon below the list of icons.

3   Browse to the Lessons > Lesson14 > Start > Icons folder and select the file named AIRicon16.png to assign the first icon.

4   Repeat Steps 2 and 3 for icon 32×32, icon 48×48, and icon 128×128. The filenames correspond to the icon sizes.

Soon you will test the AIR application and view the icons, but first you will create a digital signature.

Creating a digital signature

An AIR application requires a digital signature. The purpose of a digital signature in an AIR application, or any application, is to provide your users with some assurance as to the creator of the application. The Signature tab of the Application & Installer Settings dialog box for AIR is where the digital signature is assigned. For a high level of security, you can provide a verified digital signature for your application by purchasing one from an authorized certificate authority. You can find more information about this at the Adobe AIR Developer Center (www.adobe.com/devnet/air/). In less critical situations, you can create unverified signatures in Flash that work fine. You will do that now.

1 In the Application & Installer Settings dialog box, click the Signature tab (second from the left).

2 In the Application Digital Signature dialog box, click the New button.

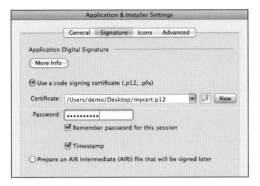

3 Fill in the project information in the Create Self-Signed Digital Certificate dialog box however you like. Since security is not a priority for this file, choose a password that is short and easy to remember. You can leave the default encryption of 1024-RSA (2048-RSA is more secure, but again, this is not a high-security situation).

4 Browse to the Lessons > Lesson14 folder to indicate the location to store the digital certificate.

A simple dialog box should appear telling you that the certificate has been created.

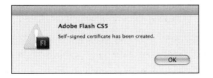

5 Click OK to return to the Application & Installer Settings dialog box.

6 In the Password field, enter the password you just created.

7 Select Remember Password For This Session.

8 Leave the rest of the AIR settings at their defaults.

Now you will use the settings you just applied to publish an AIR application from this project.

Creating an AIR application

When you publish an AIR project, an AIR (.air) file is created. This is an installer file which, when opened, steps the user through a fairly standard process of installing the application on a local hard drive. You do not need to go through this publishing process every time you want to test your AIR file—the Flash testing environment and Test Movie command work fine with AIR projects—but it is worth publishing at least once to see what to expect from the process and to see in action the custom icons that you installed.

Continuing from the previous steps, you should still be in the Application & Installer Settings dialog box preparing to create an AIR application from the lesson14_start.fla file.

1 Click the General tab in the Application & Installer Settings dialog box, and choose the browse folder next to the Output File field.

2 Browse to select the Lessons > Lesson14 folder and click Save.

3 At the bottom of the Application & Installer Settings dialog box, click the Publish button.

An AIR file is now created.

4 Click OK twice to close the Application & Installer Settings and the Publish Settings dialog boxes.

5 Navigate to the Lessons > Lesson14 folder and locate the lesson14_start.air file and double-click it. This is the installer file for the project that you just created.

6 In the Application Install dialog box that appears, notice that because the digital signature is unverified, the publisher is listed as unknown. Click the Install button.

7 Click the browse folder next to the Installation Location field and choose the location on your hard drive where you want to install the application. The default location is the Applications (Mac) or Program Files (Windows) folder. You may want to change this to the Lessons > Lesson14 folder.

8 Make sure that the Start Application After Installation option is selected and then click Continue.

Your AIR application is installed in the location that you selected and launches automatically.

Notice that this is a true application with standard window controls for maximizing, minimizing, and closing that are appropriate to your operating system. If you are on a Mac, you should also see the default File, Edit, and Window menus.

Application menus in AIR

If you want to experiment with ActionScript for AIR, you will find AIR classes in the ActionScript 3.0 Reference guide that let you code your own custom menus and write functions that respond when menu items are selected. You can also create context menus for interactive objects, and even create custom menus for the dock or taskbar icons. There are many other ways that you can customize your AIR applications with ActionScript to make them behave like other applications you have used.

9 Before closing the application, notice your dock (Mac) or taskbar (Windows). You should see the custom icon that you assigned, indicating that the application is running.

Also notice that the features in this application are the same as those you added to the Lesson 13 project. The email and print functions still work. A few graphical changes have been made, but otherwise this is the same basic file and code that you have already worked with. You will add some AIR-specific ActionScript to this file to give it some functionality that would not be available to SWF files.

10 Quit the application and return to Flash.

Examining the starting file

As mentioned earlier, the lesson14_start.fla file is a slightly modified version of the completed Lesson 13 file. As the project stands now, it would work perfectly well in Flash Player as a SWF file, and as you just saw, this file was also easily turned into an AIR application.

Soon you will add some drag-and-drop functionality to this file that will work only in AIR, but first take a moment to familiarize yourself with a few differences between this file and the Lesson 13 file.

If you completed Lesson 13, you should notice changes to the layout of the graphics and text on the screen. The layout changes are mainly to accommodate the additional UILoader instance on the left side of the Stage. This UILoader component and the preexisting note_txt field have both been embedded in a MovieClip symbol.

1 With the Properties panel visible, select either the UILoader component or the large text field to the right of it on the Stage. You will see in the Properties panel that they are both part of a movie clip with an instance name of workArea_mc.

2 With the workArea_mc clip still selected, choose Edit > Edit Symbols.

You will see that this clip stores a UILoader component with an instance name of imgLoader, an input text field named note_txt, and a UIScrollBar component with an instance name of scroller.

Soon you will use the AIR classes in ActionScript to allow the user to drag text documents into the note_txt field and image files from their desktop or other open applications into the imgLoader component. These clips are put together in a MovieClip instance so that they can both be part of the same drag operation and so that the image and text can be printed together—recall from the previous lesson that the addPage() method of the PrintJob class lets you easily send the contents of a movie clip to the printer.

3 Return to the Edit menu and choose Edit Document to return to the main Flash Timeline.

Now take a closer look at the ActionScript file.

4 Select Frame 1 of the actions layer in the Timeline and view the ActionScript file in the Actions panel. In addition to the changes to the Lesson 13 file already mentioned, a few modifications have been made to the completed code.

If you completed the Lesson 13 project, most of the code in the ActionScript file should be familiar. If you compare it to the completed Lesson 13 file, you will see that the code that formatted the background of the text fields has been removed. This was done solely to simplify the code for this project. Feel free to add your own text-formatting code.

The code in the onSubmit() function that is used to send email is identical to what you saw in Lesson 13.

The main changes to the code are in the onPrint() function, to accommodate the new UILoader component and the workArea_mc clip and to make sure that this clip prints accurately when the user clicks the Print button.

One change you should note is on lines 36 to 38. These lines create a new instance of a class called PrintJobOptions. One of the properties of this class allows a print job to be sent to the printer as a bitmap graphic rather than as a vector graphic (the default). Since this project sends text and images to the printer, this property is set to true. In line 38, the PrintJobOptions instance is added as the third parameter when the addPage() method sends the page to the printer. The rest of the PrintJob instance's ActionScript here should be familiar from the previous lesson.

```
36    var options:PrintJobOptions = new PrintJobOptions();
37    options.printAsBitmap = true;
38    printNote.addPage(workArea_mc, null, options);
```

Controlling printing with AIR

A new feature in AIR 2 files is the capability to set the properties of the user's printer in an ActionScript print job and to optionally bypass the operating system's Print > Options dialog box. This is one of many instances in which an AIR application has more access to the operating system than a SWF file.

Of course, in many cases it is preferable to let the users control their own printer settings, but if you need an AIR application to control all aspects of the way that a document is printed, it is now possible using AIR-only PrintJob properties and methods. You will make a few modifications to the onPrint() function in this file to try out this functionality.

1   With Frame 1 selected in the actions layer of the Timeline, open the Actions panel and locate the onPrint() function.

2   Within the onPrint() function, locate the line that creates the new PrintJob instance named printNote:

```
var printNote:PrintJob = new PrintJob();
```

3   Below this code, add the following lines:

```
printNote.selectPaperSize(PaperSize.LETTER);
printNote.orientation = PrintJobOrientation.LANDSCAPE;
```

These and other settings that would typically be made in the operating system's Print > Options dialog box can now be set by an AIR application. As mentioned in Lesson 13, the `start()` method of the `PrintJob` class opens the user's Print dialog box and initiates printing. A new AIR-only method called `start2()` is an alternative to the `start()` method. The first parameter of the `start2()` method lets you indicate which options will appear in the Print dialog box, and the second parameter controls whether the Print dialog box is displayed. In this example, you will set the second parameter to `false` to bypass the system's Print dialog box altogether, and you will set the first option to `null` since the operating system's Print dialog box will not be needed.

4   Within the `onPrint()` function, locate the line that reads:

```
if(printNote.start()) {
```

5   Alter this code so that it now reads:

```
if (printNote.start2(null,false)) {
```

6   Test your movie in the usual manner. (When the publish settings are set to create an AIR application, the `Test Movie` command creates an AIR application instead of a SWF file in the testing environment.)

7   Type some text in the text field and click the Print button.

The printing should take place immediately. The print job should print a letter-sized page in landscape mode on the default printer. Remember that this function can be implemented only in an AIR application and would cause errors in a SWF file.

8   Close the test file to return to the authoring environment.

You will not need to make any other changes to the printing or email functions that are already in the file. Instead, you will add two functions to this file that will add drag-and-drop capabilities to the project so that users can drag external text and image files into your AIR application. You will take advantage of a number of ActionScript AIR classes to do this, including the `NativeDrag` class, the `File` class, and the `Clipboard` class.

Listening for drag events

The `NativeDragEvent` class is used to keep track of drag-and-drop events in AIR applications. In this project, you will use events in this class to respond when a file is initially dragged over the `workArea_mc` clip and when a file is dropped on this clip. The two events you will use are called NATIVE_DRAG_ENTER and NATIVE_DRAG_DROP. They work in the same basic way as all the other ActionScript events you have used.

1 Below all the existing code in Frame 1 of the actions layer, add listeners for the NATIVE_DRAG_ENTER and NATIVE_DRAG_DROP events with this code:

```
workArea_mc.addEventListener(NativeDragEvent.
¬NATIVE_DRAG_ENTER, onDragEnter);
workArea_mc.addEventListener(NativeDragEvent.NATIVE_DRAG_DROP,
¬onDragDrop);
```

2 Add the shells for the two functions that these events will trigger:

```
function onDragEnter(e:NativeDragEvent):void {

}
function onDragDrop(e:NativeDragEvent):void {
}
```

Using ClipboardFormats

Drag-and-drop capabilities (and copy-and-paste capabilities) in AIR projects use the operating system's clipboard to perform their tasks. There are ActionScript classes that let AIR applications take advantage of nearly all the native operating system's clipboard functionality, including dragging and dropping.

One useful clipboard feature offers the ability to check the type of data stored on the clipboard. When a file is dragged, copied, or cut to the clipboard, you can determine whether the data on the clipboard is text, bitmap, HTML, or some other type of data. Being able to check what is on the clipboard is useful when writing ActionScript in order to determine when and how the clipboard's contents are used.

Often, a single file on the clipboard contains multiple types of data. When one or more files are placed on the clipboard, one of the types of data is file data, which contains a list of the files placed on the clipboard. The onDragEnter() function checks to see whether the clipboard contains file-list data. If the clipboard does contain file information, then a method of the NativeDragManager class called acceptDragDrop() is used to allow the workArea_mc clip to receive files that are dropped on it.

Add code to the onDragEnter() function so that the full function now reads:

```
function onDragEnter(e:NativeDragEvent):void {
 if(e.clipboard.hasFormat(ClipboardFormats.FILE_LIST_FORMAT)) {
  NativeDragManager.acceptDragDrop(workArea_mc);
 }
}
```

Now that the workArea_mc clip is set to receive files that are dropped on it, you will use the onDragDrop() function to determine what is done with those dropped files.

Adding the onDragDrop() function

In the onDragEnter() function, you added code that checked whether file-list data had been dragged over the workArea_mc clip. Now, if the user drops the items over the workArea_mc clip, the first thing you want to have happen is to store (in a local array) the names of the file or files that were dropped.

1 Between the curly braces of the onDragDrop() function, add this code to create a new array:

```
var cbFiles:Array = e.clipboard.getData(
¬ClipboardFormats.FILE_LIST_FORMAT,
¬ClipboardTransferMode.CLONE_ONLY) as Array;
```

The clipboard.getdata() method retrieves the data on the clipboard only if it's in the format indicated in its first parameter. In this case, the data is of the type ClipboardFormats.FILE_LIST_FORMAT. The second parameter indicates whether a reference to the original files or a copy of the files is retrieved. CLONE_ONLY indicates that a copy of the file data is retrieved.

You want to load compatible images into the imgLoader instance and text files into the note_txt field. To accomplish this, you will create two arrays. The first will contain the possible suffixes for compatible image files, and the second the possible suffixes for text files. Then you will create two for loops, which will be used to discover whether the file dropped on the workArea_mc clip has any of the suffixes stored in the arrays and to determine what to do with the data.

First, you'll create the two arrays of file types.

2 Above the closing brace of the onDragDrop() function, add these lines:

```
var imageTypes:Array = new Array("jpg", "jpeg", "png", "gif");
var textTypes:Array = new Array("txt", "html", "htm", "xml",
¬"as", "php", "rtf");
```

Next you will store a reference to the first file that was dropped on the workArea_mc clip and to that file's name. These references will check whether the file is one of the file types stored in the imageTypes and textTypes arrays.

3 Add this code below the last lines that you typed:

```
var file:File = cbFiles[0];
var str:String = cbFiles[0].name.toLowerCase();
```

Notice that when storing the name of the file that was dropped, the toLowerCase() method is called. This is so that the name of the file is stored in all lowercase characters. Now a file with the suffix "html" is treated the same as a file with the suffix "HTML," which will make the file easier to work with in the coming steps.

About the File and FileStream classes

The file variable you just created stores an instance of the File class. Soon you will use the FileStream class to read the data in that file.

The File and FileStream classes are two of the most useful AIR-specific ActionScript classes. They can be used to open, create, and save files and write data to existing files. If you plan to create your own AIR applications, it would be valuable to make a thorough study of these two classes.

At this point, the onDragDrop() function should look like this:

```
function onDragDrop(e:NativeDragEvent):void {
 var cbFiles:Array = e.clipboard.getData(
 ¬ClipboardFormats.FILE_LIST_FORMAT,
 ¬ClipboardTransferMode.CLONE_ONLY) as Array;

 var imageTypes:Array = new Array(".jpg", ".jpeg", ".png", ".gif");
 var textTypes:Array = new Array(".txt", ".html", ".xml", ".as",
 ¬".php", "rtf");

 var file:File = cbFiles[0];
 var str:String = cbFiles[0].name;
}
```

Looping through the file-type arrays

Next, you will add two separate for loops within the onDragDrop() function. The first will cycle through all the suffixes in the imageTypes array to see whether the name of the file that was dragged in contains any of those suffixes. The second loop will do the same for the textTypes array.

1 Above the closing brace of the onDragDrop() function, add this for loop:

```
for(var i:int = 0; i < imageTypes.length; i++) {
}
```

Within the braces of this for loop, you will add a conditional statement to check each element in the imageTypes array against the name of the file that was dragged in. The indexOf() method of the String class will search for the file suffixes in the imageTypes array.

2 Within the braces of the `for` loop you just created, add code so that the loop reads:

```
for(var i:int = 0; i < imageTypes.length; i++) {
 if(str.indexOf(imageTypes[i], 0) != -1) {
  workArea_mc.imgLoader.source = file.url;
 }
}
```

The first parameter of the `indexOf()` method represents the characters that are being searched for. Each time the loop repeats, it will search for a different string from the `imageTypes` array. The second parameter represents the first character in the string to begin searching. In this case, the search starts at the first character in the `str` instance and searches the whole string for the `imageType` elements. If the search finds the characters it is looking for, then a number will be returned representing the location of the string that was found. If the string is not found, the method will return −1, so the `if` statement checks whether `indexOf()` does not return -1.

If there is a match, then the file that was dragged onto the `workArea_mc` clip is one of the image types that the `UILoader` instance supports, in which case that `UILoader` instance's `workArea_mc.imgLoader.source` property is set to the file that was dropped. This will cause the dropped image to appear in the `UILoader` instance.

Finally, a second `for` loop will be added to perform a similar function for the text file types.

3 Below the closing brace of the `for` loop you just typed and above the closing brace of the `onDragDrop()` function, add the second `for` loop with this code:

```
for(var j:int = 0; j < textTypes.length; j++) {
}
```

Like the first `for` loop, this one will use a conditional statement to see whether the name of the dropped file contains one of the strings stored in an array, only this time it will be the `textTypes` array.

4 Between the braces of the new `for` loop, add a conditional statement so that the `for` loop now reads:

```
for(var j:int = 0; j < textTypes.length; j++) {
 if(str.indexOf(textTypes[j], 0) != -1) {
 }
}
```

If the conditional statement that you just added returns `true`, then you know that the user dropped a file that contains text onto the `workArea_mc` clip, in which case you use the `FileStream` class to stream the byte data from the text file into Flash. You will then store this data in a new variable named `data` and display that string in the `note_txt` text field.

5 Add code to the current `for` loop so that it reads:

```
for(var j:int = 0; j < textTypes.length; j++) {
 if(str.indexOf(textTypes[j], 0) != -1) {
   var fs:FileStream = new FileStream();
   fs.open(file, FileMode.READ);
   var data:String = fs.readUTFBytes(fs.bytesAvailable);
   fs.close();

   workArea_mc.note_txt.text = data;
 }
}
```

The line that reads:

```
var fs:FileStream = new FileStream();
```

creates a new `FileStream` instance. The next line:

```
fs.open(file, FileMode.READ);
```

uses the `open()` method to open the data in a `file` object. The first parameter points to a `file` instance, and the second parameter determines how the data will be used; in this case, the data will be read. This method can also be used to write data, which is how files can be both created and saved in AIR applications.

The next line:

```
var data:String = fs.readUTFBytes(fs.bytesAvailable);
```

stores all of the byte data from the text file in a new local variable, named `data`, as a string.

After the data has been stored, the `close()` method is used to close the file stream.

Finally, the text data from the dropped file is placed onstage in the `note_txt` field:

```
workArea_mc.note_txt.text = data;
```

The full `onDragDrop` function should read:

```
function onDragDrop(e:NativeDragEvent):void {
 var cbFiles:Array = e.clipboard.getData(
 ¬ClipboardFormats.FILE_LIST_FORMAT,
 ¬ClipboardTransferMode.CLONE_ONLY) as Array;
 var imageTypes:Array = new Array(".jpg", ".jpeg", ".png",
 ¬"gif");
 var textTypes:Array = new Array(".txt", ".html", ".htm",
 ¬".xml", "as", "php", "rtf");
 var file:File=cbFiles[0];
 var str:String=cbFiles[0].name;
```

```
for (var i:int = 0; i < imageTypes.length; i++) {
  if (str.indexOf(imageTypes[i],0) != -1) {
    workArea_mc.imgLoader.source = file.url;
  }
}
for (var j:int = 0; j < textTypes.length; j++) {
  if (str.indexOf(textTypes[j],0) != -1) {
    var fs:FileStream = new FileStream();
    fs.open(file, FileMode.READ);
    var data:String = fs.readUTFBytes(fs.bytesAvailable);
    fs.close();
    workArea_mc.note_txt.text = data;
  }
 }
}
```

6 Test your movie. The file should look about the same as the last time you tested it.

7 Try dragging a JPEG, GIF, or PNG file from the desktop or any open application over the UILoader instance in your project. Drag and drop a text file (in one of the formats stored in the textTypes array). The text should appear in the note_txt field. When you click the Print button, the most recent image and text that you selected (along with the date and user name) will print.

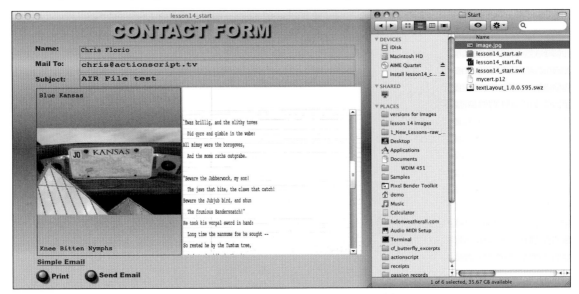

If you publish the file, you could create and distribute an installer that includes your file with the settings and icons you set earlier in this lesson. This file would install and run on Macintosh, Windows, and Linux computers.

As mentioned at the beginning of the lesson, this is just a taste of the capabilities available for AIR applications using ActionScript. Hopefully, it will lead you to a deeper study of the creative possibilities that this technology offers.

Some suggestions to try on your own

There are countless ways you could expand on the file from this lesson. Here are a few ideas:

- The scroll bar in the `workArea_mc` movie clip is always visible in this lesson. Use the techniques demonstrated in Lesson 8, "Creating and Formatting Text with ActionScript," to show and hide the scroll bar as text is added or removed from the text field.

- Create your own custom icons in your favorite graphics application and set them as the icons for the AIR application. Remember that they need to be saved as PNG files at the exact sizes described in this lesson.

- Use the filter techniques covered in Lesson 12, "Delving Deeper into Graphics and Animation with ActionScript," to apply a filter to the image that you drag into the project from this lesson. Print files with the filters applied to them.

- Use a `TextFormat` object to format text that you drag into this application.

- Add a `Camera` object to the `workArea_mc` clip and include that in your printouts.

- Create AIR applications from some of the other lesson projects that you've completed. Try creating AIR applications from some of your own Flash projects.

Review questions

1 How is a Flash project turned into an AIR application?

2 What is the purpose of a digital signature in an AIR application?

3 What are the requirements for the four graphics files to be used as an AIR application's icons?

4 Which ActionScript 3.0 classes work with AIR?

5 What event is dispatched when a file is dragged onto an object in an AIR application? What event is dispatched when the file is dropped?

6 Which AIR-specific ActionScript classes are used to read and write files?

Review answers

1 An AIR application can be created from a Flash CS5 file by choosing Adobe AIR 2 as the Player format in the Publish Settings dialog box (File > Publish Settings) for that file.

2 A digital signature in an AIR application identifies the publisher of the application, as a security measure for the end user.

3 The four graphics files to be used as an AIR application's icons must be PNG files. Their dimensions must be 128 × 128, 48 × 48, 32 × 32, and 16 × 16 pixels.

4 All of the ActionScript 3.0 language works with Adobe AIR applications. In addition to the normal ActionScript classes, there are many ActionScript classes, methods, properties, and events that are specific to AIR and that will not work with SWF files. (These AIR-only classes are called out in the ActionScript 3.0 Language and Components Reference within Flash Help.)

5 `NativeDragEvent.NATIVE_DRAG_ENTER` is dispatched when a file is dragged onto an object in an AIR application. `NativeDragEvent.NATIVE_DRAG_DROP` is dispatched when the file is dropped.

6 The `File` and `FileStream` classes are AIR-specific ActionScript classes used to read and write files.

15 USING THIRD-PARTY LIBRARIES TO EXTEND ACTIONSCRIPT

Lesson overview

In this lesson, you will learn to do the following:

- Download and install third-party ActionScript libraries.

- Use Papervision3D to add 3D capabilities to ActionScript and Flash CS5.

- Create a 3D scene with Papervision3D and add 3D objects to it.

- Add bitmaps, movie clips, and video as surface materials to 3D objects.

- Use Papervision3D methods to render a 3D scene.

- Control the movement of a 3D object with the mouse and keyboard.

- Use the Caurina Transitions library to add tweens to 3D objects.

- Use the `NetConnection`, `NetStream`, and `Video` classes to control video entirely with ActionScript.

 This lesson will take approximately 3.5 hours.

Third-party libraries such as Papervision3D and
Caurina Transitions can add powerful capabilities to
Flash CS5 and ActionScript 3.0.

If you have made it this far in the lesson files, you are by now aware of the vast capabilities of the built-in ActionScript classes. The first 14 lessons introduced techniques that only hint at the possibilities in the classes that were covered, and there are literally hundreds of additional ActionScript classes that have not been touched on in the lessons. At this point, you should be comfortable enough with the fundamentals of ActionScript 3.0 and have the knowledge you need to explore these additional capabilities.

In addition to the built-in ActionScript classes, third-party ActionScript libraries provide a wealth of capabilities that can dramatically increase the power of ActionScript in Flash CS5. Many developers have spent significant amounts of time developing powerful and useful ActionScript classes that enhance or streamline the capabilities of Flash, and a surprising number of these libraries are available for free. A quick Google search for free ActionScript 3.0 libraries returns thousands of results. Of course you want to be careful about using third-party ActionScript in your projects, but by spending time at the Adobe Flash developers center (http://www.adobe.com/devnet/ActionScript/) and at other respected ActionScript websites, you will soon get a sense of which third-party libraries are useful and reliable additions to your ActionScript toolkit.

In this lesson, you will use two of the most popular third-party ActionScript libraries: Caurina Transitions and Papervision3D.

The Caurina Transitions library (http://code.google.com/p/tweener/) is used to create and control transitions and contains a class called Tweener. This class works very similarly to the Tween class that you worked with in Lesson 3, "Creating Animation with ActionScript," but offers many more options, including the ability to tween the properties of custom classes.

Papervision3D (http://blog.papervision3d.org) is a very popular 3D engine for the Flash platform that allows you to create interactive 3D worlds in Flash.

Entire volumes could be (and have been) dedicated to Caurina Transitions and Papervision3D, and in this lesson you will just begin to learn about their capabilities. Hopefully, once you learn to use these two libraries you will be inspired to study both of them in greater depth.

Downloading and installing third-party ActionScript libraries

There are many websites where third-party ActionScript libraries can be obtained. A good starting point is Adobe's Flash Exchange (http://www.adobe.com/cfusion/exchange/index.cfm?event=productHome&exc=2). Often when downloading a third-party ActionScript library, you will be given the choice of downloading uncompiled source code as a ZIP (.zip) file, uncompiled source code using a Subversion (SVN) client, or precompiled source code as a SWC (.swc) file. There are pros and cons to all of these options, but for this lesson you will work with ActionScript libraries that have been downloaded from their host sites as uncompiled code in ZIP files.

For your convenience, these Papervision3D and Caurina Transitions libraries are included in the Lesson15 folder of this book's CD. You will find them in the Lessons > Lesson15 > Papervision_Caurina_libraries folder.

Setting Flash CS5 preferences to recognize external libraries

There are a number of ways to indicate to Flash the location of third-party ActionScript libraries that you are using. For libraries that you plan to use frequently, the easiest approach is to use the Flash CS5 preferences settings. This is the technique you will use in this lesson.

You may want at some point to place both the Papervision3D and Caurina Transitions libraries in a location that is more permanent and logical, such as in a folder that you create for custom libraries in your Flash CS5 application folder. However, for this lesson you will leave the libraries in their current location in the Lesson15 folder and set the Flash preferences to that location.

1 If it is not open, launch Flash CS5.

2 Open the preferences settings (Edit > Preferences in Windows; Flash > Preferences on the Mac) and in the Category menu choose ActionScript.

3 In the Language area at the bottom of the ActionScript Preferences screen, click the ActionScript 3.0 Settings button.

4 In the dialog box that appears, click the directory icon for the Source Path field.

5 In the Choose A Folder dialog box that appears, navigate to the Lessons > Lesson15 folder and select the folder named Papervision_Caurina_libraries.

6 Click Choose to select this folder and then click OK twice to close the Flash CS5 Preferences screen.

The libraries that you will be using for this lesson are now available to Flash CS5.

Testing the installed libraries

To be sure that the Papervision3D and Caurina Transitions libraries that you identified in the Flash Preferences are being recognized by Flash and working properly, use the test file provided in the Lesson15 folder.

1 Open TestFile.fla file from the Lessons > Lesson15 > TestFile folder.

2 Test the movie.

3 If the Papervision3D and Caurina Transitions classes are recognized and working, you should see a spinning sphere with text in it. If an error message appears, then check your preferences to make sure that the path to the Papervision_Caurina_libraries folder is set correctly and test the movie once more.

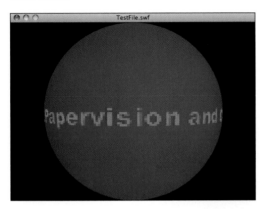

4 Once you have confirmed that the Papervision3D and Caurina Transitions libraries are available and working, close the TestFile.swf and TestFile.fla files.

Examining the completed file

To see what you will be creating in this lesson, you can examine the completed version of the lesson project.

1 Open the lesson15_complete.fla file in the Lessons > Lesson15 > Complete folder.

2 Test the movie. You should hear audio and see what looks like a full-screen image. This is actually one side of a 3D cube.

3 Click anywhere on the image and the cube will rotate 90 degrees using a 3D tween and reveal another side of the cube. Each additional click will animate the cube to another side.

4 Hold down the spacebar. While the spacebar is held down, the cube will spin away from you.

5 Release the spacebar. The cube will quickly spin back to its original location.

6 Close the lesson15_complete.swf file and then close the lesson15_complete.fla file.

This is the functionality that you will create in the lesson15_start.fla file.

Examining the starting files

To begin this lesson, you'll open the project's start file and examine it.

1 Open lesson15_start.fla, in the Lessons > Lesson15 > Start folder.

2 With the Flash Timeline visible, notice that the project has just a single layer, called background, which contains static images. As the layer name implies, these are background images, and they will not have code associated with them.

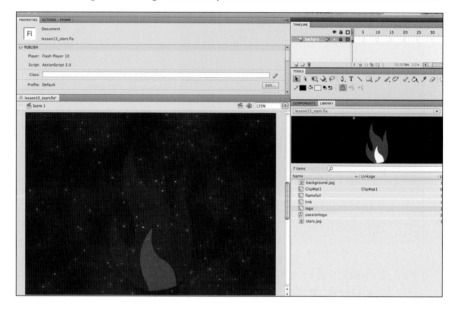

● **Note:** If you need to review the basics of creating an instance of a movie clip from the library using its linkage identifier, see Lesson 7, "Using Arrays and Loops in ActionScript 3.0."

3 If it is not already visible, open the Library panel. The library contains a number of items all of which are parts that make up the movie clip named ClipMat1. Notice that this movie clip has its linkage identifier set to ClipMat1. You will write ActionScript to assign this clip as the material for the surface of one side of a Papervision3D cube.

For many types of projects, it makes sense to write all the code for the project in external ActionScript files. This approach enables members of a team to work on design and code independently. It also allows developers to write their ActionScript in other applications besides Flash if they choose. In this project, all code for the project will be in a file called Cube3D.as. The skeleton of this file is provided for you in the Lesson15 > Start folder. Before you examine this file, you will set it as the main class for the lesson15_start.fla file.

Setting the main class file in Flash CS5

In Lesson 4, "Creating ActionScript in External Files," you wrote code in an external class file and then added ActionScript in the Flash Timeline to create instances of your ActionScript class. In this lesson, all of the code that you will write for the entire lesson will be in an external class file; there will be no code at all added to the Timeline. In a situation like this, in which an external class replaces the Timeline as the location of the main code for the project, you can indicate that the external class will be used as the main class in the Flash Property inspector.

In this lesson, the name of the main class you will use will be Cube3D. You will assign Cube3D as the main class for the lesson15_start.fla file now.

1 In Flash, make sure that the Property inspector is visible.

2 Make sure that nothing is selected onstage by clicking in the gray workspace outside the Stage area.

3 In the Property inspector, in the Publish settings area, locate the empty field named Class, and type Cube3D in this field.

The Cube3D class now becomes the main class for this file. Notice that you typed "Cube3D," which is the name of the class, not "Cube3D.as," which is the name of the file that contains the class.

Examining the Cube3D.as class file

After you have assigned an existing class file as the main class file of a FLA file you can easily access this file in the Property inspector.

1 In the Property inspector, next to the field where you just typed the class name Cube3D, click the pencil icon. This step launches the Cube3D.as file (if it is not already open) in Flash and makes it the active file. If you have Flash Builder on your machine, you may be prompted to choose between launching the file in Flash Builder or Flash Professional. For now, choose Flash Professional.

Note: If you need to review the basics of this structure, see Lesson 4.

2 Notice that a lot of code has already been created for you in this file including the package tags, a number of import statements, and the shell for a class named Cube3D.

3 Notice that the first series of import statements that have been added to this file are all from the flash package. Many of these are for classes that you have already used. When you work with these built-in classes in the Flash CS5 Timeline, import statements may be added for you automatically, but code in the Timeline will work with or without these import statements. Remember that this is not the case in external ActionScript files. Any classes that are referenced in an external ActionScript file must be imported. If you are not used to working with external class files, you may need to develop the habit of importing all the classes you use in your own files.

4 In this project, you will also use the Tweener class from the Caurina Transitions library. Notice the import statement for the caurina.transitions.Tweener class.

5 This project uses many Papervision3D classes. Notice that these also have been imported for you. Each of these classes will be discussed as you add code that uses them later in the lesson, starting with the `BasicView` class, which is one of the most useful Papervision3D classes.

Using the Papervision3D BasicView class

Papervision3D is a very popular open source 3D ActionScript library originally developed by Carlos Ulloa. It is a full-blown 3D engine for Flash that allows you to add 3D scenes to a Flash project that can include models, cameras, lights, and a variety of materials and shading types. It even allows external 3D models created in third-party 3D programs such as 3DStudioMax to be added to your Flash projects and manipulated with ActionScript. Papervision3D allows objects to be controlled in three dimensions, which are then rendered and translated to the 2D coordinate system of the Flash Stage.

A Flash Papervision3D project consists of a number of elements, each of which has a corresponding Papervision3D class. These elements include 3D scenes, where the three-dimensional parts of the Flash project take place; cameras, which are used to view a scene; a viewport, which determines which part of the scene is rendered; and a render engine, which actually does the work of rendering your project to the Flash Stage. All of these elements need to be added to a Papervision3D project before 3D objects can be added, manipulated, and viewed.

Adding all these elements would mean creating instances of the `Scene3D`, `Camera3D`, `ViewPort3D`, and `BasicRenderEngine` classes—except that Papervision3D also includes a class called `BasicView`, which automatically creates instances of all these basic elements of a Papervision3D scene. If a class that you create extends the Papervision3D `BasicView` class, then your class will already include a scene, camera, viewport, and render engine. You will modify the `Cube3D` class so that it extends the `BasicView` class.

Extending the BasicView class

As discussed in Lesson 4, you use the keyword `extends` to set one class as a child of another class. After you do this, the child class inherits all of the methods, properties, and events of the parent class. You will set the `Cube3D` class to extend the `BasicView` class, making `Cube3D` a child of `BasicView`.

In the Cube3D.as file, locate the line

```
public class Cube3D
```

and modify it so that it now reads as follows:

```
public class Cube3D extends BasicView
```

The Cube3D class will now automatically create instances of Papervision3D's Scene3D, Camera3D, ViewPort3D, and BasicRenderEngine classes. You can now begin adding 3D objects and materials to this project and render them using the rendering methods that are built into the BasicView class.

Keep in mind that the parent, or super, class of the Cube3D class is now the BasicView class. You can call the methods of a parent class from within a child class by using the keyword super, which you will do soon, after you create some variables and the constructor function for the Cube3D class.

Creating variables for the Cube3D class

Typically in an ActionScript class, the first things that are written in the file after the class declarations are the variables that will be available to the entire class. You will use two such variables. This project will work with a 3D cube, so you will create a variable named cube that will be used to reference an instance of the Cube class. You will also create a Boolean named zooming that will be used later in the file to determine whether or not the cube is currently being tweened away from the user. You will add these variables now.

1 Below the opening curly brace of the Cube3D class, create the cube variable by inserting this line:

```
private var cube:Cube;
```

Notice that the data type is set to Cube. The Cube class is part of the Papervision3D library. A cube is one of seven types of "primitive" 3D objects that can be created with Papervision3D. For more information about the other primitives, see the Papervision3D reference (http://docs.pv3d.org).

Soon you will create an instance of the Cube class and store it in this variable. By declaring it here, you will be able to reference the cube everywhere in the Cube3D class.

2 Below the line you just inserted, create the zooming variable:

```
private var zooming:Boolean = false;
```

Later you will create event listeners that will zoom a 3D cube when the user presses the spacebar. Since the cube will not be zooming when the project launches, the initial value of the zooming variable is set to false.

Now you will create the constructor function for this class.

Creating the constructor function for the Cube3D class

In Lesson 4, you learned that the constructor function in an ActionScript class file is a function that is given the same name as the class and is called automatically when the class is instantiated. In this file, that would mean that the constructor would be called `Cube3D()`.

You will create that function now and then add code to it that will be executed as soon as the class is run.

1 Below the last line of code that you added, create the constructor function by typing the following code:

```
public function Cube3D()
 {

 }
```

The constructor function you just created will perform a number of tasks, but the first thing it will do is call the constructor function of the parent class. You can call the constructor function of a parent class by calling the method `super()` within a class's constructor function.

When one class extends another class, the parent class's constructor function is called automatically. However, when you want to pass specific parameters to the parent's constructor function, you will want to use the `super()` method to call the parent's constructor explicitly.

The parent class of this file is `BasicView`. You will explicitly set four of the parameters of the `BasicView` class when you call its constructor. Do this now by calling the `super()` method.

2 Between the curly braces of the `Cube3D` constructor function, add this code:

```
super(stage.stageWidth,stage.stageHeight,true,true);
```

The first two parameters of the `BasicView` class's constructor set the width and height of the scene's viewport. In the code you just typed, you set the viewport to match the Flash Stage.

The third parameter is a Boolean that determines whether the `BasicView` instance will scale to match the Flash Stage. You set this to `true`.

The fourth parameter is also a Boolean and is used to set the `interactive` property of a `BasicView` instance. This allows the entire scene to detect interactions.

Materials within the scene also have an `interactive` property that must be set to `true` for every material that will need to respond to ActionScript events. Later in the lesson you will set this property for the materials that you use.

Note: In the context of an ActionScript class, methods are the same as functions. In this lesson, the two terms are used interchangeably.

You will now add code so that the Cube3D constructor will call two additional functions. One is a function called makeCube() that you will create soon. This function will be used to create a cube and set its properties. Add a call to this function now.

3 Below the last line of code you typed, add the following line:

```
makeCube();
```

The second function that you will call already exists. It is the startRendering()function, which is part of the parent BasicView class. This function works similarly to an ENTER_FRAME listener and is used to render the BasicView instance at the frame rate of the Flash project.

4 Below the line you just added, type the following code:

```
startRendering();
```

When the startRendering() method is called, a function of the BasicView class named onRenderTick() automatically begins executing on every frame and will render the scene. You will add some additional functionality to this onRenderTick() function using the super keyword later in the lesson.

The final elements that you add to the constructor function are event listeners for the KEY_UP and KEY_DOWN events. These are the same events that you have used in previous lessons. You will see that in a Papervision3D project, all of the ActionScript that you have already learned works in the usual way. Also, most Papervision3D-specific code works similarly to built-in ActionScript code.

5 Above the closing curly brace of the Cube3D constructor function, add these lines:

```
stage.addEventListener(KeyboardEvent.KEY_DOWN, onKeyD);
stage.addEventListener(KeyboardEvent.KEY_UP, onKeyU);
```

The entire constructor function should now read as follows:

```
public function Cube3D()
  {
    super(stage.stageWidth,stage.stageHeight,true,true);
    makeCube();
    startRendering();
    stage.addEventListener(KeyboardEvent.KEY_DOWN, onKeyD);
    stage.addEventListener(KeyboardEvent.KEY_UP, onKeyU);
  }
```

Next you will start to create the makeCube() method, which, not surprisingly, will create a cube.

Creating and modifying a 3D cube

You will use the makeCube() method to create an instance of the Papervision3D Cube() class. A Papervision3D cube is a six-sided 3D object. Using Papervision3D methods and properties, you animate a cube and add a separate surface material to each side of the cube.

First you will create the shell for the makeCube() method.

1 Below the closing curly brace of the Cube3D constructor function, insert the following code:

```
private function makeCube():void
{

}
```

All 3D primitives in Papervision3D are given a material or materials that determine what the surface of the object will be. A Papervision3D object can have a simple wireframe material or a solid-color material. A material can also be a bitmap image, a movie clip, or a video file.

If the primitive has just a single side, then it will have only a single material property. Since a 3D cube has six sides, it can have up to six materials, which are referenced in its MaterialsList property. A Papervision3D materials list is similar to an ActionScript array in that it can store a list of items. The MaterialsList property for a cube can store a list of up to six materials that can be assigned to the six sides of the cube.

Before you create the actual cube, you will first create a MaterialsList instance and populate it with a single material.

2 Below the opening curly brace of the makeCube() function, add this code:

```
    var materials:MaterialsList = new MaterialsList();
```

Now you will create a material that will be used on the cube. As mentioned, one of the materials that can be used on a Papervision3D object is a bitmap file. Papervision3D has a data type called BitmapFileMaterial that can be used to load an external bitmap file to use as a material. You will create a BitmapFileMaterial instance to store a reference to an external JPEG file that you will apply as a material to your cube.

3 On the line below the code you just added, type:

```
var imageMat1:BitmapFileMaterial = new BitmapFileMaterial
¬ ("../assets/back.jpg");
```

When this code runs, a file named back.jpg will be loaded from the Assets folder of the Lesson15 folder.

Now you will set this material's `interactive` property to `true` so that later in the lesson you can add a CLICK event for this material.

4   On a new line below the code you just added, type:

```
imageMat1.interactive = true;
```

Now you will add this material to the `materials` list you created using the `addMaterial()` method of the `MaterialsList` class.

5   On a line below the code from the previous step, add this code:

```
materials.addMaterial(imageMat1,"all");
```

The first parameter for the `addMaterial()` method is the name of the material added to the materials list.

The second parameter is a string that indicates the side of the cube to which this material will be added. For now, this property has been set to `"all"`. The bitmap material will be assigned to all six sides of the cube when you create it. Later in the lesson, you will add other materials to the materials list.

Now that you have your materials ready, you will create a Papervision3D cube in the `cube` instance.

6   Below the last line you typed, add the following code:

```
cube = new Cube(materials,640,640,480,4,4,4);
```

The cube has a number of parameters. The first determines the materials list that will be used on the cube. The next three set the width, depth, and height of the cube; these were set to 640, 640, and 480 units, respectively.

All Papervision3D objects are made from a mesh of triangles. The more triangles in a model, the higher quality the model and the more processor-intensive the model will be to render. The final three parameters that were set for the cube determine the number of triangles used to create the width, height, and depth of the cube. These were all set to 4.

Next, you will add an `OBJECT_CLICK` event listener to the cube. You will use a Papervision3D `OBJECT_CLICK` event that works in the same way as the usual ActionScript `CLICK` event listener.

7   On a line below the last line you typed, add this code:

```
cube.addEventListener(InteractiveScene3DEvent.OBJECT_CLICK,
¬onClick);
```

Notice that this CLICK event is not a MouseEvent event but is a Papervision3D InteractiveScene3Devent event. In all other ways, the syntax should be familiar to you. Soon you will create the onClick() function, and then later you will use that function to animate the cube.

Your next step, though, is to add the cube you created to the scene.

Placing the cube in the scene

You place a Papervision3D object into a scene in the same way that you place any object on the Flash Stage, using the addChild() method. This will be the last code you add to the makeCube() function for the time being.

1 Add this line below the code you just typed:

```
scene.addChild(cube);
```

In Papervision3D as in ordinary ActionScript, the z-axis represents the depth of an object. Higher z values represent distances farther from the viewer, and lower values bring the object closer and make it appear larger. The default z value of 3D objects is zero.

2 Below the last line you typed, add a line to bring the cube closer to the viewer:

```
cube.z = -300;
```

The entire makeCube() function at this point should read as follows:

```
private function makeCube():void
{
 var materials:MaterialsList = new MaterialsList();
 var imageMat1:BitmapFileMaterial = new
¬BitmapFileMaterial("../assets/back.jpg");
 imageMat1.interactive = true;
 materials.addMaterial(imageMat1,"all");
 cube = new Cube(materials,640,640,480,4,4,4);
 cube.addEventListener(InteractiveScene3DEvent.OBJECT_CLICK,
¬onClick);
 scene.addChild(cube);
 cube.z = -300;
}
```

If you tested the movie at this point, you would receive error messages because three functions were referred to that do not yet exist. To be able to test what you have done so far, you will need to create the shell for the onClick(), onKeyD(), and onKeyU() functions.

3 On a new line below the closing curly brace for the `makeCube()` function, add the shell for all three functions:

```
private function onKeyD(e:KeyboardEvent):void
  {

  }

private function onKeyU(e:KeyboardEvent):void
  {

  }

private function onClick(e:InteractiveScene3DEvent):void
  {
  }
```

4 Save the Cube3D.as file and test the movie. If you see what looks like a full-screen bitmap image, you have been successful so far.

This would have been a lot of work if the result were just a single bitmap image, but what you are actually viewing is a 3D cube with the image mapped as a material onto the surface of its sides. Soon you will add code to animate the cube so that you can see it in all its three-dimensional glory.

Animating the 3D cube

As mentioned, a method of the `BasicView` class called `onRenderTick()` will be taking place repeatedly at the frame rate of the Flash file. You will create a local version of that function and add some code to it to animate the cube when the spacebar is pressed. First, however, you will add some code to the `OnKeyD()` function to determine whether the spacebar has been pressed and to set the zooming property to true when it has been pressed.

1   Within the curly braces of the onKeyD() function, add the following code:

```
if (e.keyCode == Keyboard.SPACE)
  {

  }
```

2   Between the curly braces of the conditional statement you just added, insert this line:

```
zooming = true;
```

The full onKeyD() function should read as follows:

```
function onKeyD(e:KeyboardEvent):void
  {
    if (e.keyCode == Keyboard.SPACE)
    {
      zooming = true;
    }
  }
```

Overriding the onRenderTick() function

Next you will use the zooming property to determine when to animate the cube. You will do this in the onRenderTick() function.

Recall that the onRenderTick() method is part of the BasicView class, and that it was set to start executing with the startRender() call you added earlier in the lesson. The reason that 3D graphics were drawn on the Stage when you tested the movie a few steps back is because the onRenderTick() method was executed.

Frequently in a Papervision3D project that uses a class that extends BasicView, it is helpful to add some functionality to the onRenderTick() method. You can do this by overriding the parent class's method and then making your own version of the onRenderTick() method. You use the keyword Override when you want to create a function that replaces the parent function of the same name. You will add your version of the onRenderTick() function now.

1   Below the shell for the onClick() function and above the final two closing curly braces, add the shell for the new onRenderTick() function:

```
override protected function onRenderTick(e:Event=null):void
  {
  }
```

Often when you override a function from a parent class, you do so because you want to add to the parent method's functionality rather than replace it. When this is the case, you can retain all of the parent function's actions by calling the original function from within the overriding function using the keyword `super`. You will do this now to retain all of the rendering functionality in the `BasicView` class's `onRenderTick()` function.

2   Between the curly braces of the `onRenderTick()` function, add this line:

```
super.onRenderTick();
```

Next you will add a conditional statement that checks to see if the `zooming` property is `true`. Remember that this property will be set to `true` when the spacebar is being pressed.

3   Below the last line that you added, insert the following code:

```
if (zooming)
  {

  }
```

While the spacebar is being pressed (`zooming`), you will animate two properties of the cube. You will make the cube move away from the screen by adding to its z property, and you will make the cube spin on its own y-axis by adding to a Papervision3D property called `localRotationY`.

4   Below the opening curly brace of the conditional statement you just created, insert the following code:

```
cube.z +=  5;
cube.localRotationY++;
```

The full `onRenderTick()` function should now read as follows:

```
override protected function onRenderTick(e:Event=null):void
  {
   super.onRenderTick();
   if (zooming)
   {
     cube.z +=  5;
     cube.localRotationY++;
   }
  }
```

5   Save the Cube3D.as file and test the movie. When the lesson15_start.swf file appears, press the spacebar. The cube should rotate away from you.

At this point, the cube will continue to rotate away even after the spacebar is released, but soon you will add code to animate the cube back when the spacebar is released, using the `onKeyU()` function.

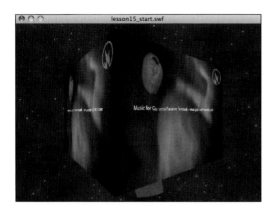

6 Close the lesson15_start.swf file to return to the Flash authoring environment.

Using Caurina Tweener to animate the 3D Cube

In the last step, you created code that makes the cube spin into the distance when the spacebar is pressed. Now you will write code to make the cube spin back to its original position whenever the spacebar is released. You already created a function that will respond to KEY_UP events, so you will write this code in that function.

Before you add code to animate the cube back to its starting point, you will turn off the animation that was set in motion when the spacebar was pressed. The animation occurs when the zooming property is true, so the first thing you will do when the Key_UP event occurs is set this property to false.

1 Locate the onKeyU() function, and in between this function's curly braces, add the following line:

```
zooming = false;
```

Rather than simply changing properties of the cube when a key is released, you will use the Tweener class to animate the cube. The Tweener class works very similarly to the built-in Tween class that you used in Lesson 3. In fact, both Tweener and the built-in Tween class are based on code originally created by Grant Skinner. However, the Tweener class, which was created by Zhe Fernando, allows you to create tweens that can animate any type of object using properties of any class, including custom classes. This capability enables Tweener to animate the unique properties of 3D objects found in the Papervision3D classes.

You will add two tweens using a Tweener class for each of the properties you animated in the onRenderTick() method. The first tween is the z property of the cube.

2 Below the code you just added, insert the following line:

```
Tweener.addTween(cube,{z:-300,time:2});
```

This line calls the addTween() method directly from the Tweener class. The first parameter between the parentheses is the name of the object to be tweened.

After this parameter are curly braces that contain two name:value pairs. The first one indicates the parameter that will be tweened (z) and the value to which it will be tweened (–300). This setting will return the cube to its original z position. The second name:value pair indicates that this process will take place over two seconds.

Now add a similar tween to animate the cube's localRotationY property.

3   On a line below the code you just added, insert the following code:

```
Tweener.addTween(cube,{localRotationY:0,time:2});
```

This line also uses the addTween() method, this time to animate the localRotationY property of the cube to return the cube to its original position of zero over two seconds.

4   Test the movie to try the tweens you just added. Pressing the spacebar will still animate the cube away from you, but now releasing the spacebar will cause the cube to spin back to its original position over two seconds.

5   Close the lesson15_start.swf file to return to your code.

In the next task, you will add another addTween() method. This time you place the tween within the onClick() method. You will write this code so that each time the cube is clicked, it will rotate 90 degrees from its current position to reveal a different face.

Rotating the cube when it is clicked

You have already created an onClick() function that responds when the cube is clicked. Now you will add a tween within that function to rotate the cube. Since you want to be sure that each click will rotate the cube exactly 90 degrees, you do not want the user to be able to set multiple tweens in motion at the same time. You will therefore create the tween inside a conditional statement that prevents more than one tween from occurring simultaneously.

1   Locate the onClick() function. Between the curly braces of the onClick() function, add this conditional statement:

```
if (! Tweener.isTweening(e.displayObject3D))
    {

    }
```

This statement checks the isTweening property of the Tweening class and will execute the code in the conditional statement only if a tween is not (!) occurring.

2 To tween the cube 90 degrees over two seconds when the cube is clicked, add this code between the braces of the conditional statement you just added:

```
Tweener.addTween(cube,{localRotationY:cube.localRotationY +
¬90,time:2});
```

By now, the code for the `addTween()` method should be becoming familiar to you.

3 Test the movie once more. The spacebar still behaves as before, but now when you click the cube, it should rotate 90 degrees to reveal another face.

At this point, you can click to rotate from face to face of the cube, but the materials of all four of the visible faces are the same image. In the next tasks, you will add different types of materials to the different faces of the cube. They will include a movie clip as a material and video files as materials.

4 Close the lesson15_start.swf file to return to your code.

Adding a movie clip as a material on a 3D object

Earlier in the lesson, you assigned a JPEG image as the material for all the sides of the cube using the Papervision3D `BitmapFileMaterial` class. Now you will add some other types of materials to some of the cube's sides, starting with a movie clip.

Any Flash display object can be used as a Papervision3D material, including `MovieClip` and `Sprite` instances created in code as well as movie clip symbols in the Flash CS5 library. To use a symbol from the Flash CS5 library, you can use the Papervision3D `MovieAssetMaterial` class. Using a movie clip as a material means that your Papervision3D objects can contain any type of graphic content that Flash can display, including images, text, and animation, but it also means that materials can have their own interactivity built into them. This feature offers many powerful capabilities that would be hard to reproduce in most other 3D environments.

The ClipMat1 movie clip in the lesson15_start.fla library contains a background image and two nested movie clips: one named `logo`, containing an animated logo, and one named `link`, with some text. You will add ClipMat1 as the surface material of one of the sides of the cube and then add some code to respond when the nested `link` clip is clicked.

1 In the Cube3D.as file, locate the `makeCube()` function and find the line that reads:

```
imageMat1.interactive = true;
```

2 Below this line, create a new instance of the `MovieAssetMaterial` class:

```
var clipMat1:MovieAssetMaterial = new MovieAssetMaterial
¬("ClipMat1",false,true,false,true);
```

Parameters of the MovieAssetMaterial class

The variable you just created, called `clipMat1`, stores a reference to a new `MovieAssetMaterial` instance with five parameters that have been set.

The first parameter is a string that contains the linkage identifier of the movie clip in the Flash library that will be used as a material (for a review of how to use movie clip symbols in the library with ActionScript, see Lesson 7).

The second parameter is a Boolean for `transparency`, which is set to `false` because the movie clip that is being used has no transparency.

The third parameter is another Boolean, for `animation`. This is set to `true` because the movie clip contains animation that needs to be rendered on each frame. Keep in mind that rendering `MovieAssetMaterial` animation is more processor-intensive than just drawing the movie clip material once on a 3D object.

The fourth parameter is a Boolean called `createUnique`, which specifies whether you want to create a new instance of the movie clip or use an existing one. This property is set to `false`.

The fifth parameter sets the `precise` parameter to `true`, which creates a better-quality rendering of the movie clip's contents but again is more processor-intensive than leaving this parameter at its default of `false`.

Before you add this `MovieAssetMaterial` instance to your materials list, set one more property to make this material interactive. This is necessary to make `MovieAssetMaterial` respond to ActionScript events.

3 Below the line you just added, insert this code:

```
clipMat1.interactive = true;
```

Now add this `MovieAssetMaterial` instance to your materials list.

4 Locate the line of code in the `makeCube()` function that reads:

```
materials.addMaterial(imageMat1,"all");
```

and below that line, insert the following code:

```
materials.addMaterial(clipMat1,"right");
```

5 Save the Cube3D.as file and test the movie. When the cube appears, click it to tween it 90 degrees. Do this three times, and you will see that one of the cube's surfaces now contains the `MovieAssetMaterial` instance that you just created.

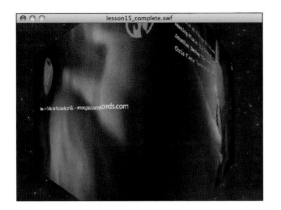

6 Close the lesson15_start.swf file to return to your code.

You will now add an event listener to respond when the movie clip named link within the ClipMat1 clip is clicked.

Adding a CLICK event to a movie clip nested in MovieAssetMaterial

If you use a movie clip in a `MovieAssetMaterial` instance in Papervision3D and set its `interactive` property to `true` as you did in the previous steps, then this clip and any nested objects it contains can receive and respond to events the way they normally do in ActionScript. You will take advantage of this feature by creating a `navigateToURL()` method that executes when the user clicks the nested `link` clip in the `clipMat1` object.

To do this, you will first create a variable within the `makeCube()` function that stores a reference to the link clip.

1 In the `makeCube()` function, locate the line that reads:

```
cube.z = -300;
```

and below this line, insert the following code.

```
var clip:MovieClip = MovieClip(MovieClip(clipMat1.movie).
¬getChildByName("link"));
```

The `clip` variable you just created stores a reference to the link instance using an ActionScript method called `getChildbyName()`.

Now you can add a listener to the referenced clip.

2 Below the line that you just inserted, type the following code:

```
clip.addEventListener(MouseEvent.CLICK,link);
```

You will now of course need to create a function named `link()` to respond when the clip is clicked. Since this code should be very familiar by now, you will write the entire function in a single step.

3 Below the closing curly brace of the makeCube() function, insert the following code:

```
private function link(e:Event):void
  {
  navigateToURL(new URLRequest("http://www.passionrecords.
  ¬com"),"_blank");
  }
```

4 Save the Cube3D.as file and test the movie. When the cube appears, click it to rotate it 90 degrees, and repeat this until the surface with the movie clip material appears. Then click the text in the upper-left corner of the movie clip material. Your default browser should navigate to the URL in the link() function.

5 Close the lesson15_start.swf file and return to the Cube3D.as file.

Next you will add some video files as materials to sides of the cube. To do this, you will need to delve a little deeper into the process of controlling video with ActionScript.

Adding video as a material on a 3D object

Using video as a Papervision3D material is easy and very similar to using a movie clip asset. Instead of using the Papervision3D MovieAssetMaterial class, you use the VideoStreamMaterial class. In previous lessons, when you controlled video you used the FLVPlayback component. This very useful component can save a lot of coding; however, when you're using video as a Papervision3D material, you may find it more efficient to bypass the FLVPlayback component and work with video using only ActionScript. To do this requires the use of three ActionScript classes that you have not been introduced to yet: the NetConnection class, the NetStream class, and the Video class.

About the NetConnection, NetStream, and Video classes

The NetConnection, NetStream, and Video classes work together to enable ActionScript to load and play video files and control them in many ways. An in-depth study of all three classes will yield a broad range of tools for working with streaming media.

You can think of a NetConnection instance as a large pipeline that enables multiple streams of content to flow into a compiled Flash file. After a NetConnection instance is established, NetStream instances send individual streams of content through the NetConnection instance. Each NetStream instance can, for example, contain one streaming video file. The NetStream class contains many properties and methods for controlling video.

The Video class extends the DisplayObject class and is basically a container for displaying video. After a video file is streamed into Flash using a NetStream instance, it can be displayed on the Stage using a Video instance.

Thus, the process of viewing streaming video with ActionScript in Flash is to create a NetConnection instance, send one or more NetStream instances through the NetConnection instance, and then display the streaming video data in a Video instance. In this lesson, you use these three classes to stream two distinct video files into Flash so that they can be used as Papervision3D materials.

Creating NetConnection, NetStream, and Video instances

Within the makeCube() function, you will use NetConnection, NetStream, and Video instances to stream video into the lesson file and then use the Papervision3D VideoStreamMaterial class to turn the video into materials for sides of the cube.

Start by creating a new NetConnection instance.

1   In the makeCube() function, locate the line that reads:

```
clipMat1.interactive = true;
```

and below that line insert a new NetConnection instance with this code:

```
var nc:NetConnection = new NetConnection;
```

Note: For more information about Flash Media Server, visit http://www.adobe.com/products/flashmediastreaming/.

2   On a line below the code you just added, call the `connect` method of the `NetConnection` instance that you just created:

```
nc.connect(null);
```

The parameter for the `connect()` method is always set to `null` unless you are connecting to live streaming server software such as Flash Media Server.

Next you will create two `NetStream` instances: one for each of two video files that you will use as materials.

3   On a line below the code you just added, insert the following lines:

```
var ns1:NetStream = new NetStream(nc);
var ns2:NetStream = new NetStream(nc);
```

Notice that the parameter for both `NetStream` instances was set to the `NetConnection` instance named `nc` that you just created. As mentioned, multiple `NetStream` instances can flow through a single `NetConnection` instance.

Now you will play specific video clips in each `NetStream` instance.

4   Below the code you just typed, add this code:

```
ns1.play("../assets/left.f4v");
ns2.play("../assets/front.f4v");
```

Two video files from the Lesson 15 Assets folder will now be loaded and play through the two `NetStream` instances.

The next step may seem a little obscure. The purpose of the `client` property of the `NetStream` class is to indicate the location to store any metadata that is included in content that is being streamed. If a client for this metadata is not assigned, an error will occur when the metadata arrives from a `NetStream`.

Even though you will not be using the metadata from the streaming video files in this lesson, you still need to set the `client` property for each of the `NetStream` instances to avoid errors. Do this now.

5   Below the code you just typed, add the following lines:

```
ns1.client = new Object();
ns2.client = new Object();
```

A new object has been created to store each `NetStream` instance's metadata. Again, this metadata will not be needed for this lesson, but the step is required nonetheless.

Next you will create two new `Video` instances to display the `NetStream` instances.

6   On lines below the last code you added, insert this code:

```
var vid1:Video = new Video();
var vid2:Video = new Video();
```

7 The `attachNetSream()` method of the `Video` class is what connects a `NetStream` instance to a `Video` instance. Add code below the lines you just typed that calls this method on your `Video` instances.

```
vid1.attachNetStream(ns1);
vid2.attachNetStream(ns2);
```

8 In a normal Flash project, you would just use the `addChild()` method to display the video clips on the Flash Stage. However, in this case, the video files will be used as Papervision3D materials, so you will instead create two instances of the `VideoStreamMaterial` class. On a line below the last code you added, enter this code:

```
var vidMat1:VideoStreamMaterial = new
¬VideoStreamMaterial(vid1,ns1);
var vidMat2:VideoStreamMaterial = new
¬VideoStreamMaterial(vid2,ns2);
```

Notice that each `VideoStreamMaterial` instance takes a parameter that indicates a `Video` instance and a second parameter that indicates the `NetStream` instance that streams content to the `Video` instance.

Next set both the `animated` and `interactive` properties for each `VideoStreamMaterial` instance to `true`.

9 Below the code you just inserted, add these lines:

```
vidMat1.animated = true;
vidMat1.interactive = true;
vidMat2.animated = true;
vidMat2.interactive = true;
```

Finally you will add these two `VideoStreamMaterial` instances to the materials list so they will appear as sides of the cube.

10 Locate the line within the `makeCube()` function that reads:

```
materials.addMaterial(clipMat1,"right");
```

and below that line, insert the following code:

```
materials.addMaterial(vidMat1,"left");
materials.addMaterial(vidMat2,"front");
```

The full `makeCube()` function should now read as follows:

```
private function makeCube():void
  {
    var materials:MaterialsList = new MaterialsList();

    var imageMat1:BitmapFileMaterial = new
    ¬BitmapFileMaterial("../assets/back.jpg");
```

(code continues on next page)

```
imageMat1.interactive = true;

var clipMat1:MovieAssetMaterial = new
¬MovieAssetMaterial("ClipMat1",false,true,false,true);
clipMat1.interactive = true;

var nc:NetConnection = new NetConnection;
nc.connect(null);
var ns1:NetStream = new NetStream(nc);
var ns2:NetStream = new NetStream(nc);
ns1.client = new Object();
ns2.client = new Object();
ns1.play("../assets/left.f4v");
ns2.play("../assets/front.f4v");
var vid1:Video = new Video();
var vid2:Video = new Video();
vid1.attachNetStream(ns1);
vid2.attachNetStream(ns2);

var vidMat1:VideoStreamMaterial = new
¬VideoStreamMaterial(vid1,ns1);
var vidMat2:VideoStreamMaterial = new
¬VideoStreamMaterial(vid2,ns2);

vidMat1.animated = true;
vidMat1.interactive = true;
vidMat2.animated = true;
vidMat2.interactive = true;


materials.addMaterial(imageMat1,"all");
materials.addMaterial(clipMat1,"right");
materials.addMaterial(vidMat1,"left");
materials.addMaterial(vidMat2,"front");


cube = new Cube(materials,640,640,480,4,4,4);
cube.addEventListener(InteractiveScene3DEvent.OBJECT_CLICK,
¬onClick);

scene.addChild(cube);
cube.z = -300;

var clip:MovieClip = MovieClip(MovieClip(clipMat1.movie).
¬getChildByName("link"));
clip.addEventListener(MouseEvent.CLICK,link);
}
```

11 Save the Cube3D.as file and test the movie. As soon as the lesson15_start.swf file appears, you should hear audio. This is from the audio track of one of the video files. Click the cube to rotate it; do this four times, and you should see the JPEG material, the movie clip material, and each of the two video materials. Press the spacebar, and the cube should rotate to reveal all four materials while the video files continue to play. Release the spacebar, and the cube animates back to its original position.

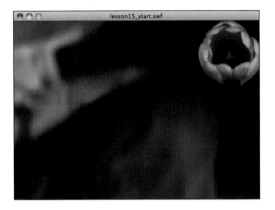

Here is the entire completed code for this project:

```
package
{

  import flash.display.MovieClip;
  import flash.events.*;
  import flash.media.Video;
  import flash.net.NetConnection;
  import flash.net.NetStream;
  import flash.net.navigateToURL;
  import flash.net.URLRequest;
  import flash.display.Stage;
  import flash.ui.Keyboard;

  import caurina.transitions.Tweener;

  import org.papervision3d.events.InteractiveScene3DEvent;
  import org.papervision3d.materials.BitmapFileMaterial;
  import org.papervision3d.materials.VideoStreamMaterial;
  import org.papervision3d.materials.MovieAssetMaterial;
  import org.papervision3d.materials.utils.MaterialsList;
  import org.papervision3d.objects.DisplayObject3D;
  import org.papervision3d.objects.primitives.Cube;
  import org.papervision3d.view.BasicView;
```

(code continues on next page)

```
public class Cube3D extends BasicView
{

 private var cube:Cube;
 private var zooming:Boolean = false;


 public function Cube3D_reference()
 {
  super(stage.stageWidth,stage.stageHeight,true,true);
  makeCube();
  startRendering();
  stage.addEventListener(KeyboardEvent.KEY_DOWN, onKeyD);
  stage.addEventListener(KeyboardEvent.KEY_UP, onKeyU);
 }

 private function makeCube():void
 {
  var materials:MaterialsList = new MaterialsList();

  var imageMat1:BitmapFileMaterial = new
  ¬BitmapFileMaterial("../assets/back.jpg");
  imageMat1.interactive = true;

  var clipMat1:MovieAssetMaterial = new MovieAssetMaterial
  ¬("ClipMat1",false,true,false,true);
  clipMat1.interactive = true;

  var nc:NetConnection = new NetConnection;
  nc.connect(null);
  var ns1:NetStream = new NetStream(nc);
  var ns2:NetStream = new NetStream(nc);
  ns1.client = new Object();
  ns2.client = new Object();
  ns1.play("../assets/left.f4v");
  ns2.play("../assets/front.f4v");
  var vid1:Video = new Video();
  var vid2:Video = new Video();
  vid1.attachNetStream(ns1);
  vid2.attachNetStream(ns2);

  var vidMat1:VideoStreamMaterial = new
  ¬VideoStreamMaterial(vid1,ns1);
  var vidMat2:VideoStreamMaterial = new
  ¬VideoStreamMaterial(vid2,ns2);

  vidMat1.animated = true;
```

```
  vidMat1.interactive = true;
  vidMat2.animated = true;
  vidMat2.interactive = true;


  materials.addMaterial(imageMat1,"all");
  materials.addMaterial(clipMat1,"right");
  materials.addMaterial(vidMat1,"left");
  materials.addMaterial(vidMat2,"front");


  cube = new Cube(materials,640,640,480,4,4,4);
  cube.addEventListener(InteractiveScene3DEvent.OBJECT_CLICK,
  ¬onClick);
  scene.addChild(cube);
  cube.z = -300;


  var clip:MovieClip = MovieClip(MovieClip(clipMat1.movie).
  ¬getChildByName("link"));
  clip.addEventListener(MouseEvent.CLICK,link);
}


private function link(e:Event):void
{
navigateToURL(new URLRequest("http://www.passionrecords.
¬com"),"_blank");
}

function onKeyD(e:KeyboardEvent):void
{
 if (e.keyCode == Keyboard.SPACE)
 {
  zooming = true;
 }
}

function onKeyU(e:KeyboardEvent):void
{
 zooming = false;
 Tweener.addTween(cube,{z:-300,time:2});
 Tweener.addTween(cube,{localRotationY:0,time:2});
}
```

(code continues on next page)

```
private function onClick(e:InteractiveScene3DEvent):void
{
 if (! Tweener.isTweening(e.displayObject3D))
 {
 Tweener.addTween(cube,{localRotationY:cube.localRotationY +
 ¬90,time:2});
 }
}



 override protected function onRenderTick(e:Event=null):void
 {
  super.onRenderTick();
  if (zooming)
  {
   cube.z +=  5;
   cube.localRotationY++;
  }
 }
 }
 }
```

If you have successfully completed this lesson, you can now incorporate
Papervision3D into your Flash projects and know how to get started with any
third-party ActionScript library.

Some suggestions to try on your own

This lesson introduces a number of ActionScript tools that you can pursue more deeply. Try some of these suggestions for taking this lesson's topics further:

- Consult the Papervision3D documentation (http://docs.pv3d.org/) and learn how to add primitives to the scene created in this lesson.

- Try adding materials to your Papervision3D objects.

- Consult the Papervision3D documentation about the use of other Papervision3D features. Explore how to work with cameras, shaders, and external models.

- Explore the documentation for the Caurina `Tweener` class (http://hosted.zeh. com.br/tweener/docs/en-us/) and experiment with additional ways to create tweens using a variety of object properties.

- Search the web for other popular ActionScript libraries and see what additional ActionScript tools are available. Begin your exploration at the ActionScript Libraries section of Adobe's Flash Exchange (http://www.adobe.com/cfusion/exchange/index.cfm?s=5&from= 1&o=desc&cat=52&l=-1&event=productHome&exc=2).

- Look up the `NetConnection`, `NetStream`, and `Video` classes in the ActionScript 3.0 Reference and explore other properties, events, and methods that are available for working with video and streaming media in Flash CS5.

Review questions

1 Name two free third-party ActionScript libraries that are available for Flash CS5.

2 Name four types of objects that are found in a Papervision3D basic view.

3 Name five types of materials that can be applied to a Papervision3D model.

4 What is the class from the Caurina Transitions library that can create tweens from custom objects and properties?

5 To display streaming video using only ActionScript, what three ActionScript classes would be used?

Review answers

1 There are many free third-party ActionScript libraries available. The two that were used in this lesson are Papervision3D and Caurina Transitions.

2 A Papervision3D basic view would include a scene, a camera, a viewport, and a render engine.

3 A Papervision3D material can be a wireframe, a solid color, a bitmap, a movie clip, or a video.

4 The Caurina Tweener class can create tweens from custom objects and properties.

5 To display streaming video in Flash CS5 using only ActionScript, you would use the NetConnection, NetStream, and Video classes.

INDEX

Contributor

Chris Florio is an interactive media artist and teacher. He has been working with and teaching Flash and ActionScript as long as they have existed. Chris is a faculty member of the New England Institute of Art's Web Design and Interactive Media Department. He teaches courses in ActionScript, AIR development, Flash video, game programming, audio for gaming, and interactive performance. Students in his interactive performance classes have used ActionScript and other tools in live concerts with the Metrowest Symphony Orchestra, Club d'Elf, and other ensembles.

Chris is also a composer and the director of Passion Records (www.passionrecords.com). He has released five albums under his name and has composed music for many orchestras and ensembles. He lives in Ipswich, Massachusetts, with his wife Helen, dog Katy, and horse Sally. When not writing ActionScript or making music, he keeps sane by going for long walks with his wife, drinking good beer, and reading Terry Pratchett and history books.

Dedication   This book is dedicated to my wife Helen, who of course had to live through months of my ActionScript explorations and still seems to love me.

Acknowledgments   Thanks to a terrific editorial team: Rebecca Freed, Angela Nimer, Judy Ziajka, Matthew Newton, Connie Jeung-Mills, and Naomi Adler Dancis, who were all great to work with and saved me from embarrassing myself countless times. Thanks to many others who helped make the process successful and enjoyable, particularly Christine Yarrow, Victor Gavenda, and Danielle Foster.

This book exists because of the amazing work of the Flash and ActionScript teams at Adobe. Thanks to them all. Special thanks for help on this book and support with the prerelease versions of Flash CS5 to Kevin Lynch, Rusty Williams (my "beta buddy"), Nivesh Rajbhandari, Justin Everett-Church, Mally Gardiner, Anton de Jong, Jody Elizabeth Bleyle, Jay Armstrong, Dave Jacowitz, Jeff Swartz, Richard Galvan, Ashu Mittal, and Kristan Jiles. Thanks to the excellent Web Design and Interactive Media Department (WDIM) at the New England Institute of Art (NEIA), whose faculty members provide an inspiring environment for creating and learning. Thanks in particular to WDIM chair Lauri Stevens, and all the administration at NEIA, for giving me the space to work on this book.

Appreciation to all my ActionScript students at NEIA, for inspiring me to dig deeper into ActionScript and for kicking my butt on a regular basis. Thanks to Max Jackson, Derek Tran, and Kyle Kellogg, former students and serious ActionScripters who gave feedback and/or inspiration for the lessons.

It is due to the generous members of the Flash community that I and countless others stay abreast of the latest and coolest ActionScript techniques. Since there are too many to mention, I salute them all. Thanks to Keith Peters, Chris Allen, and Michelle Yaiser, who run the Boston Flash User Group and keep the standards high.

My gratitude to Rattana Ouch for the use of his artwork and Helen Weatherall for use of her photographs. Special thanks to Passion Records, Jonathan Keezing, David Horton, Peter Cokkinias, Mimi Rabson, Thomas Sanger-Elnaes, Hiro Honshuko, and Mike Rivard for permission to use their music and/or performances in the audio and video files for the lessons.

Thanks to my mother Marianne Florio and all my family: I love you all.

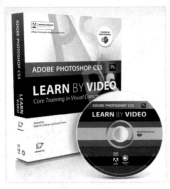

Learn Adobe Photoshop CS5 by Video:
Core Training in Visual Communication
(ISBN 9780321719805)

Learn Adobe Flash Professional CS5 by Video:
Core Training in Rich Media Communication
(ISBN 9780321719829)

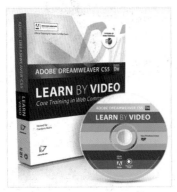

Learn Adobe Dreamweaver CS5 by Video:
Core Training in Web Communication
(ISBN 9780321719812)

The **Learn by Video** series from video2brain and Adobe Press is the only Adobe-approved video courseware for the Adobe Certified Associate Level certification, and has quickly established itself as one of the most critically-acclaimed training products available on the fundamentals of Adobe software.

Learn by Video offers up to 19 hours of high-quality HD video training presented by experienced trainers, as well as lesson files, assessment quizzes and review materials. The DVD is bundled with a full-color printed book that provides supplemental information as well as a guide to the video topics.

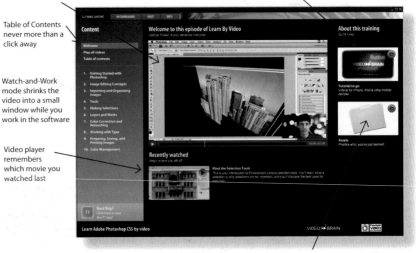

Up to 19 hours of high-quality video training

Tutorials-to-Go! Transfer selected movies to your iPhone, iPod, or compatible cell phone

Table of Contents never more than a click away

Watch-and-Work mode shrinks the video into a small window while you work in the software

Video player remembers which movie you watched last

Lesson files are included on the DVD

Additional Titles

- **Learn Adobe Photoshop Elements 8 and Adobe Premiere Elements 8 by Video** (ISBN 9780321685773)
- **Learn Photography Techniques for Adobe Photoshop CS5 by Video** (ISBN 9780321734839)
- **Learn Adobe After Effects CS5 by Video** (ISBN 9780321734860)
- **Learn Adobe Flash Catalyst CS5 by Video** (ISBN 9780321734853)
- **Learn Adobe Illustrator CS5 by Video** (ISBN 9780321734815)
- **Learn Adobe InDesign CS5 by Video** (ISBN 9780321734808)
- **Learn Adobe Premiere Pro CS5 by Video** (ISBN 9780321734846)

For more information go to **www.adobepress.com/learnbyvideo**